The carbon world

Planet Earth is a carbon-based world. All living creatures are made of molecules based on carbon atoms. It is strange to think that humans are based on carbon, the same element that diamond is made of, the hardest natural element in the world. Diamond is made only of carbon whilst humans are made of many other elements and molecules.

Why is a diamond so hard? The answer lies in its structure, the way the carbon atoms are arranged inside the diamond. Its tetrahedral structure is very strong — the diagram only shows a few of the millions of carbon atoms making up diamond. Atoms are very tiny particles and have never been seen — so how do we know how the carbon atoms are arranged in diamond?

Chemistry is a science based upon atoms — how they are constructed, how they are arranged in elements and molecules and how they behave. The structure of diamonds was one of the first to be discovered by a technique called x-ray crystallography.

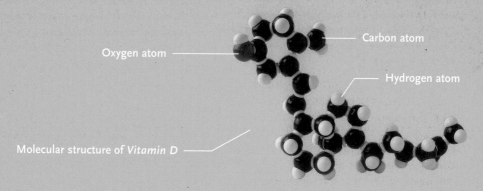

Oxygen atom

Carbon atom

Hydrogen atom

Molecular structure of *Vitamin D*

William Collins' dream of knowledge for all began with the publication of his first book in 1819. A self-educated mill worker, he not only enriched millions of lives, but also founded a flourishing publishing house.

Today, staying true to this spirit, Collins books are packed with inspiration, innovation and practical expertise. They place you at the centre of a world of possibility and give you exactly what you need to explore it.

Collins

DO MORE

Published by Collins
An imprint of HarperCollinsPublishers
77 – 85 Fulham Palace Road, Hammersmith,
London W6 8JB

Browse the complete Collins Education catalogue at

www.collinseducation.com

©HarperCollinsPublishers Limited 2006

10 9 8 7 6 5 4 3

ISBN-10: 0-00-775545-7
ISBN-13: 978-0-00-775545-5

Sam Goodman and Chris Sunley assert their moral rights
to be identified as the authors of this work

British Library Cataloguing in Publication Data
A Catalogue record for this publication is available from the British Library

Cover design by White-Card, London
Cover Illustration by IFA-design, Plymouth
Text page design by Sally Boothroyd/Wendi Watson
New artwork by Jerry Fowler
Printed and bound by Printing Express, Hong Kong

Acknowledgements:
The Authors and Publishers are grateful to the following for permission to reproduce copyright material:

University of Cambridge International Examinations: pp 48 – 53, 96 – 103, 139 – 147, 170 – 179, 208 - 213

University of Cambridge International Examinations bears no responsibility for the example answers to questions taken from its past question papers which are contained in this publication.

Photographs

B Barby/Magnum Photos 152 (T); Corbis 32; Lesley Garland Photo Library 70; GeoScience Photos 86 (L); Getty Images 111, 123 (T); GSF Photo Library 22; Jupiterimages Corporation © 2006 64, 68, 72, 114, 117, 119, 127, 152 (B); 216 – 219; Andrew Lambert Photographs 11, 20, 28 (B), 33, 79, 84, 86 (R), 87, 110, 113, 126; Andrew McClenaghan 27; Lawrence Migdale 34; Cordelia Molloy 159; Panos Pictures/P Fryer 161: Alfred Pasieka 26; P Plailly 19; C & S Thompson 76; David Vincent 13, 14, 15, 35, 63, 82, 88, 89, 90, 91; South American Pictures 160; Still Pictures/M Edwards 128, 129; Tony Waltham/Geophotos 122; 123 (B)

Inside Front Cover spread: Diamond in rock – DK Images/ Harry Taylor © Dorling Kindersley; Layer structure of graphite – DK Images/ Andy Crawford, Tim Ridley © Dorling Kindersley; Vitame D – DK Images © Dorling Kindersley; Molecular structure of diamond – DK Images/ Andy Crawford, Tim Ridley © Dorling Kindersley; Man and woman – Getty Images/ Rubberball; Palm tree – Getty Images/ Jon Shireman

Section spreads: pp6/7 Whiteboard – Getty Images/ Ryan McVay; Floating Atoms – Joerg Hartmannsgruber; pp54/55 Wood-burning fire – Alexander Lowry/ Science photo Library; Triangle Diagram – Joerg Hartmannsgruber; pp104/105 Periodic table – Joerg Hartmannsgruber; pp 148/149 Refinery © Macduff Everton/CORBIS; Distillation tower – Joerg Hartmannsgruber

Every effort has been made to contact the holders of copyright material, but if any have been inadvertently overlooked, the Publishers will be pleased to make the necessary arrangements at the first opportunity.

Cambridge IGCSE
CHEMISTRY

by Sam Goodman and Chris Sunley

Collins

GETTING THE BEST FROM THE BOOK

Welcome to Cambridge IGCSE Chemistry. This textbook and the accompanying CD-ROM have been designed to help you understand all of the requirements needed to succeed in the Cambridge IGCSE Chemistry course. There are four sections in the textbook: Principles of Chemistry, Chemistry of the Elements, Inorganic Chemistry and Organic Chemistry. Each section in the book covers the essential knowledge and skills you need. The textbook also has some very useful features which have been designed to really help you understand all the aspects of Chemistry which you will need to know for this specification.

To be able to do well in the subject you will need to know how to complete chemical calculations. The worked examples in the text take you through the question step-by-step to help you really understand.

This section has been designed to challenge those who want to achieve the very top grades. The A* extra feature is normally an extra piece of information or a tip.

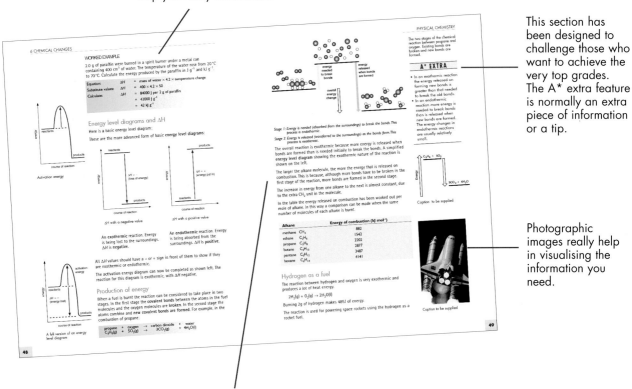

Photographic images really help in visualising the information you need.

Coverage of each topic is linked closely to the Cambridge specification so that you build a powerful knowledge-base with which to succeed in the examination.

There will be three stages to your assessment on the course because Cambridge IGCSE Chemistry is assessed in the following manner:

Paper 1 – Compulsory Multiple Choice Paper – this is worth 30% of the marks

Paper 2 – Core Curriculm – this is worth 50% of the marks

OR

Paper 3 – Extended curriculum – this is worth 50% of the marks

Paper 4 – Coursework – this is worth 20% of the marks

OR

Paper 5 – Practical Test – this is worth 20% of the marks

OR

Paper 6 – Alternative to Practical – this is worth 20% of the marks.

Collins Cambridge IGCSE Chemistry covers all of the topics and skills you will need to achieve success, whichever assessment pathway you are entered for.

Lots of clear illustrations to help you simplify and understand the complexities of chemical processes in the chemical world.

Throughout the book chemical reactions are displayed separately from the rest of the text. You'll need to know many of these reactions so they are clearly illustrated to help you.

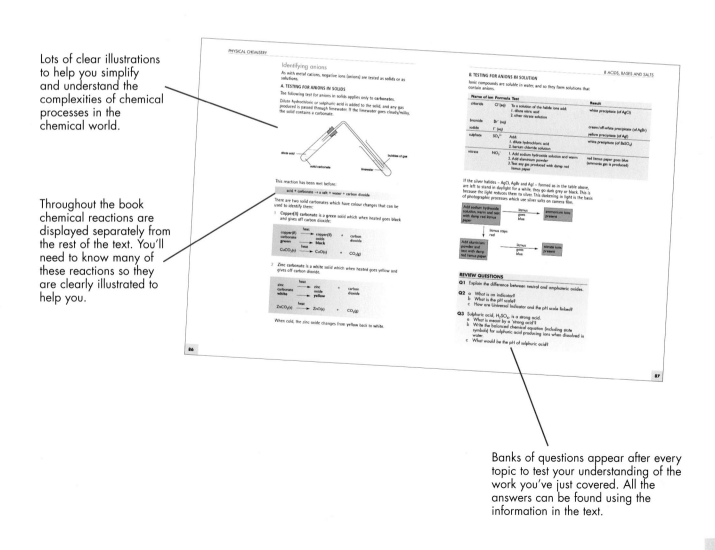

Banks of questions appear after every topic to test your understanding of the work you've just covered. All the answers can be found using the information in the text.

IGCSE Chemistry CD-ROM

To help you through the course we have added this unique CD-ROM which may be able to be used in class or by yourself as part of your private study. To allow you to really understand the subject as you progress through the course we have added the following features to the CD-ROM:

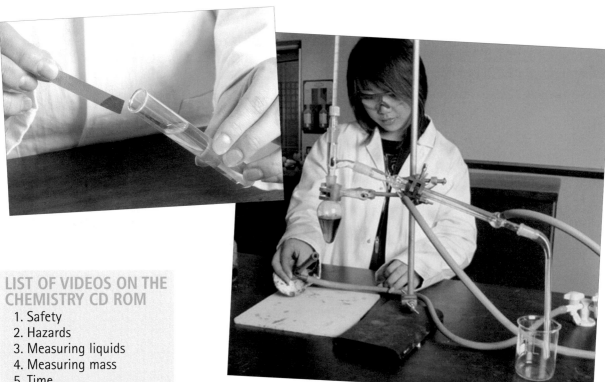

LIST OF VIDEOS ON THE CHEMISTRY CD ROM

1. Safety
2. Hazards
3. Measuring liquids
4. Measuring mass
5. Time
6. Temperature
7. Chromatography
8. Filtration
9. Evaporation
10. Titration
11. Distillation
12. Identifying unknown compounds
13. Identifying gases
14. Flame tests
15. Identifying metals in solution
16. Identifying ammonium compounds
17. Identifying non-metals
18. Salts
19. Reduction and oxidation
20. Thermal decomposition

VIDEO FILMS

Chemistry is a practical subject and to reinforce your studies the CD-ROM has 20 short films which cover experiments and practical work. Each of the films covers an area which you need to know well for the practical section of the course. The information in the films will also help you with the knowledge required in other parts of the specification. You can use the films to help you understand the topic you are currently studying or perhaps come back to them when you want to revise for the exam.

Each of the films has sound too so if you are watching them in a library or quiet study area you may need headphones.

QUESTION BANK

"Practice makes perfect", so the saying goes, and we have included a large bank of questions related to the Chemistry specification to help you understand the topics you will be studying.

Just like the films your teacher may be able to use this in class or you may want to try the questions in your private study sessions.

These questions will reinforce the knowledge you have gained in the classroom and through using the textbook and could also be used when you are revising for your examinations. Don't try to do all the questions at once though; the most effective way to use this feature is by trying some of the questions every now and then to test yourself. In this way you will know where you need to do a little more work. The questions are not full 'exam-type' questions that you will be set by your IGCSE examiners. Some of the questions test underlying principles that are not specifically mentioned in your specification.

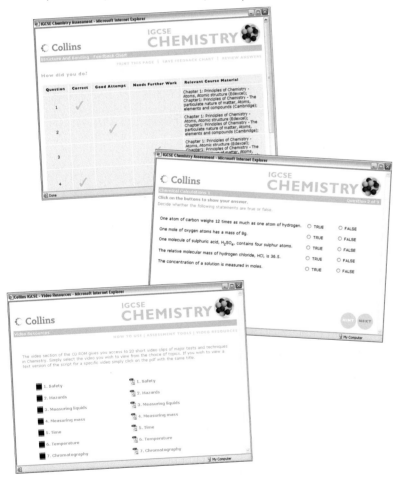

Good luck with your IGCSE chemistry studies. This book and the CD-ROM provide you with stimulating, interesting and motivating learning resources that we are sure will help you succeed in your chemistry course.

OPERATING SYSTEMS REQUIRED AND SET-UP INSTRUCTIONS.

Mac System requirements
500 MHz PowerPC G3 and later
Mac OS X 10.1.x and above
128MB RAM
Microsoft Internet Explorer 5.2, Firefox 1.x, Mozilla 1.x, Netscape 7.x and above, Opera 6, or Safari 1.x and above
(Mac OS X 10.2.x only)
325 MB of free hard disc space.

To run the program from the CD
1 Insert the CD into the drive
2 When the CD icon appears on the desktop, double-click it
3 Double-click Collins IGCSE Biology.html

To install the program to run from the hard drive
1 Insert the CD into the drive
2 When the CD icon appears on the desktop, double-click it to open a finder window
3 Drag Collins IGCSE Biology.html to the desktop
4 Drag Collins IGCSE Biology Content to the desktop.

PC System requirements
450 MHz Intel Pentium II processor (or equivalent) and later
Windows 98/ME/NT/2000/XP
128MB RAM
Microsoft Internet Explorer 5.5, Firefox 1.x, Mozilla 1.x, Netscape 7.x and above, Opera 7.11 and above
325 MB of hard disc space

To run the program from the CD
1 Insert the CD into the drive
2 Double-click on the CD-ROM drive icon inside My Computer
3 Double-click on Collins IGCSE Biology.html

To install the program to run from the hard drive
1 Insert the IGCSE Biology disc into your CD-ROM drive
2 Double-click on the CD-ROM drive icon inside My Computer
3 Double-click on the SETUP.EXE
4 Follow onscreen instructions. These include instructions concerning the Macromedia Flash Player included with and required by the program.
5 When the installation is complete, remove the CD from the drive.

For free technical support, call our helpline on: Tel.: + 44 141 306 3322 or send an email to: it.helpdesk@harpercollins.co.uk.

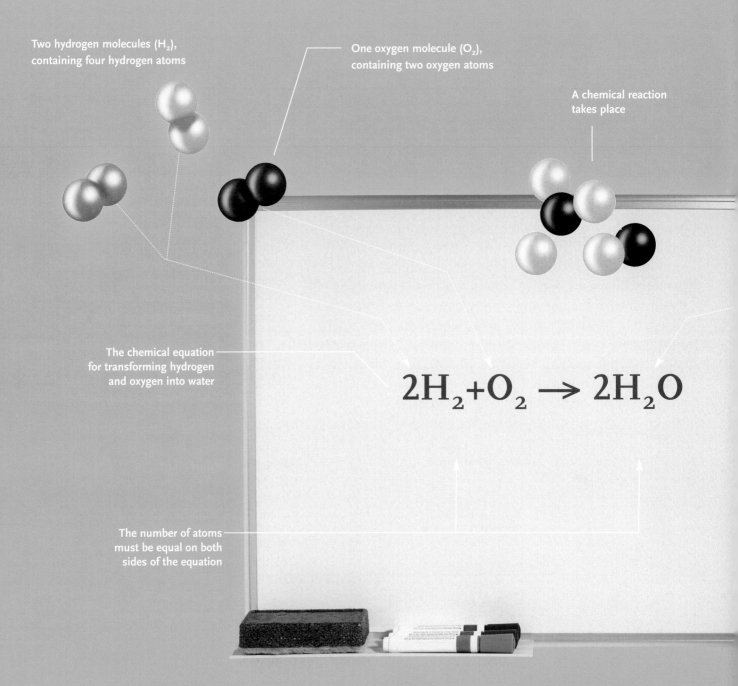

Two hydrogen molecules (H_2), containing four hydrogen atoms

One oxygen molecule (O_2), containing two oxygen atoms

A chemical reaction takes place

The chemical equation for transforming hydrogen and oxygen into water

The number of atoms must be equal on both sides of the equation

$$2H_2 + O_2 \rightarrow 2H_2O$$

A universal language

All over the world people use different languages to communicate. Chemistry has its own language. Every chemical element has a symbol, like O for oxygen; when writing you join letters together to make words; in chemistry you join element symbols together to make formulae.

A water molecule has two hydrogen atoms and one oxygen atom. The formula for water is H_2O. Water is a 'compound'. When elements or compounds interact with each other to produce different substances this is called a chemical reaction.

To describe a chemical reaction we write an equation – equations are the 'sentences' of chemistry. The language of chemistry is universal, which means that scientists from Asia to the Americas, from the Arctic to the Antarctic, can understand the equations others have written.

PRINCIPLES OF CHEMISTRY

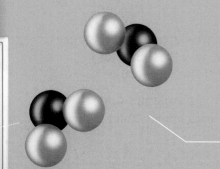

Two water molecules (H$_2$O)

1 THE PARTICULATE NATURE OF MATTER

States of matter

WHAT ARE THE STATES OF MATTER?

All matter is made of atoms and they are arranged differently in the three states of matter – **solids, liquids** and **gases**. The way the atoms (or particles) are arranged explains the **properties** of the three states.

In **solids**, the particles are held tightly together in a **fixed position**, so solids have a **definite shape**. However, the particles are **vibrating** about their fixed positions because they have energy.

In **liquids**, the particles are held tightly together and have enough energy to **move around**. Liquids have **no definite shape** and will take on the shape of the container they are in.

In **gases**, the particles are further apart and have enough energy to **move apart** from each other. Gases can **expand** to fill the container they are in. Gases can be compressed to form liquids by using high pressure and cooling.

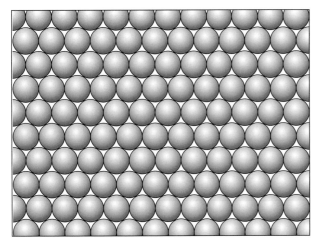

Particles in a solid.

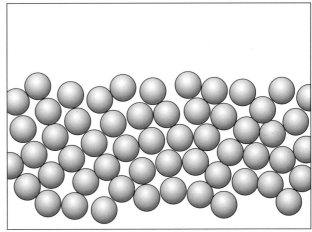

Particles in a liquid.

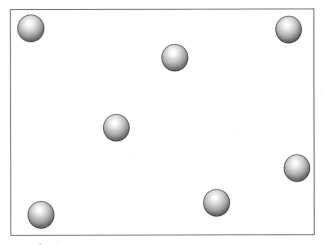

Particles in a gas.

HOW DO SUBSTANCES CHANGE FROM ONE STATE TO ANOTHER?

To change solids → liquids → gases, **heat** must be put in. The heat provides the particles with enough energy to overcome the forces holding them together. The particles move **further apart** as they change from one state to another.

These are **endothermic** processes, meaning that energy is absorbed.

To change gases → liquids → solids involves **cooling**, so removing energy. This makes the particles come **closer together** as they change from one state to another.

These are **exothermic** processes, meaning that energy is being given out.

The **temperatures** at which one state changes to another have specific names:

Name of temperature	Change of state
melting point	solid → liquid
boiling point	liquid → gas
freezing point	liquid → solid
condensation point	gas → liquid

The particles in a **liquid** can move around. They have different energies, so some are moving faster than others. The faster particles have enough energy to escape from the surface of the liquid and change into gas molecules – also called vapour molecules. This process is **evaporation**. The rate of evaporation increases with **temperature** since heating gives more particles the energy to be able to escape from the surface.

The diagram summarises the changes in states of matter:

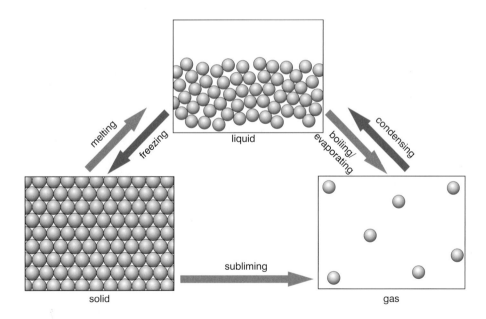

Changes of state.

The diagram on the next page shows how forces between particles in solids, liquids and gases change as the temperature increases and they change from one state into another.

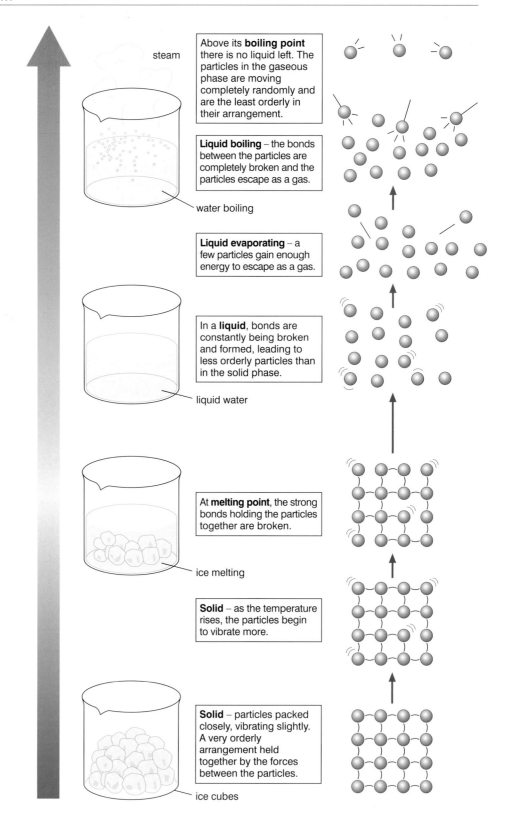

steam

Above its **boiling point** there is no liquid left. The particles in the gaseous phase are moving completely randomly and are the least orderly in their arrangement.

Liquid boiling – the bonds between the particles are completely broken and the particles escape as a gas.

water boiling

Liquid evaporating – a few particles gain enough energy to escape as a gas.

In a liquid, bonds are constantly being broken and formed, leading to less orderly particles than in the solid phase.

liquid water

At **melting point**, the strong bonds holding the particles together are broken.

ice melting

Solid – as the temperature rises, the particles begin to vibrate more.

Solid – particles packed closely, vibrating slightly. A very orderly arrangement held together by the forces between the particles.

ice cubes

Diffusion

You will have noticed how the smell of some foods being cooked in the kitchen spreads into other rooms. This is because the gas particles from the food spread out from the kitchen. The gas particles are moving, and the movement of gas particles from one place to another is called **diffusion**.

Diffusion can be demonstrated in the laboratory using a gas jar of air placed over a gas jar of brown bromine vapour. In a very short time the brown bromine vapour fills both gas jars. This is not because the bromine is light and 'floating upwards' (bromine molecules are heavier than the molecules in the air).

The reason the bromine and air mix is because all the gas particles are moving.

Another example showing the diffusion of gases is when a gas jar of hydrogen is put over a gas jar of air as the diagram below shows. The lighter hydrogen molecules are found in the lower jar and the heavier air molecules move into the upper jar.

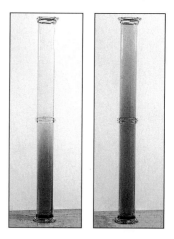

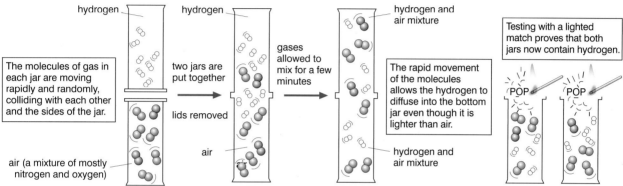

hydrogen

hydrogen

hydrogen and air mixture

The molecules of gas in each jar are moving rapidly and randomly, colliding with each other and the sides of the jar.

two jars are put together

lids removed

gases allowed to mix for a few minutes

air

The rapid movement of the molecules allows the hydrogen to diffuse into the bottom jar even though it is lighter than air.

Testing with a lighted match proves that both jars now contain hydrogen.

POP POP

air (a mixture of mostly nitrogen and oxygen)

hydrogen and air mixture

Diffusion is evidence for the **kinetic theory of matter** which says matter is made of tiny, invisible particles which are in constant motion in gases and liquids.

The gas and liquid particles are constantly moving in a random way. Evidence for this is shown in smoke cells viewed under a microscope (called 'Brownian motion').

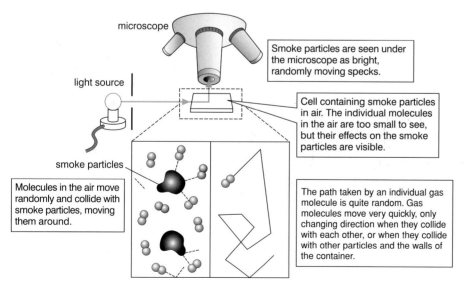

microscope

Smoke particles are seen under the microscope as bright, randomly moving specks.

light source

Cell containing smoke particles in air. The individual molecules in the air are too small to see, but their effects on the smoke particles are visible.

smoke particles

Molecules in the air move randomly and collide with smoke particles, moving them around.

The path taken by an individual gas molecule is quite random. Gas molecules move very quickly, only changing direction when they collide with each other, or when they collide with other particles and the walls of the container.

Diffusion takes place in liquids as well but slower because of the slower speed of liquid particles. You can see this yourself by dropping instant coffee particles into a cup of hot water and not stirring it. The brown colour of the coffee slowly spreads through all the water.

Another example is using potassium manganate (VII) crystals in a beaker of water.

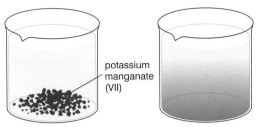

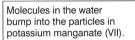
potassium
manganate
(VII)

Molecules in the water bump into the particles in potassium manganate (VII).	As the particles are spread out by the movement of the water molecules, the colour slowly diffuses through the liquid.	After a few days the particles have mixed completely with the water.

Diffusion occurs more rapidly if the liquid is hot. This is because the particles in a hot liquid have more energy than a cold liquid. They move around more rapidly so spreading the particles more quickly throughout the liquid.

The lighter the gas particles the faster they move. This is shown by using ammonia solution and hydrochloric acid (both concentrated). Cotton wool is soaked in each liquid and put at either end of a long glass tube. When ammonia (NH_3) meets hydrogen chloride (HCl) they form solid ammonium chloride as a white powder:

$$NH_3(g) + HCl(g) \rightarrow NH_4Cl(s)$$

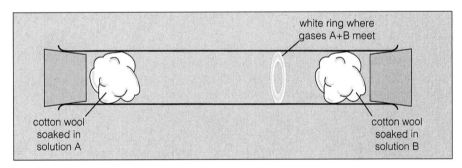

white ring where gases A+B meet

cotton wool soaked in solution A

cotton wool soaked in solution B

Diffusion of the gases will produce ammonium chloride

REVIEW QUESTIONS

Q1 In which state of matter do particles have the most energy? Explain your answer.

Q2 Sodium (melting point 98 °C) and aluminium (melting point 660 °C) are both metals and are solids at room temperature. From their different melting points, what can you deduce about the forces in the metals?

Q3 What is diffusion?

Q4 Explain what the kinetic theory says.

Q5 Why does diffusion take place more slowly in liquids than gases?

Q6 Comparing bromine molecules (mass = 160) and ammonia molecules (mass = 17), which will diffuse fastest and why?

More questions on the CD ROM

Examination questions are on page 48.

2 EXPERIMENTAL TECHNIQUES

Measurement

In your study of chemistry you will carry out practical work. It is essential to use the right apparatus for the task.

Time is measured with clocks, such as a wall clock. The clock should be accurate to about 1 second. You may be able to use your own wristwatch if you prefer.

Temperature is measured using a thermometer. The range of the thermometer should be -10°C to +110°C with intervals of 1°C.

Mass is measured with a balance or scales. Your teacher may show you how to measure the mass of solids and liquids.

Volume of liquids can be measured with burettes, pipettes and measuring cylinders. Your teacher will show you how to use these accurately.

Measuring equipment

Criteria of purity

PAPER CHROMATOGRAPHY

Paper chromatography is a way of separating solutions or liquids which are mixed together.

The diagrams below show how it is used to find the colours that make up a black ink.

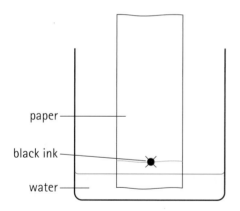

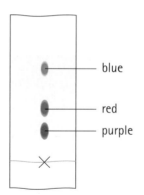

blue

red

purple

A piece of filter paper is marked with black ink and dipped into water in a beaker

A bit of ink is placed on the X spot and the paper is put into water. As the water rises up the paper the different dyes travel different distances and so are separated on the **chromatogram**.

Even colourless liquids can be separated using this technique. The difference is that the chromatogram paper is white/colourless at the end. To see the pattern of dots, the paper is sprayed with a liquid **locating agent** that shows up the dots as colours that can then be seen.

Paper chromatography can be used to identify what an unknown liquid is made of, i.e. interpreting a chromatogram.

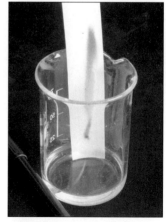

After a few minutes the chromatogram has been created by the action of the water on the ink

The diagram below shows how this technique works.

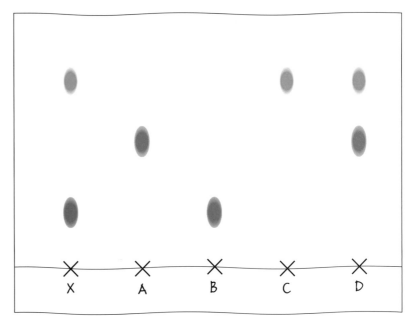

The unknown liquid X is compared with known liquids, in this case A to D.

X must be made of B and C because the pattern of their dots matches the pattern shown by X.

THE PURITY OF SOLIDS AND LIQUIDS

It is very important that manufactured foods and drugs only contain the substances the manufacturers want in them, i.e. they must be pure and not contain any contaminants.

The simplest way of checking the purity of solids and liquids is using heat to find the temperatures at which they melt or boil.

An impure solid will have a **lower melting point** than the pure solid.

A liquid containing a dissolved solid (solute) will have a **higher boiling point** than the pure liquid solvent.

The best example to remember these facts is water and ice.

Pure water boils at 100°C. Salted water for boiling vegetables in boils at about 102°C.

Pure ice melts at 0°C. Ice with salt added to it melts at about -4°C.

Methods of purification

Techniques in purifying solids and liquids rely on finding different properties between the substances that make up the impure mixture.

PURIFYING IMPURE SOLIDS

The method is:

(a) add a solvent that the solid that is wanted is soluble in, and dissolve it,

(b) filter the mixture to remove the insoluble impurity,

(c) heat the solution to remove some solvent and leave to crystallise,

(d) filter off the crystals, wash with a small amount of cold solvent and dry them – this is the pure solid.

Filtration of copper hydroxide

An example of using this technique would be separating 'rock salt' (the impure form of sodium chloride, NaCl). Water is added to dissolve the salt but leave the other solids undissolved. Filter off the insoluble impurities, warm the salt solution and leave it to crystallise to form salt crystals.

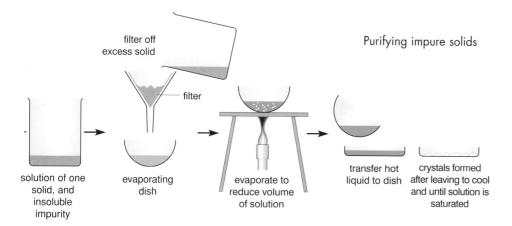

Purifying impure solids

filter off excess solid

filter

solution of one solid, and insoluble impurity

evaporating dish

evaporate to reduce volume of solution

transfer hot liquid to dish

crystals formed after leaving to cool and until solution is saturated

PURIFYING IMPURE LIQUIDS

There are two methods:

(a) Liquids contaminated with soluble solids dissolved in them.

The method is **distillation**.

The solution is heated, the liquid boils and turns into a vapour, it is condensed back to the pure liquid and collected.

This is the technique used in **desalination plants**, i.e. the production of pure drinking water from sea water. The solids are left behind after boiling off the water.

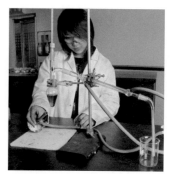

Distillation

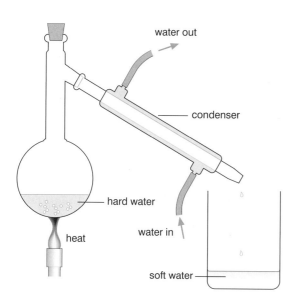

water out

condenser

hard water

heat

water in

soft water

(b) Liquids contaminated with other liquids.

In this case **fractional distillation** is used, which uses the difference in boiling points of the different liquids mixed together.

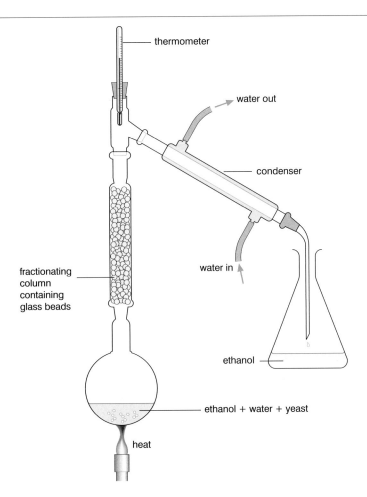

thermometer

water out

condenser

fractionating column containing glass beads

water in

ethanol

ethanol + water + yeast

heat

Apparatus for fractional distillation of alcohol.

The mixture is boiled, and the liquid with the lowest boiling point turns to a vapour first, comes off and is condensed back to liquid at the top of the fractionating column. The next lowest boiling point liquid comes off, and so on until all the liquids have been separated. You can identify the fraction you want to 'save' by the temperature reading on the thermometer.

Fractional distillation is the method used in the separation of crude oil and collecting ethanol from the fermentation mixture (above) (see page 147).

WHICH METHOD TO USE

Which of the three methods to use depends on the mixture to be separated and so purified.

Sugar contaminated with sand would be solvent/filtration/crystallisation. Sugar is soluble in water, sand is insoluble in water.
Obtaining water from copper sulphate solution would be distillation. Copper sulphate is a soluble solid dissolved in water ('the solution').
Obtaining ethanol from wine is fractional distillation because only liquids are involved in 'wine'.

REVIEW QUESTIONS

Q1 What separation technique would be used to identify the food colouring used in a sweet?

Q2 Pure liquid X has a boiling point of 87°C. What is its likely boiling point if it contains dissolved solids as impurities?

Q3 Why does putting salt onto ice make it melt?

More questions on the CD ROM

Examination questions are on page 48.

3 ATOMS, ELEMENTS AND COMPOUNDS

Atomic structure and the Periodic Table

A substance that is made up of only one type of atoms is called an element. An element cannot be broken down into simpler substances by chemical means

The smallest amount of an element that still behaves like that element is an **atom**. Each element has its own unique type of atom. Atoms are made up of smaller, sub-atomic particles. The three main sub-atomic particles are: **protons**, **neutrons** and **electrons**.

These particles are very small and have very little mass. However, it is possible to compare their masses using a **relative scale**. Their charges can also be compared in a similar way. The proton and neutron have the **same** mass, and the proton and electron have equal but **opposite** charges.

Sub-atomic particle	Relative mass	Relative charge
proton	1	+1
neutron	1	0
electron	approx. $\frac{1}{2000}$	−1

Protons and neutrons are found in the centre of the atom, in a cluster called the **nucleus**. The electrons form a series of 'shells' around the nucleus.

WHAT ARE ATOMIC NUMBER AND MASS NUMBER?

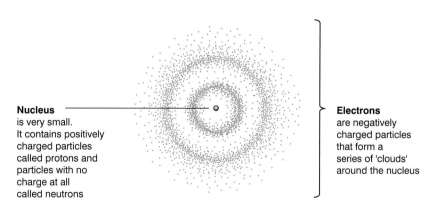

Nucleus
is very small.
It contains positively charged particles called protons and particles with no charge at all called neutrons

Electrons
are negatively charged particles that form a series of 'clouds' around the nucleus

In order to describe the numbers of protons, neutrons and electrons in an atom, scientists use two numbers. These are called the **proton number** and the **nucleon number**.

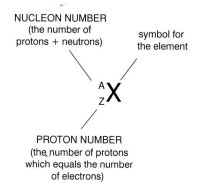

NUCLEON NUMBER
(the number of
protons + neutrons)

symbol for
the element

$$_{Z}^{A}X$$

PROTON NUMBER
(the number of protons
which equals the number
of electrons)

The atomic number is used to order the elements in the periodic table. The atomic structures of the first twenty elements are shown here.

Element	Proton number	Nucleon number	Number of protons	Number of neutrons	Number of electrons
Hydrogen	1	1	1	0	1
Helium	2	4	2	2	2
Lithium	3	7	3	4	3
Beryllium	4	9	4	5	4
Boron	5	10	5	5	5
Carbon	6	12	6	6	6
Nitrogen	7	14	7	7	7
Oxygen	8	16	8	8	8
Fluorine	9	19	9	10	9
Neon	10	20	10	10	10
Sodium	11	23	11	12	11
Magnesium	12	24	12	12	12
Aluminium	13	27	13	14	13
Silicon	14	28	14	14	14
Phosphorus	15	31	15	16	15
Sulphur	16	32	16	16	16
Chlorine	17	35.5	17	18 or 20	17
Argon	18	40	18	22	18
Potassium	19	39	19	20	19
Calcium	20	40	20	20	20

Hydrogen is the only atom that has **no neutrons**.

Isotopes

Atoms of the same element with the same number of protons and electrons but different numbers of neutrons are called **isotopes**.
For example, there are three isotopes of hydrogen:

Isotope	Symbol	Number of neutrons
normal hydrogen	^1_1H	0
deuterium	^2_1H	1
tritium	^3_1H	2

Isotopes have the same chemical properties but slightly different physical properties.

Some isotopes are **radioactive**. They emit radioactivity from the nucleus and **decay** i.e. if the radioactivity is alpha-particles or beta-particles they change into other atoms with different numbers of protons and/or neutrons.

Isotopes that do not decay and emit radiation are classed as non-radioactive isotopes.

Radioactive isotopes emit radioactivity of one of the following types:

Alpha-particles (α) are helium nuclei, they contain 2 protons and 2 neutrons.

Beta-particles (β) are fast moving electrons.

Gamma-rays (γ) are high-energy electromagnetic rays.

The gamma-rays from some radioactive isotopes are the most dangerous of the three types of radiation because they penetrate furthest. However, they are also the most useful. In medicine they are used to sterilise equipment and in radiotherapy to treat cancer tumours.

Industry uses radioactive isotopes as 'tracers' to detect leaks in pipes.

Radioactive isotopes used in medicine.

How are electrons arranged in the atom?

The electrons are arranged in shells around the nucleus. The shells do not all contain the same number of electrons – the shell nearest to the nucleus can only take two electrons, whereas the next one further from the nucleus can take eight.

Oxygen has a proton number of 8, so has 8 electrons. Of these, 2 will be in the first shell and 6 will be in the second shell. This arrangement is written 2, 6. A phosphorus atom with a proton number of 15 has 15 electrons, arranged 2, 8, 5.

The electron arrangements are very important as they determine the way that the atom reacts chemically.

Electron shell	Maximum number of electrons
I	2
2	8
3	8

Atom diagrams

The atomic structure of an atom can be shown simply in a diagram.

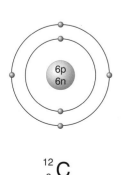

$${}^{12}_{6}\text{C}$$

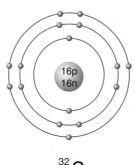

$${}^{32}_{16}\text{S}$$

Atom diagrams for carbon and sulphur showing the number of protons and neutrons, and the electron arrangements.

Name	Symbol
Helium	He
Neon	Ne
Argon	Ar
Krypton	Kr
Xenon	Xe
Radon	Rn

THE NOBLE GASES

This is a group of **very unreactive** non-metals. They used to be called the inert gases as it was thought that they didn't react with anything! But scientists later managed to produce fluorine compounds of some of the noble gases. As far as your school laboratory work is concerned, however, they are completely unreactive.

This can be explained in terms of their electronic structures. The atoms all **have complete outer electron shells**. They don't need to lose electrons (as metals do), or gain electrons (as most non-metals do).

VALENCY ELECTRONS

When atoms combine into compounds they try to complete their outer shells. For metals to do this it is easier to lose electrons than to gain them. For non-metals it is easier to gain electrons than to lose them. Alternatively, elements can share electrons in their outer shells to form compounds.

The number of electrons in the outer shell (orbit) are called the valency electrons, and this number is the same as the Group number of the element in the Periodic Table.

For example, carbon has 4 electrons in the outer shell so it would share 4 electrons to make a completed shell of 8 electrons. We say that the valency number of carbon is 4.

Bonding: the structure of matter

In 1808, the British chemist **John Dalton** published a book outlining his **theory of atoms**. These were the main points of his theory:

1 All matter is made of small, indivisible spheres called atoms.

2 All the atoms of a given **element** are identical and have the **same mass**.

3 The atoms of **different elements** have **different masses**.

4 Chemical **compounds** are formed when **atoms join together**.

5 All molecules of a chemical compound have the **same type** and **number of atoms**.

A **mixture** contains more than one substance (elements or compounds). In a mixture, the separate substances can be separated by simple means. This is because the substances in a mixture have not combined chemically.

Most elements can be classified as either **metals** or **non-metals**. In the periodic table, the metals are arranged on the left and in the middle, and the non-metals are on the right.

Metalloid elements are between metals and non-metals. They have some properties of metals and some of non-metals. Examples of metalloids are silicon and germanium.

Metals and non-metals have quite different physical and chemical properties.

Non-metals. Clockwise from top left: sulphur, bromine, phosphorus, carbon, iodine

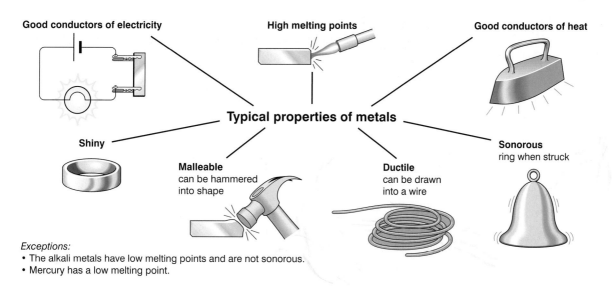

Typical properties of metals

Good conductors of electricity

High melting points

Good conductors of heat

Shiny

Malleable
can be hammered
into shape

Ductile
can be drawn
into a wire

Sonorous
ring when struck

Exceptions:
• The alkali metals have low melting points and are not sonorous.
• Mercury has a low melting point.

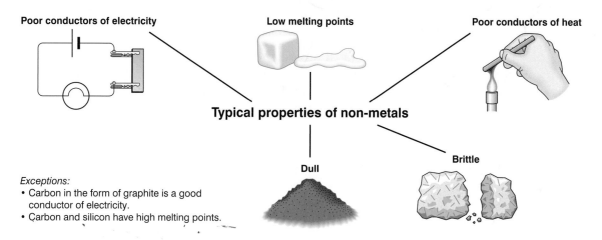

Typical properties of non-metals

Poor conductors of electricity

Low melting points

Poor conductors of heat

Dull

Brittle

Exceptions:
• Carbon in the form of graphite is a good
  conductor of electricity.
• Carbon and silicon have high melting points.

ALLOYS

An **alloy** is when a metal is mixed with other elements.

Common examples are:

Alloy   Constituents

Brass   Copper (70%), zinc (30%)

Bronze Copper (90%), tin (10%)

Steel   Iron and various small amounts of carbon

Solder   Tin (50%), lead (50%)

How do atoms combine?

Atoms bond together with other atoms in a chemical reaction to make a compound. For example, sodium will react with chlorine to make sodium chloride; hydrogen will react with oxygen to make water.

This reactivity is due to the electron arrangements in atoms. If atoms have incomplete electron shells they will usually react with other atoms. Only atoms with complete electron shells tend to be unreactive. The noble gases, atoms in group 0 of the periodic table, fall into this category.

When atoms combine they try to achieve full outer electron shells. They do this either by gaining electrons to fill the gaps in the outer shell or by losing electrons from the outer shell to leave an inner complete shell.

There are two different ways in which atoms can bond together: ionic bonding and covalent bonding.

What happens in ionic bonding?

Ionic bonding involves **electron transfer** between metals and non-metals. Both metals and non-metals try to achieve complete outer electron shells.

Metals lose electrons from their outer shells and form **positive** ions. This is an example of **oxidation**.

Non-metals gain electrons into their outer shells and form **negative** ions. This is an example of **reduction**.

The ions are held together by strong electrical (electrostatic) forces.

The bonding process can be represented in **dot-and-cross diagrams**. Look at the reaction between sodium and chlorine as an example.

Crystals of sodium chloride

Sodium is a metal. It has a proton number of 11 and so has 11 electrons, arranged 2, 8, 1. Its atom diagram looks like this:	Chlorine is a non-metal. It has a proton number of 17 and so has 17 electrons, arranged 2, 8, 7. Its atom diagram looks like this:

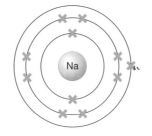 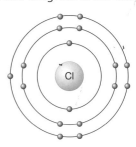

Sodium has one electron in its outer shell. It can achieve a full outer shell by losing this electron. The sodium atom transfers its outermost electron to the chlorine atom.

Chlorine has seven electrons in its outer shell. It can achieve a full outer shell by gaining an extra electron. The chlorine atom accepts an electron from the sodium.

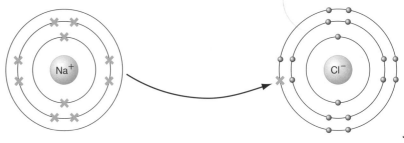

The sodium is no longer an atom; it is now an ion. It does not have equal numbers of protons and electrons, it is no longer neutral. It has one more proton than it has electrons, so it is a positive ion with a charge of 1+. The ion is written as Na^+.

The chlorine is no longer an atom; it is now an ion. It does not have equal numbers of protons and electrons, it is no longer neutral. It has one more electron than protons, so it is a negative ion with a charge of 1–. The ion is written as Cl^-.

METALS CAN TRANSFER MORE THAN ONE ELECTRON TO A NON-METAL

Magnesium combines with oxygen to form **magnesium oxide**. The magnesium (electron arrangement 2, 8, 2) transfers two electrons to the oxygen (electron arrangement 2, 6). Magnesium therefore forms a Mg^{2+} ion and oxygen forms an O^{2-} ion.

Dot and cross diagram for magnesium oxide, MgO

Aluminium has an electron arrangement 2, 8, 3. When it combines with fluorine with an electron arrangement 2, 7, three fluorine atoms are needed for each aluminium atom. The formula of **aluminium fluoride** is therefore AlF_3. Aluminium forms an Al^{3+} ion and fluorine forms F^- ions.

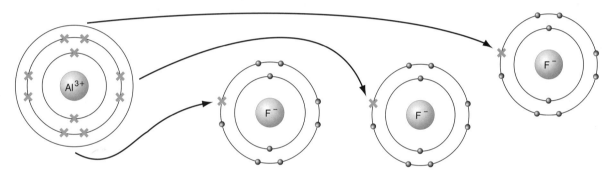

What ions can an element form?

The ion formed by an element can be worked out from the position of **the element in the periodic table**. The elements in group 4 and group 0 generally do not form ions.

Group number	1	2	3	4	5	6	7	0
Ion charge	1+	2+	3+	X	3–	2–	1–	X

What is covalent bonding?

Covalent bonding involves electron sharing. It occurs between atoms of non-metals. It results in the formation of a **molecule**. The non-metal atoms try to achieve complete outer electron shells.

A **single covalent bond** is formed when two atoms each contribute one electron to a **shared pair** of electrons. For example, hydrogen gas exists as H_2 molecules. Each hydrogen atom wants to fill its electron shell. They can do this by sharing electrons.

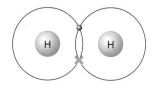

represented as

H — H

The dot-and-cross diagram and displayed formula of H_2.

A single covalent bond can be represented by a single line. The formula of the molecule can be written as a **displayed formula**, H—H. The hydrogen and oxygen atoms in water are also held together by single covalent bonds.

Water contains single covalent bonds.

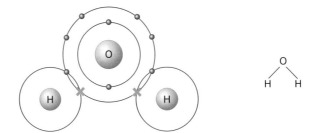

Some molecules contain **double covalent bonds**. In carbon dioxide, the carbon atom has an electron arrangement of 2, 4 and needs an additional four electrons to complete its outer electron shell. It needs to share its four electrons with four electrons from oxygen atoms (electron arrangement 2, 6). Two oxygen atoms are needed, each sharing two electrons with the carbon atom.

Carbon dioxide contains double bonds.

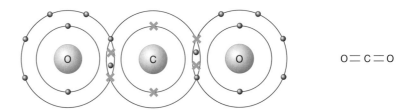

The following are examples of the arrangement of electrons in other, and sometimes more complex, covalent molecules. Note that only the outer electron shells/orbits are shown for each atom.

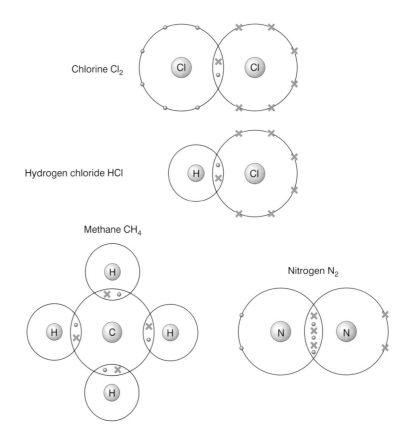

Chlorine Cl₂

Hydrogen chloride HCl

Methane CH₄

Nitrogen N₂

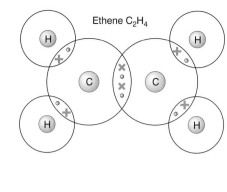

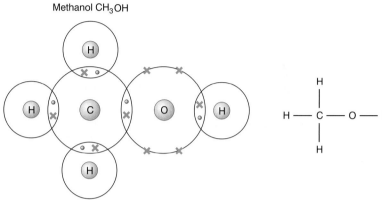

Compounds containing covalent bonds have very different properties from compounds that contain ionic bonds. These differences are considered in the next section.

How many covalent bonds can an element form?

The number of covalent bonds a non-metal atom can form is linked to its position in the periodic table. Metals (groups 1, 2, 3) do not form covalent bonds. The noble gases in group 0 are unreactive and usually do not form covalent bonds.

Group in the periodic table	1	2	3	4	5	6	7	0
Covalent bonds formed	X	X	X	4	3	2	1	X

What structures do ionic compounds form?

Ionic compounds form **giant lattice structures**. For example, when sodium chloride is formed by ionic bonding, the ions do not pair up. Each sodium ion is surrounded by six chloride ions, and each chloride ion is surrounded by six sodium ions.

The electrostatic attractions between the ions are very strong. The properties of sodium chloride can be explained using this model of its structure.

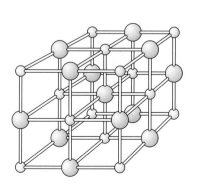

○ chloride ion ○ sodium ion

In solid sodium chloride, the ions are held firmly in place – they are not free to move. Ionic compounds have giant ionic lattice structures like this.

Properties of sodium chloride	Explanation in terms of structure
Hard crystals	Strong forces between the ions
High melting point (801°C)	Strong forces between the ions
Dissolves in water	The water is also able to form strong electrostatic attractions with the ions – the ions are 'plucked' off the lattice structure
Does not conduct electricity when solid	Strong forces between the ions prevent them from moving
Does conduct electricity when molten or dissolved in water	The strong forces between the ions have been broken down and so the ions are able to move

Covalent molecules

Covalent bonds are also strong bonds. They are **intramolecular** bonds – formed within each molecule. Much weaker **intermolecular forces** attract the individual molecules to each other.

The properties of covalent molecules can be explained using a simple model involving these two types of bond or forces.

Properties of hydrogen	Explanation in terms of structure	
Hydrogen is a gas with a very low melting point (−259 °C)	The intermolecular forces between the molecules are weak	
Hydrogen does not conduct electricity	There are no ions or free electrons present. The covalent bond (intramolecular bond) is a strong bond and the electrons cannot be easily removed from it	

Macromolecules

Some covalently bonded compounds do not exist as simple molecular structures in the way that hydrogen does. Diamond, for example, exists as a **giant structure** with each carbon atom covalently bonded to four others. The bonding is extremely strong – diamond has a melting point of about 3730°C. Diamond is the hardest naturally-occurring material in the world. Its hardness and high melting point make it ideal for industrial drill bits e.g. drilling for oil and gas. Another form of carbon is graphite. Graphite has a different giant structure as seen in the diagram. Different forms of the same element are called **allotropes**.

(a) In diamond, each carbon atom forms four strong covalent bonds.

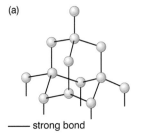

(a)

—— strong bond

In graphite, carbon atoms form layers of hexagons in the plane of their strong covalent bonds. The weak bonds are between the layers. Because the layers can slide over each other, graphite is flaky and can be used as a lubricant. Graphite can conduct electricity because the electrons are free to move along the layers.

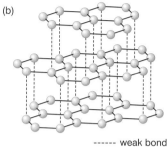

(b)

------ weak bond

(b) In graphite, each carbon atom forms three strong covalent bonds and one weak bond.

Silicon(IV) oxide (silicon dioxide, SiO_2) is another giant covalent molecule.

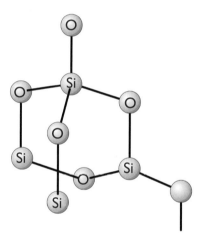

You can see from its structure that every silicon atom has four covalent bonds arranged tetrahedrally. The structure is similar to the diamond structure above, which is why silicon(IV) oxide has a high melting point and is hard like diamond.

Structures can usually be identified as being giant or molecular from their melting points.

Structure	Atom	Molecule	Ion
Giant	Diamond, graphite, metals High melting points	Sand (silicon(IV) oxide molecules) High melting point	All ionic compounds, e.g. sodium chloride High melting points
Simple molecular	Noble gases, e.g. helium Low melting points	Carbon dioxide, water Low melting points	None

Metallic bonding

Metals are giant structures with high melting and boiling points.

Metallic bonds are quite strong, which means that metal atoms can be hard to pull apart (so explaining their melting and boiling points). The malleability of metals is due to the nature of the forces holding metals together. Since there is no net force or attraction between the cations, they can be moved from one lattice site to another as the metals are bent or shaped.

Many parts of aircraft are constructed of aluminium or some of its alloys. This is because it is strong but light. The atoms in aluminium are held together by strong metallic bonds and form a giant structure of atoms.

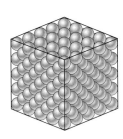

Metal atoms are closely packed in the giant structure and this accounts for the physical properties of metals e.g. malleability

Metal atoms give up one or more of their electrons to form positive ions, called cations. The electrons they give up form a 'sea of electrons' surrounding the positive metal ions, and the negative electrons are attracted to the positive ions, holding the structure together.

The electrons are free to move through the whole structure, which is why metals conduct electricity. The electrons are **delocalised**, meaning they are not fixed in one position.

Ions and electrons in a metal.

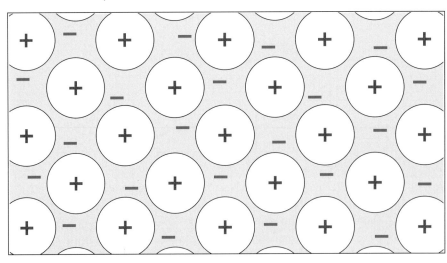

The metal cations are in a closely packed lattice – much closer than the diagram above shows.

Metals. Clockwise from top left: zinc, silver foil, lead shot, copper crystals.

REVIEW QUESTIONS

Q1 What happens to an isotope when it emits radioactivity and decays?

Q2 Where does all radioactivity come from in a radioactive isotope?

Q3 Name the three types of radioactivity?

Q4 What two metals make the alloy brass?

Q5 Why do silicon dioxide and diamond have similar properties?

More questions
on the CD ROM

Examination questions are on page 48.

4 STOICHIOMETRY

Videos & questions on the CD ROM

How are chemical formulae written?

All substances are made up from simple building blocks called **elements**. Each element has a unique **chemical symbol**, containing one or two letters. Elements discovered a long time ago often have symbols that don't seem to match their name. For example, silver has the chemical symbol Ag. This is derived from the Latin name for silver – 'argentum'.

When elements chemically combine they form **compounds**. A compound can be represented by a **chemical formula**.

Simple compounds

Many compounds contain just two elements. For example, when magnesium burns in oxygen a white ash of magnesium oxide is formed. To work out the chemical formula of magnesium oxide:

1 Write down the name of the compound.

2 Write down the chemical symbols for the elements in the compound.

3 Use the periodic table to find the 'combining power' of each element (see opposite). Write the combining power of each element under its symbol.

4 If the numbers can be cancelled down, do so.

5 Swap over the combining powers. Write them after the symbol, slightly below the line (as a 'subscript').

6 If any of the numbers are 1, you do not need to write them.

Magnesium oxide has the chemical formula you would have probably guessed.

What about calcium chloride?

1 Write down the name of the compound.

2 Write down the chemical symbols for the elements in the compound.

3 Use the periodic table to find the 'combining power' of each element. Write the combining power of each element under its symbol.

4 If the numbers can be cancelled down, do so.

5 Swap over the combining powers. Write them after the symbol, slightly below the line (as a subscript).

6 If any of the numbers are 1, there is no need to write them.

The chemical formula of a compound is not always immediately obvious, but if you follow these rules you will have no problems.

magnesium   oxide

Mg   O

2   2

1   1

Mg_1 O_1

MgO

calcium   chloride

Ca   Cl

2   1

(They don't cancel)

Ca_1 Cl_2

$CaCl_2$

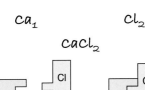

'Combining powers' of elements

There is a simple relationship between an element's **group number** in the periodic table and its combining power. Groups are the vertical columns in the periodic table.

Group number	I	2	3	4	5	6	7	0
Combining power	I	2	3	4	3	2	I	0

RULES FOR DETERMINING COMBINING POWER

Groups 1–4: combining power = group number.

Groups 5–0: combining power = 8 – (group number).

If an element is not in one of the main groups, its combining power will be included in the name of the compound containing it. For example, copper is a transition metal and is in the middle block of the periodic table. In copper(II) oxide, copper has a combining power of 2.

Sometimes an element does not have the combining power you would predict from its position in the periodic table. The combining power of these elements is also included in the name of the compound containing it. For example, phosphorus is in group 5, so you would expect it to have a combining power of 3, but in phosphorus(V) oxide its combining power is 5.

The only exception is hydrogen. Hydrogen is often not included in a Group, nor is its combining power given in the name of compounds containing hydrogen. It has a combining power of 1.

The combining power is linked to the **number of electrons** in the outer shell of the atom of the element.

Compounds containing more than two elements

Some elements exist bonded together in what is called a **radical**. For example, in copper(II) sulphate, the sulphate part of the compound is a radical.

There are a number of common radicals, each having its own combining power. You cannot work out these combining powers easily from the periodic table – you have to learn them. The shaded ones in the table below are the ones you are most likely to encounter at IGCSE.

Combining power = I		Combining power = 2		Combining power = 3	
hydroxide	OH	carbonate	CO_3	phosphate	PO_4
hydrogencarbonate HCO_3		sulphate	SO_4		
nitrate	NO_3				
ammonium	NH_4				

The same rules apply to radicals as to elements. For example:

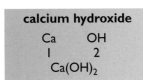

copper(II) sulphate		potassium nitrate	
Cu	SO$_4$	K	NO$_3$
2	2	1	1
CuSO$_4$		KNO$_3$	

If the formula contains **more than one radical unit**, the radical must be put in brackets. For example:

calcium hydroxide

Ca	OH
1	2
Ca(OH)$_2$	

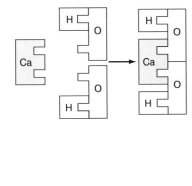

The brackets are used just as they are used in maths – the number outside the bracket multiplies everything inside it. Be careful how you use the brackets – for example, do not be tempted to write calcium hydroxide as CaOH$_2$ rather than Ca(OH)$_2$. This is incorrect.

CaOH$_2$ contains one Ca, one O, two H ✗

Ca(OH)$_2$ contains one Ca, two O, two H ✓

Writing chemical equations

In a **chemical equation** the starting chemicals are called the **reactants** and the finishing chemicals are called the **products**.

Follow these simple rules to write a chemical equation.

1   Write down the **word equation**.

2   Write down the **symbols** (for elements) and **formulae** (for compounds).

3   **Balance the equation**, to make sure there are the same number of each type of atom on each side of the equation.

Many elements are **diatomic**. They exist as molecules containing two atoms

Element	Form in which it exists
hydrogen	H$_2$
oxygen	O$_2$
nitrogen	N$_2$
chlorine	Cl$_2$
bromine	Br$_2$
iodine	I$_2$

The reaction between hydrogen and oxygen produces a lot of energy as well as water – enough to launch a rocket.

WORKED EXAMPLES

1 When a lighted splint is put into a test tube of hydrogen the hydrogen burns with a 'pop'. In fact the hydrogen reacts with oxygen in the air

Word equation: hydrogen + oxygen → water

Symbols and formulae: $H_2 + O_2 \rightarrow H_2O$

Balance the equation: $2H_2 + O_2 \rightarrow 2H_2O$

For every two molecules of hydrogen that react, one molecule of oxygen is needed and two molecules of water are formed.

$2H_2$	+	O_2	→	$2H_2O$
two molecules		one molecule		two molecules

(the reactants) to form water (the product). Write the chemical equation for this reaction.

2 What is the equation when natural gas (methane) burns in air to form carbon dioxide and water?

Word equation: methane + oxygen → carbon dioxide + water

Symbols and formulae: $CH_4 + O_2 \rightarrow CO_2 + H_2O$

Balance the equation: $CH_4 + 2O_2 \rightarrow CO_2 + 2H_2O$

Methane is burning in the oxygen in the air to form carbon dioxide and water.

Balancing equations

Balancing equations can be quite tricky. Basically it is done by trial and error. However, the golden rule is that **balancing numbers can only be put in front of the formulae.**

For example, to balance the equation for the reaction between methane and oxygen:

	Reactants	Products
Start with the unbalanced equation.	$CH_4 + O_2$	$CO_2 + H_2O$
Count the number of atoms on each side of the equation.	1C ✓, 4H, 2O	1C ✓, 2H, 3O
There is a need to increase the number of H atoms on the products side of the equation. Put a '2' in front of the H_2O.	$CH_4 + O_2$	$CO_2 + 2H_2O$
Count the number of atoms on each side of the equation again.	1C ✓, 4H ✓, 2O	1C ✓, 4H ✓, 4O
There is a need to increase the number of O atoms on the reactant side of the equation. Put a '2' in front of the O_2.	$CH_4 + 2O_2$	$CO_2 + 2H_2O$
Count the atoms on each side of the equation again.	1C ✓, 4H ✓, 4O ✓	1C ✓, 4H ✓, 4O ✓

No atoms have been created or destroyed in the reaction. The equation is balanced!

The number of each type of atom is the same on the left and right sides of the equation.

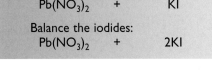

$$CH_4 + 2O_2 \rightarrow CO_2 + 2H_2O$$

In balancing equations involving **radicals** you can use the same procedure. For example, when lead(II) nitrate solution is mixed with potassium iodide solution, lead(II) iodide and potassium nitrate are produced.

1 Words:
   lead(II) nitrate + potassium iodide → lead(II) iodide + potassium nitrate

2 Symbols:
   $Pb(NO_3)_2$ + KI → PbI_2 + KNO_3

3 Balance the nitrates:
   $Pb(NO_3)_2$ + KI → PbI_2 + $2KNO_3$

   Balance the iodides:
   $Pb(NO_3)_2$ + 2KI → PbI_2 + $2KNO_3$

This reaction occurs simply on mixing the solutions of lead(II) nitrate and potassium iodide. Lead iodide is an insoluble yellow compound.

Ionic equations

Ionic equations show reactions involving **ions** (atoms or radicals that have lost or gained electrons). The size of the charge on an ion is the same as the combining power – whether it is positive or negative depends on which part of the periodic table the element is placed in.

In many ionic reactions some of the ions play no part in the reaction. These ions are called **spectator ions**. A simplified ionic equation can therefore be written, using only the important, reacting ions. In these equations, **state symbols** are often used and appear in brackets.

The equation must **balance** in terms of chemical symbols and charges.

State	State symbol
solid	(s)
liquid	(l)
gas	(g)
solution	(aq)

States and their symbols.

WORKED EXAMPLES

1 In the reaction given to produce lead(II) iodide, the potassium and nitrate ions are spectators – the important ions are the lead(II) ions and the iodide ions.

The simplified ionic equation is:

$Pb^{2+}(aq) + 2I^-(aq) \rightarrow PbI_2(s)$

Balance the equation:

	Reactants	Products
	$Pb^{2+}(aq) + 2I^-(aq)$	$PbI_2(s)$
symbols	1Pb ✓, 2I ✓	1Pb ✓, 2I ✓
charges	2^+ and $2^- = 0$ ✓	0 ✓

The equation shows that any solution containing lead(II) ions will react with any solution containing iodide ions to form lead(II) iodide.

2 Any solution containing copper(II) ions and any solution containing hydroxide ions can be used to make copper(II) hydroxide, which appears as a solid:

$$Cu^{2+}(aq) + 2OH^-(aq) \rightarrow Cu(OH)_2(s)$$

	Reactants	**Products**
	$Cu^{2+}(aq) + 2OH^-(aq)$	$Cu(OH)_2(s)$
symbols	1Cu ✓, 2O ✓, 2H ✓	1Cu ✓, 2O ✓, 2H ✓
charges	2^+ and $2^- = 0$ ✓	0 ✓

Copper hydroxide

Half equations

In electrolysis, the reactions at the electrodes can be shown as **half equations**.

For example, when copper is deposited at the **cathode** the half equation can be written as:

$$Cu^{2+}(aq) + 2e^- \rightarrow Cu(s)$$

The symbol e^- stands for an **electron**. At the cathode, positive ions gain electrons and become neutral. The equation must **balance** in terms of symbols and charges.

A typical reaction at the **anode** during electrolysis would be:

$$2Cl^-(aq) \rightarrow Cl_2(g) + 2e^-$$

In this reaction two chloride ions combine to form one molecule of chlorine, releasing two electrons.

Atomic masses and the mole

Atoms are far too light to be weighed. Instead scientists have developed a relative atomic mass scale. Initially the hydrogen atom, the lightest atom, was chosen as the unit that all other atoms were weighed in terms of.

On this scale, a carbon atom weighs the same as 12 hydrogen atoms, so carbon's relative atomic mass was given as 12.

Using this relative mass scale you can see, for example, that:

- 1 atom of magnesium has 24 × the mass of 1 atom of hydrogen
- 1 atom of magnesium has 2 × the mass of 1 atom of carbon
- 1 atom of copper has 2 × the mass of 1 atom of sulphur.

	Hydrogen	Carbon	Oxygen	Magnesium	Sulphur	Calcium	Copper
Symbol	H	C	O	Mg	S	Ca	Cu
Relative atomic mass	1	12	16	24	32	40	64

Recently, the reference point has been changed to carbon and the relative atomic mass is defined as:

> the mass of an atom on a scale where the mass of a carbon atom is 12 units.

This change does not really affect the work that is done at IGCSE. The relative atomic masses are not changed.

The mole concept

A mole is an amount equal to the number of atoms in 12g of ^{12}C. The mole is also a number of particles contained within a substance that is approximately 6×10^{23}, i.e. 600 000 000 000 000 000 000 000

6×10^{23} atoms of hydrogen have a mass of 1 g.

6×10^{23} atoms of carbon have a mass of 12 g.

6×10^{23} atoms of magnesium have a mass of 24 g.

These will all contain 1 mole of atoms

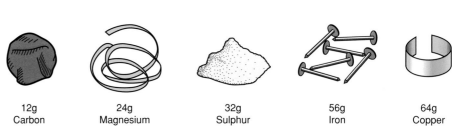

| 12g Carbon | 24g Magnesium | 32g Sulphur | 56g Iron | 64g Copper |

Calculations can be done using the simple equation:

$$\text{moles of atoms} = \frac{\text{mass}}{A_r}$$

1 How many moles of atoms are there in 72 g of magnesium?
(A_r of magnesium = 24)

Write down the formula:	moles	=	$\dfrac{mass}{A_r}$
Rearrange if necessary:			(None needed)
Substitute the numbers:	moles	=	$\dfrac{72}{24}$
Write the answer and units:	moles	=	3 moles

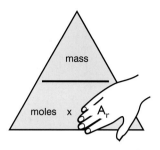

Put your finger over the quantity you are trying to work out.
The triangle will then tell you whether to multiply or divide the other quantities.

2 What is the mass of 0.1 moles of carbon atoms?
(A_r of carbon = 12)

Write down the formula:	moles	=	$\dfrac{mass}{A_r}$
Rearrange if necessary:	mass	=	moles $\times A_r$
Substitute the numbers:	mass	=	0.1×12
Write the answer and units:	mass	=	1.2 g

How do we work out chemical formulae?

When chemists are investigating a compound, one of the first things they want to know is its chemical formula. One way of doing this is to find the mass of each element in the compound and then use the mole to find out the chemical formula. An example of how this is done is shown below.

Making magnesium oxide

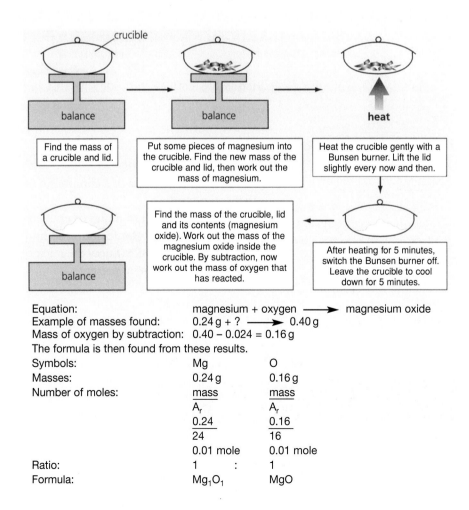

Equation: magnesium + oxygen ⟶ magnesium oxide
Example of masses found: 0.24 g + ? ⟶ 0.40 g
Mass of oxygen by subtraction: 0.40 − 0.024 = 0.16 g
The formula is then found from these results.

Symbols:	Mg	O
Masses:	0.24 g	0.16 g
Number of moles:	$\dfrac{mass}{A_r}$	$\dfrac{mass}{A_r}$
	$\dfrac{0.24}{24}$	$\dfrac{0.16}{16}$
	0.01 mole	0.01 mole
Ratio:	1 :	1
Formula:	Mg_1O_1	MgO

WORKED EXAMPLES

1 Find the formula of the oxide of carbon formed when 0.3 g carbon reacts with 0.8 g oxygen (C=12, O=16)

symbols	C		O
masses:	0.3 g		0.8 g
moles:	$\dfrac{0.3}{12}$		$\dfrac{0.8}{16}$
	0.025		0.05
ratio:	1	:	2
formula:		CO_2	

2 A compound was found to contain 52.2% carbon, 13.0% hydrogen and 34.8% oxygen by mass. Find its simplest formula (C = 12, H = 1, O = 16).

When a question gives a percentage by mass, assume that 100 g of the compound is present, and use the individual percentage figures to calculate the number of moles.

symbols:	C		H		O
masses:	52.2 g		13.0 g		34.8 g
number of moles:	$\dfrac{52.2}{12}$		$\dfrac{13.0}{1}$		$\dfrac{34.8}{16}$
	4.35		13.0		2.18
ratio:	2	:	6	:	1
formula:	C_2H_6O				

What is the difference between empirical and molecular formulae?

The **empirical formula** of a compound is the simplest ratio of elements in that compound.

The actual number of moles of each element in one mole of a compound is known as the **molecular formula**. To find the molecular formula of a compound, you need to know the mass of one mole as well as the amount of each individual element present.

WORKED EXAMPLE

A sugar with a molar mass of 180 was found to contain 40.0% carbon, 6.67% hydrogen and 53.33% oxygen by mass. Find its empirical formula and its molecular formula (C = 12, H = 1, O = 16).

symbols:	C		H		O
mass:	40.0 g		6.67 g		53.33 g
moles:	$\dfrac{40.0}{12}$		$\dfrac{6.67}{1}$		$\dfrac{53.33}{16}$
	3.33		6.67		3.33
ratio:	1	:	2	:	1

empirical formula (simplest ratio): CH_2O

find mass of empirical formula: $\dfrac{12 + 2 + 16}{30}$

compare with M_r: 180

M_r is six times the mass of the empirical formula

molecular formula is therefore six times the empirical formula: $C_6H_{12}O_6$

Can the mole be applied to molecules?

Substances that have molecular structures can also be measured in moles. A mole of molecules always contains 6.023×10^{23} molecules, and its mass can be calculated from the relative molar mass of the substance.

Cl_2
35.5 + 35.5
71 g = M_r

one mole of chlorine molecules contains 6.023×10^{23} molecules

H_2O
1 + 1 + 16
M_r = 18 g

one mole of water molecules contains 6.023×10^{23} molecules

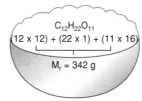

$C_{12}H_{22}O_{11}$
(12 x 12) + (22 x 1) + (11 x 16)
M_r = 342 g

one mole of sugar molecules contains 6.023×10^{23} molecules

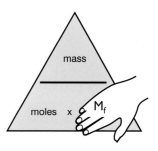

mass

moles x M_f

Put your finger over the quantity you are trying to work out.

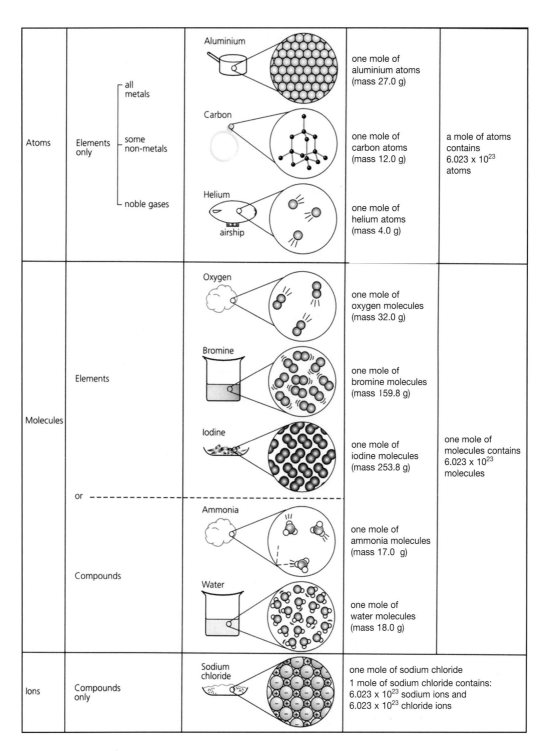

Atoms	Elements only	all metals / some non-metals / noble gases	Aluminium	one mole of aluminium atoms (mass 27.0 g)	a mole of atoms contains 6.023×10^{23} atoms
			Carbon	one mole of carbon atoms (mass 12.0 g)	
			Helium — airship	one mole of helium atoms (mass 4.0 g)	
Molecules	Elements		Oxygen	one mole of oxygen molecules (mass 32.0 g)	one mole of molecules contains 6.023×10^{23} molecules
			Bromine	one mole of bromine molecules (mass 159.8 g)	
			Iodine	one mole of iodine molecules (mass 253.8 g)	
	or Compounds		Ammonia	one mole of ammonia molecules (mass 17.0 g)	
			Water	one mole of water molecules (mass 18.0 g)	
Ions	Compounds only		Sodium chloride	one mole of sodium chloride 1 mole of sodium chloride contains: 6.023×10^{23} sodium ions and 6.023×10^{23} chloride ions	

Chemists working in the laboratory need to measure out many different amounts of compounds. Varying amounts of compounds can be measured in moles in a similar way to previous calculations by using the formula

$$\text{number of moles} = \frac{\text{mass}}{M_r}$$

This can be arranged to give:

$$\text{mass} = \text{number of moles} \times M_r$$

WORKED EXAMPLES

1　How many moles are there in 27 g of water, formula H_2O?

These calculations involve two steps. The first step is to calculate the M_r. The second is to use this value to find the number of moles.

find the M_r of water:　H_2　　　　O
　　　　　　　　　　(1+1)　+　16
　　　　　　　　　　　　18

find moles of water:　moles　=　$\dfrac{\text{mass}}{M_r}$

　　　　　　　　　　　　=　$\dfrac{27}{18}$

　　　　　　　　　　　　=　1.5 moles

2　What is the mass of 0.025 moles of calcium carbonate, formula $CaCO_3$?

find the M_r:　　　Ca　　C　O_3
　　　　　　　　　40　　12　(3 x 16)
　　　　　　　　　　　　100

find mass:　　　mass　=　moles x M_r
　　　　　　　　　　=　0.025 x 100
　　　　　　　　　　=　2.5 g

5　Calculate the mass of:

a　0.02 moles of water, H_2O

b　0.004 moles of calcium carbonate, $CaCO_3$

c　2.5 moles of sulphuric acid, H_2SO_4

The mole in gases and solutions

HOW CAN THE NUMBER OF MOLES OF A GAS BE CALCULATED?

In many chemical reactions gases react or are given off. If the number of moles of a gas can be found then formulae and equations for reactions involving gases can be written.

It is possible to find the mass of a gas, and turn this into moles using the equations described earlier in the chapter. For a dense gas like carbon dioxide, this can be quite accurate, but for gases of a low density like hydrogen the measurements might not be very accurate.

The most useful way to measure the amount of a gas is to find its volume at a particular temperature. At 273 K and one atmosphere of pressure one mole of any gas occupies 22.4 dm^3 (or 22 400 cm^3). These conditions are known as standard temperature and pressure (often shortened to 'STP'). At room temperature and pressure (this is usually taken to be 293 K and one atmosphere pressure) one mole of any gas will occupy 24 dm^3.

One mole of gas occupies ...

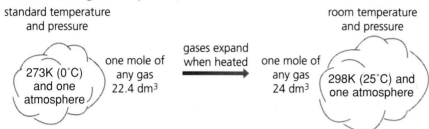

One mole of any gas.

One mole of any gas will always contain Avogadro's number (6.023×10^{23}) of atoms or molecules. Equal volumes of all gases at the same temperature and pressure will always contain equal numbers of molecules. This is known as **Avogadro's law.**

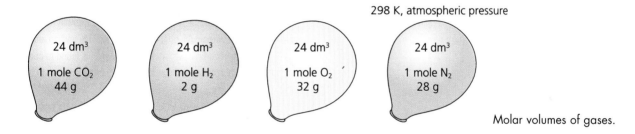

Molar volumes of gases.

$$\text{The number of moles of a gas} \quad = \quad \frac{\text{volume of gas}}{\text{volume of 1 mole}}$$

At room temperature and pressure one mole of a gas:

$$\text{mole of a gas} \quad = \quad 24\ 000\ (\text{cm}^3)$$

This equation can be rearranged as follows:

$$\text{volume} \quad = \quad \text{moles} \times 24\ 000$$

WORKED EXAMPLES

1 How many moles are present in 336cm^3 of nitrogen gas?

$$\text{Number of moles} \quad = \quad \frac{\text{volume}}{24\ 000}$$

$$= \quad \frac{336}{24\ 000}$$

$$= \quad 0.014\ \text{moles}$$

2 What volume is occupied by 0.02 moles of carbon dioxide gas at room temperature and pressure?

volume = moles x 24 000

   = 0.02 x 24 000

   = 480 cm^3

How are moles measured in solutions?

Many chemicals are used in the laboratory as aqueous solutions – that is, dissolved in water. Chemists usually measure how concentrated a solution is by finding out how many moles of a substance are dissolved in each litre of solvent.

The number of moles of substance contained in each litre of a solution is called its concentration. If one mole of any substance is dissolved in water and then made up to a volume of one litre it produces a '1 mol/dm^3 solution'. By dissolving different amounts of solid in water and making the volume up to one litre solutions of different concentrations can be prepared.

Making a 1 mol/dm^3 solution.

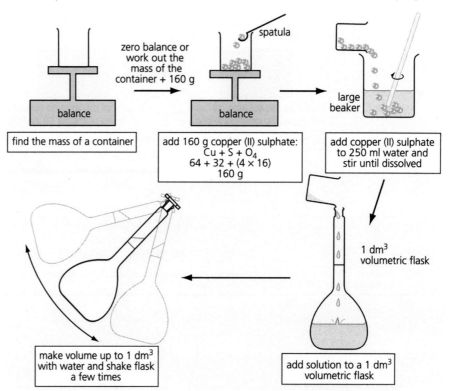

The following equation can be used to find the number of moles of substance in an aqueous solution:

$$\text{number of moles} = \frac{\text{volume of solution (cm}^3\text{)} \times \text{mol/dm}^3}{1000}$$

this can be rearranged to give

$$\text{volume of solution (cm}^3\text{)} = \frac{\text{moles} \times 1000}{\text{mol/dm}^3}$$

or

$$\text{mol/dm}^3 = \frac{\text{moles} \times 1000}{\text{volume}}$$

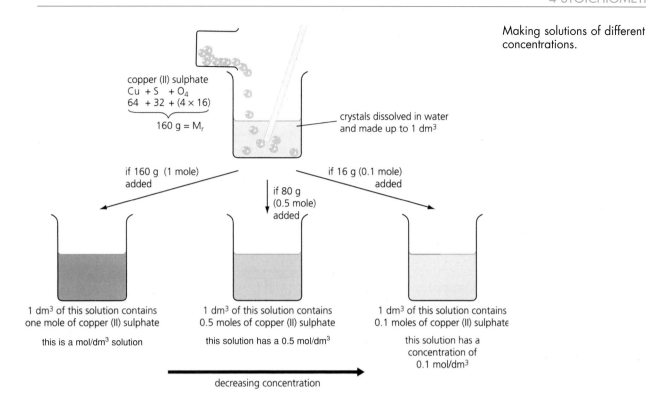

Making solutions of different concentrations.

copper (II) sulphate
$Cu + S + O_4$
$64 + 32 + (4 \times 16)$
$160 \text{ g} = M_r$

crystals dissolved in water and made up to 1 dm³

if 160 g (1 mole) added

if 80 g (0.5 mole) added

if 16 g (0.1 mole) added

1 dm³ of this solution contains one mole of copper (II) sulphate

this is a mol/dm³ solution

1 dm³ of this solution contains 0.5 moles of copper (II) sulphate

this solution has a 0.5 mol/dm³

1 dm³ of this solution contains 0.1 moles of copper (II) sulphate

this solution has a concentration of 0.1 mol/dm³

decreasing concentration

WORKED EXAMPLES

1 How many moles are present in 200cm³ of a 2.0 mol/dm³ solution of hydrochloric acid?

$$\text{moles} = \frac{\text{volume} \quad x \quad \text{mol/dm}^3}{1000}$$

$$\frac{200 \quad x \quad 2.0}{1000}$$

$$= \quad 0.4 \text{ moles}$$

2 What volume of 0.25 mol/dm³ copper (II) sulphate solution would contain 0.5 moles?

$$\text{volume} = \frac{\text{moles} \quad x \quad 1000}{\text{mol/dm}^3}$$

$$= \frac{0.5 \quad x \quad 1000}{0.25}$$

$$= \quad 2000 \text{ cm}^3 \text{ or 2 dm}^3$$

3 What is the concentration of 100 cm³ of a solution of sodium chloride containing 0.04 moles?

$$\text{mol/dm}^3 = \frac{\text{moles} \quad x \quad 1000}{\text{volume}}$$

$$= \frac{0.04 \quad x \quad 1000}{100} \quad = \quad 0.4 \text{ M}$$

4 What is the concentration of 200 cm^3 of an aqueous solution containing 2.02g of potassium nitrate (KNO_3)?

First find the number of moles of potassium nitrate:

M_r

K   N O_3

39 + 14 + (3 x 16)

101

moles = $\dfrac{mass}{M_r}$

= $\dfrac{2.02}{101}$

= 0.02 moles

mol/dm^3 = $\dfrac{moles \quad x \quad 1000}{volume}$

= $\dfrac{0.02 \quad x \quad 1000}{200}$

= 0.1 mol/dm^3

How can concentration be calculated using titration?

Sulphuric acid can be neutralised by alkalis such as sodium hydroxide as follows:

$$H_2SO_4(aq) \ + \ 2NaOH(aq) \ \rightarrow \ Na_2SO_4(aq) \ + \ 2H_2O(l)$$

The exact volumes of sodium hydroxide needed to neutralise a particular volume of sulphuric acid can be measured by titration (see opposite). When the concentration of one solution is known, a titration can be used to find the concentration of the other solution.

WORKED EXAMPLE

25.0 cm^3 of sodium hydroxide solution was neutralsed by 15.0cm^{3}0.10 M suphuric acid. Use this information to find the concentration of the alkali.

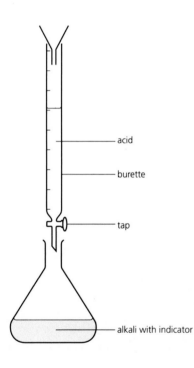

acid

burette

tap

alkali with indicator

select relevant substances from equation: $H_2SO_4 \ \rightarrow \ 2NaOH$

molar ratio: 1 : 2

find moles of acid: moles = $\dfrac{volume \ x \ mol/dm^3}{1000}$

= $\dfrac{15.0 \quad x \quad 0.1}{1000}$

= 0.0015 moles

use molar ratio to find moles of alkali: 0.0015 moles H_2SO_4 0.003 moles NaOH

find concentration of alkali: mol/dm^3 = $\dfrac{moles \ x \ 1000}{volume}$

$\dfrac{0.003 \quad x \quad 1000}{25}$

= 0.12 mol/dm^3

Percentage yield and percentage purity

When a chemical is being made by a reaction in the laboratory the general process is:

1   Turn the reactants into products. Reactants → products

2   Separate out the product you want from any others

3   Purify the product

In this process of producing the required pure product there will be some loss of the product. The amount of product made is called the **yield**.

If all the reactants were successfully converted to the product and there was no loss when it was purified there would be a '100% yield' of the product. This is rare.

There is an equation, using **moles**, that is used to calculate **percentage yield**:

$$\text{Percentage yield} = \frac{\text{actual yield}}{\text{maximum yield}} \times 100$$

The example below shows how this is done.

WORKED EXAMPLE

In the preparation of bromoethane (C_2H_5Br) from ethanol (C_2H_5OH) the reaction is:

C_2H_5OH + HBr	→	C_2H_5Br +	H_2O
I mole + I mole	→	I mole +	I mole
46 g + 8I g	→	109 g +	I8 g

so 46 g C_2H_5OH should make 109 g C_2H_5Br if it was all successfully converted.

In an experiment, starting with 10 g C_2H_5OH the amount of C_2H_5Br made was 16 g. What is the percentage yield?

$$\text{Moles } C_2H_5OH = \frac{10}{46} = 0.217$$

Since the equation is 1 mole → 1 mole, maximum yield C_2H_5Br = 0.217

$$\text{Actual yield } C_2H_5Br = \frac{16}{109} = 0.147$$

$$\text{Percentage yield} = \frac{\text{actual yield}}{\text{maximum yield}} \times 100$$

$$= \frac{0.147}{0.217} \times 100 = 67.74\%$$

In a similar way, there is a concept called **percentage purity** but this can use **masses** instead of moles.

The equation is:

$$\text{Percentage purity} = \frac{\text{mass of pure product}}{\text{mass of impure product}} \times 100$$

The following example shows how this works.

WORKED EXAMPLE

A sample of impure common salt (sodium chloride) had a mass of 5.6 g. When purified, the mass of sodium chloride produced was 4.2 g. What is the percentage purity?

$$\text{Percentage purity} = \frac{\text{pure}}{\text{impure}} \times 100$$

$$= \frac{4.2}{5.6} \times 100 = 75.0\%$$

REVIEW QUESTIONS

Q1 Work out the chemical formulae of the following compounds:
a sodium chloride
b magnesium fluoride
c aluminium nitride
d lithium oxide
e carbon oxide (carbon dioxide).

Q2 Work out the chemical formulae of the following compounds:
a iron(III) oxide
b phosphorus(V) chloride
c chromium(III) bromide
d sulphur(VI) oxide (sulphur trioxide)
e sulphur(IV) oxide (sulphur dioxide).

Q3 Work out the chemical formulae of the following compounds:
a potassium carbonate
b ammonium chloride
c sulphuric acid
d magnesium hydroxide
e ammonium sulphate.

Q4 Write symbol equations from the following word equations:
a carbon + oxygen → carbon dioxide
b iron + oxygen → iron(III) oxide
c iron(III) oxide + carbon → iron + carbon dioxide
d calcium carbonate + hydrochloric acid → calcium chloride + carbon dioxide + water.

Q5 Write ionic equations for the following reactions:
a calcium ions and carbonate ions form calcium carbonate
b iron(II) ions and hydroxide ions form iron(II) hydroxide
c silver(I) ions and bromide ions form silver(I) bromide.

Q6 Write half equations for the following reactions:
a the formation of aluminium atoms from aluminium ions
b the formation of sodium ions from sodium atoms
c the formation of oxygen from oxide ions
d the formation of bromine from bromide ions.

REVIEW QUESTIONS

Q7 Calculate the number of moles in the following:
a 56 g of silicon (Si = 28)
b 3.1 g of phosphorus (P = 31)
c 11 g of carbon dioxide, CO_2 (C = 12, O = 16)
d 50 g of calcium carbonate, $CaCO_3$ (Ca = 40, C = 12, O = 16)

Q8 Calculate the mass of the following:
a 2 moles of magnesium atoms (Mg = 24)
b 2 moles of hydrogen molecules, H_2 (H = 1)
c 0.1 moles of sulphuric acid, H_2SO_4 (H = 1, O = 16, S = 32)

Q9 Titanium chloride contains 25% titanium and 75% chlorine by mass. Work out the simplest formula of titanium chloride. (Ti = 48, Cl = 35.5)

Q10 Calculate the formulae of the following compounds:
a 2.3 g of sodium reacting with 8.0 g of bromine (Na = 23, Br = 80).
b 0.6 g of carbon reacting with oxygen to make 2.2 g of compound
c 11.12 g of iron reacting with chlorine to make 18.22 g of compound

Q11 What mass of sodium hydroxide can be made by reacting 2.3 g of sodium with water? (H = 1, O = 16, Na = 23)
$$2Na(s) + 2H_2O(l) \rightarrow 2NaOH(aq) + H_2(g)$$

Q12 Iron(III) oxide is reduced to iron by carbon monoxide. (C = 12, O = 16, Fe = 56)
$$Fe_2O_3(s) + 3CO(g) \rightarrow 2Fe(s) + 3CO_2(g)$$

a Calculate the mass of iron that could be obtained by the reduction of 800 tonnes of iron(III) oxide.
b What volume of carbon dioxide would be obtained by the reduction of 320 g of iron(III) oxide?

Q13 What mass of barium sulphate can be produced from 50 cm^3 of 0.2 M barium chloride solution and excess sodium sulphate solution?
(O = 16, S = 32, Ba = 137)
$$BaCl_2(aq) + Na_2SO_4(aq) \rightarrow BaSO_4(s) + 2NaCl(aq)$$

Q14 An impure sample of solid X has a mass of 1.20g. After purification the mass of pure X obtained was 0.80g. What was the percentage purity of the original sample?

More questions on the CD ROM

Examination questions are on page 48.

EXAMINATION QUESTIONS

Q1 The structures of some substances are shown below.

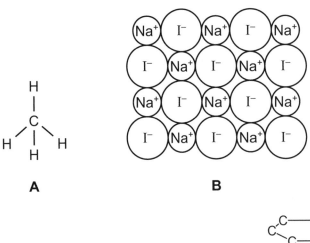

A   B   C

H — Br

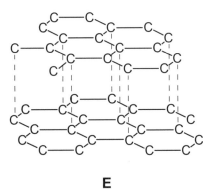

D   E

a   Answer these questions using the letters **A**, **B**, **C**, **D** or **E**.
    i   Which structure is methane? _____ [1]
    ii   Which two structures are giant structures? _____ and _____ [1]
    iii   Which two structures are hydrocarbons? _____ and _____ [1]
    iv   Which structure contains ions? _____ [1]
    v   Which two structures have very high melting points?
                          _____ and _____ [1]

b   Structure **E** is a form of carbon.
    i   What is the name of this structure? Put a ring around the correct answer.
      carbide _____ graphite _____ lead _____ poly(hexene)   [1]
    ii   Name another form of carbon.
      _____ [1]

c   Write the simplest formula for substance **B**.
    _____ [1]

d   Is substance **D** an element or a compound? Explain your answer.   [1]
    _____ [1]
    _____ [1]

Q2 A student collected some water from a polluted river.
    The water contained soluble solids and insoluble clay and had a pH of 5.
    a   How can the student separate the clay from the rest of the river water?
      _____ [1]

    b   The student uses litmus paper to show that the river water is acidic.
      What will be the result of this test?
      _____ [1]

c The student then boiled the river water to obtain the soluble solids.
   The diagram shows how she heated the water.

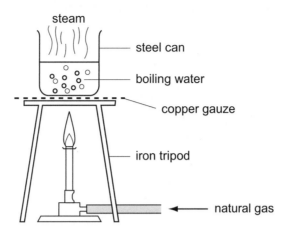

Which of the substances named in the diagram is
i   an alloy, _____ [1]
ii a compound which is liquid at room temperature, _____ [1]
iii an element, _____ [1]
iv a fuel? _____ [1]

d Name the main substance in natural gas.
   _____ [1]

e What is the normal temperature of boiling water?
   _____ [1]

f After the student boiled off the water, she analysed the white powder on the inside
   of the steel can. The table shows her results.

name of ion	formula of ion	mass of ion present /milligrams
calcium	Ca^{2+}	16
carbonate	CO_3^{2-}	35
chloride	Cl^-	8
nitrate	NO_3^-	4
sodium	Na^+	8
sulphate	SO_4^{2-}	6

i   Which positive ion had the greatest concentration in the sample of river water?
    _____ [1]

ii Complete the following equation to show how a sodium ion is formed from a
    $Na \rightarrow Na^+ +$ _____ [1]

g Instead of using natural gas, the student could have used butane to heat the water.
   The formula of butane is C_4H_{10}.
   i   What products are formed when butane burns in excess air?
       _____ [1]

   ii Name the poisonous gas formed when butane undergoes incomplete combustion.
       _____ [1]

49

Q3 A student investigated an aqueous solution of calcium hydroxide and water.
Two experiments were carried out.

Experiment 1
By using a measuring cylinder 25 cm³ of the aqueous solution of calcium hydroxide was placed in a flask. Phenolphthalein indicator was added to the flask. A burette was filled to the 0.0 cm³ mark with solution **M** of hydrochloric acid. Solution **M** was added slowly to the flask until the colour just disappeared. Use the burette diagram to record the volume in the table and complete the column.

Experiment 2
Experiment 1 was repeated using a different solution, **N**, of hydrochloric acid. Use the burette diagrams to record the volumes in the table and complete the table.

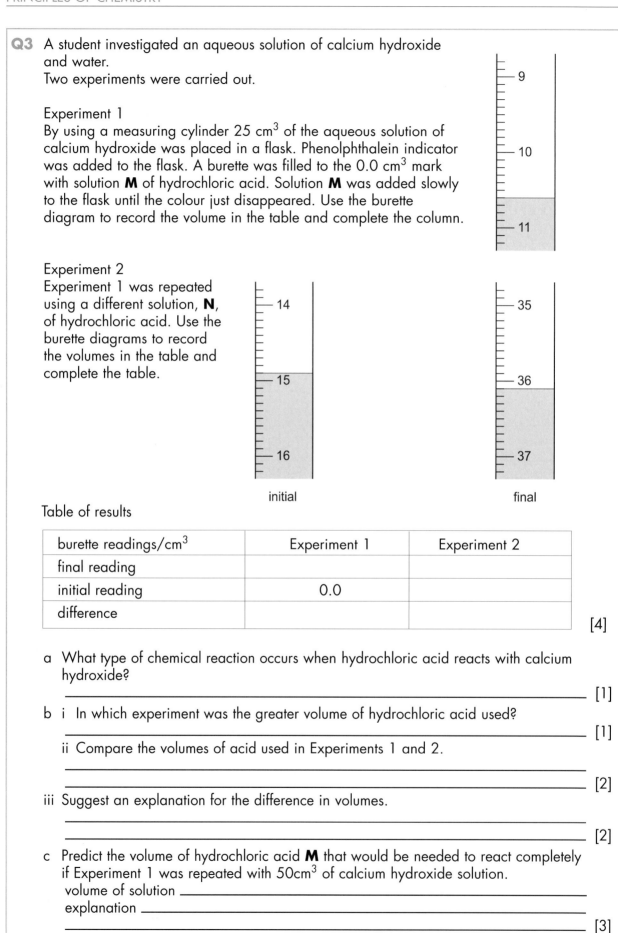

initial   final

Table of results

burette readings/cm³	Experiment 1	Experiment 2
final reading		
initial reading	0.0	
difference		

[4]

a What type of chemical reaction occurs when hydrochloric acid reacts with calcium hydroxide?

_____ [1]

b i In which experiment was the greater volume of hydrochloric acid used?

_____ [1]

ii Compare the volumes of acid used in Experiments 1 and 2.

_____
_____ [2]

iii Suggest an explanation for the difference in volumes.

_____
_____ [2]

c Predict the volume of hydrochloric acid **M** that would be needed to react completely if Experiment 1 was repeated with 50cm³ of calcium hydroxide solution.
volume of solution _____
explanation _____
_____ [3]

d Suggest **one** change you could make to the **apparatus** used in the experiments to obtain more accurate results.

_____

_____ [1]

Q4 The label below is from a bottle of concentrated lemon drink.

> **Concentrated lemon drink**
> Ingredients: Water, sugar, citric acid, preservatives, potassium sorbate (artificial sweetener). Yellow colourings E102 and E104.

a What is meant by the term *concentrated*?

_____ [1]

b Predict the pH of the lemon drink.

_____ [1]

c Describe an experiment to show that two different yellow colourings are present in the drink.

Q5 Read the following instructions for the preparation of hydrated nickel(II) sulphate $(NiSO_4.7H_2O)$, then answer the questions which follow.

1 Put 25 cm^3 of dilute sulphuric acid in a beaker.
2 Heat the sulphuric acid until it is just boiling then add a small amount of nickel(II) carbonate.
3 When the nickel(II) carbonate has dissolved, stop heating, then add a little more nickel carbonate. Continue in this way until nickel(II) carbonate is in excess.
4 Filter the hot mixture into a clean beaker.
5 Make the hydrated nickel(II) sulphate crystals from the nickel(II) sulphate solution.

The equation for the reaction is

$$NiCO_3(s) + H_2SO_4(aq) \rightarrow NiSO_4(aq) + CO_2(g) + H_2O(l)$$

a What piece of apparatus would you use to measure out 25cm^3 of sulphuric acid?

_____ [1]

b Why is the nickel(II) carbonate added in excess?

_____ [1]

c When nickel(II) carbonate is added to sulphuric acid, there is a fizzing. Explain why there is a fizzing.

_____ [1]

d Draw a diagram to describe step 4.
You must label your diagram.

_____ [3]

e After filtration, which one of the following describes the nickel(II) sulphate in the beaker?
Put a ring around the correct answer.

crystals   filtrate   precipitate   water   [1]

f Explain how you would obtain pure dry crystals of hydrated nickel(II) sulphate from the solution of nickel(II) sulphate.

_____

_____ [2]

g When hydrated nickel(II) sulphate is heated gently in a test tube, it changes colour from green to white.

   i Complete the symbol equation for this reaction.

   $NiSO_4.7H_2O(s)$ $NiSO_4(s)$ + _____ [1]

   ii What does the sign $\rightleftharpoons$ mean?

   _____ [1]

   iii How can you obtain a sample of green nickel(II) sulphate starting with white nickel(II) sulphate?

   _____ [1]

Q6 The salt copper(II) sulphate can be prepared by reacting copper(II) oxide with sulphuric acid.

Complete the list of instructions for making copper(II) sulphate using six of the words below.

blue   cool   dilute   filter   saturated   sulphate   white   oxide

Instructions

1 Add excess copper(II) oxide to [_____] sulphuric acid in a beaker and boil it.

2 [_____] to remove the unreacted copper(II) oxide.

3 Heat the solution until it is [_____].

4 [_____] the solution to form [_____] coloured crystals of copper(II). [6]

Q7 Strontium and sulphur chlorides both have a formula of the type XCl_2 but they have different properties.

property	strontium chloride	sulphur chloride
appearance	white crystalline solid	red liquid
melting point /°C	873	-80
particles present	ions	molecules
electrical conductivity of solid	poor	poor
electrical conductivity of liquid	good	poor

a The formulae of the chlorides are similar because both elements have a valency of 2. Explain why Group II and Group VI elements both have a valency of 2.

[_____]

[_____] [2]

b Draw a diagram showing the arrangement of the valency electrons in one covalent molecule of sulphur chloride. Use x to represent an electron from a sulphur atom. Use o to represent an electron from a chlorine atom.

[3]

c   Explain the difference in electrical conductivity between the following.
   i   solid and liquid strontium chloride

[1]

   ii   liquid strontium chloride and liquid sulphur chloride

[1]

Q8 a i   Write a symbol equation for the action of heat on zinc hydroxide.

[2]

   ii   Describe what happens when solid sodium hydroxide is heated strongly.

[1]

 b   What would be observed when copper(II) nitrate is heated?

[3]

 c   Iron(III) sulphate decomposes when heated. Calculate the mass of iron(III) oxide formed and the volume of sulphur trioxide produced when 10.0 g of iron(III) sulphate was heated. Mass of one mole of $Fe_2(SO_4)_3$ is 400g.

$$Fe_2(SO_4)_3 \text{ (s)} \qquad Fe_2O_3 \text{ (s)} + 3SO_3 \text{ (g)}$$

Number of moles of $Fe_2(SO_4)_3$ =

Number of moles of Fe_2O_3 formed =

Mass of iron(III) oxide formed =   g

Number of moles of SO_3 produced =

Volume of sulphur trioxide at r.t.p. = dm^3 [5]

big

small

PARTICLE SIZE
– the reactants can collide more often

TEMPERATURE
– the particles move more quickly and
collide more often

low

high

CONCENTRATION
– more particles means more chances
of collisions

low

high

Speeding up and slowing down

In villages all over Asia, people do their daily cooking over fires, which provide heat. In cooking we're using fire to control a chemical process. Without the chemical processes of cooking, we couldn't eat most meat, or plants like rice; or like cassava, which is poisonous if it's not cooked. But if you don't stop the process at the right time, the food becomes inedible again – the process of cooking is all about the rates of reaction. In addition to temperature, rates of reaction are affected by particle size, concentration, the presence of a catalyst and pressure (if gases).

PHYSICAL CHEMISTRY

5 ELECTRICITY AND CHEMISTRY

Electricity from chemical reactions

Many chemical reactions involve energy changes, and often heat or light is given off. It is possible in some cases to arrange the apparatus and chemicals so that much of this energy is turned into an electrical current. A **cell** is a simple device to turn chemical energy into electrical energy. A simple cell was invented by Daniell to use the reaction between zinc metal and copper (II) sulphate solution to provide electrical energy. When this reaction is carried out in a test tube, a displacement reaction happens and heat is given off.

Symbol equation: $Zn(s) + CuSO_4 (aq) \rightarrow ZnSO_4(aq) + Cu(s)$

Ionic equation: $Zn(s) + Cu^{2+}(aq) \rightarrow Zn^{2+}(aq) + Cu(s)$

Each zinc atom gives away two electrons to a Cu^{2+} ion. Zinc has a greater tendency to give away electrons than copper, which makes it a better reducing agent. Copper ions are reduced to copper metal and zinc atoms are oxidised into Zn^{2+} ions.

When copper and zinc are used as electrodes in a Daniell cell and the two solutions have a concentration of $1.0 mol/dm^3$, then a potential difference of about 1.1V is set up.

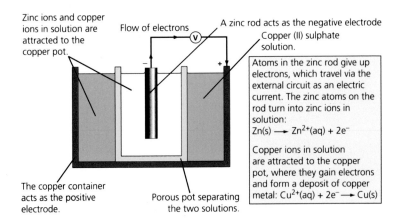

Zinc ions and copper ions in solution are attracted to the copper pot.

Flow of electrons

A zinc rod acts as the negative electrode

Copper (II) sulphate solution.

Atoms in the zinc rod give up electrons, which travel via the external circuit as an electric current. The zinc atoms on the rod turn into zinc ions in solution:
$Zn(s) \rightarrow Zn^{2+}(aq) + 2e^-$

Copper ions in solution are attracted to the copper pot, where they gain electrons and form a deposit of copper metal: $Cu^{2+}(aq) + 2e^- \rightarrow Cu(s)$

The copper container acts as the positive electrode.

Porous pot separating the two solutions.

Other pairs of metals can be used to form similar cells. The more reactive metal of the pair will lose electrons to the ions of the less reactive metal. When metals are near each other, on the reactivity series, the potential difference set up is small. For example, a cell using zinc and iron (which have similar reactivities) will set up a potential difference of only 0.32V but a cell involving magnesium and silver (which have very different reactivities) would set up a potential difference of 3.2V.

How are cells used?

LEAD ACID BATTERY

A **battery** is a series of individual cells that are combined. The battery that provides electrical energy for vehicles is known as a **lead–acid accumulator**. When the vehicle is started the battery provides an electric current to help start the engine. Once the engine is running it drives a small dynamo which produces an electric current to recharge the battery. The battery itself consists of a series of plates of lead alternating with a grid of lead packed with lead(IV) oxide. The plates dip into dilute sulphuric acid.

These batteries are very heavy, and one of the problems of electric-powered vehicles is the mass of the batteries. However, electric vehicles are quiet and do not produce harmful exhaust fumes. Although lead and its compounds are poisonous, used batteries do not normally cause pollution problems. Since lead is a valuable metal, nearly all the lead in old discarded batteries is recovered.

ZINC CARBON DRY CELLS

The everyday 'batteries' that we use to power calculators or torches are often **Zinc–carbon dry cells**. The electrolyte in a dry cell is kept just moist, and there is no risk of spilling aqueous solutions. In this cell the zinc casing acts as the negative electrode and is gradually dissolved away. When the battery is flat, the zinc is nearly all used up. It is important at this stage to remove the battery from electrical equipment, or the wet paste inside may leak out and cause damage. Once the battery has gone flat it must be thrown away.

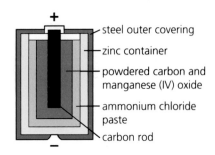

SILVER-OXIDE CELLS

The tiny 'button' cells in watches and cameras are also a type of dry cell, containing zinc and silver oxide. The high price of silver and its compounds makes these rather expensive, but they do last for a long time, because generally watches and cameras need only a small current.

ALKALINE CELLS

'Alkaline' cells are similar to zinc-carbon dry batteries, but the electrolyte contains alkaline potassium hydroxide and the zinc electrode is made slightly porous. Alkaline cells provide a greater current and last longer than zinc-carbon dry cells.

RECHARGEABLE CELLS

One type of rechargeable cell contains cadmium and nickel compounds. A redox reaction occurs to produce an electric current when the cell is in use. When the the cell is connected to a recharger an electric current is passed through. This reverses the reaction and recharges the cell.

FUEL CELLS

Fuel cells use the energy from fuels to provide electrical energy. A fuel such as hydrogen or methane is passed into the cell together with oxygen. These are made to react via the external circuit to provide an electric current. Although fuel cells are expensive to construct, provided the fuel is continually passed in, the cell will continue to provide an electric current. Fuel cells are used in spacecraft to provide a constant source of electrical energy.

The electrolysis of molten lead bromide

Lead(II) bromide, $PbBr_2$, is an ionic binary salt made of the ions Pb^{2+} and $2 \times Br^-$.

When molten, the ions are free to move and migrate to the oppositely charged electrode where the ions are turned into atoms or molecules.

The equations of electrolysis are:

Cathode (-) $Pb^{2+} + 2e^- \rightarrow Pb$

Anode (+) $2Br^- \rightarrow Br_2 + 2e^-$

The electrolysis of concentrated hydrochloric acid

Hydrochloric acid is a strong acid and ionises,

$HCl \rightarrow H^+ + Cl^-$

These ions migrate to the oppositely charged electrode and turn into molecules.

The equations of electrolysis are:

Cathode (-) $2H^+ + 2e^- \rightarrow H_2$

Anode (+) $2Cl^- \rightarrow Cl_2 + 2e-$

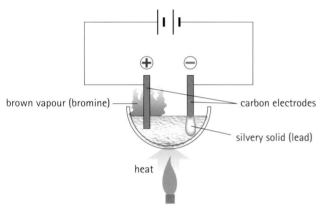

Electrolysis of molten lead bromide.

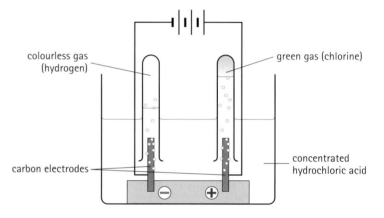

Electrolysis of concentrated hydrochloric acid.

Does the electrode material affect the outcome?

When copper (II) sulphate solution is elecrolysed using carbon electrodes, the following processes occur.

AT THE ANODE

Sulphate ions do not discharge. However, hydroxide ions from the water are attracted to the anode and discharged as oxygen gas.

$$4OH^-(aq) \rightarrow O_2(g) + 2H_2O(l) + 4e^-$$

AT THE CATHODE

Copper metal is deposited. Discharge of hydroxide ions involves four electrons, so to maintain an electrical balance two copper (II) ions must be discharged.:

$$2Cu^{2+}(aq) + 4e^- \rightarrow 2Cu(s)$$

USING COPPER ELECTRODES

When copper (II) sulphate is electrolysed using copper electrodes, a different process happens.

At the anode, copper on the anode dissolves away into solution:
$$Cu(s) \rightarrow Cu^{2+}(aq) + 2e^-$$
At the cathode, copper is deposited:
$$Cu^{2+}(aq) + 2e^- \rightarrow Cu(s)$$

The electrolysis of concentrated aqueous sodium chloride

When sodium chloride dissolves in water, its **ions** separate:

$$NaCl(aq) \rightarrow Na^+(aq) + Cl^-(aq)$$

There are also some ions from the water:

$$H_2O(l) \rightleftharpoons H^+(aq) + OH^-(aq)$$

In the process of **electrolysis**, ions are converted to atoms. In the case of brine:

Na$^+$ and H$^+$ are attracted to the cathode (−)

Cl$^-$ and OH$^-$ are attracted to the anode (+).

At the cathode (−)	**At the anode (+)**
Sodium is more reactive than hydrogen, so only the **hydrogen ions** are changed to atoms to form a molecule:	Both OH$^-$ and Cl$^-$ are attracted to the anode, but only the **chloride ions** are changed to atoms to form a molecule:
$$2H^+(aq) + 2e^- \rightarrow H_2(g)$$	$$2Cl^-(aq) \rightarrow Cl_2(g) + 2e^-$$

The remaining solution contains the ions Na$^+$ and OH$^-$, so it is sodium hydroxide solution, NaOH(aq).

Summary At the cathode: hydrogen gas
At the anode: chlorine gas
The solution: sodium hydroxide

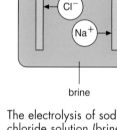

The electrolysis of sodium chloride solution (brine).

The electrolysis of brine is a very important industrial process and is the basis of the **chlor–alkali industry**, which is the large-scale production of chlorine, hydrogen and sodium hydroxide.

Conditions for electrolysis

The substance being electrolysed (the **electrolyte**) must contain ions and these ions must be free to move. In other words, the substance must either be molten or dissolved in water.

A d.c. voltage must be used. The **electrode** connected to the **positive** terminal of the power supply is known as the **anode**. The electrode connected to the **negative** terminal of the power supply is known as the **cathode**. The electrical circuit can be drawn.

How does the electrolyte change?

The negative ions are attracted to the anode and release electrons. (Loss of electrons is oxidation.) For example:

chloride ions $\rightarrow$ chlorine molecules + electrons
$$2Cl^-(aq) \quad \rightarrow \quad Cl_2(g) \quad + \quad 2e^-$$

The positive ions are attracted to the cathode and gain electrons. (Gaining electrons is reduction.) For example:

copper ions + electrons $\rightarrow$ copper atoms
$$Cu^{2+}(aq) \quad + \quad 2e^- \quad \rightarrow \quad Cu(s)$$

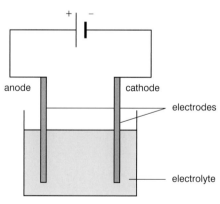

A typical electrical circuit used in electrolysis.

The electrons move through the external circuit from the anode to the cathode.

Using electrolysis to extract aluminium from aluminium oxide Al_2O_3

At the cathode **aluminium** is formed:

aluminium ions	+	electrons	$\rightarrow$	aluminium
$Al^{3+}(l)$	+	$3e^-$	$\rightarrow$	$Al(l)$

At the anode **oxygen** is formed:

oxide ions	$\rightarrow$	oxygen molecules	+	electrons
$2O^{2-}(l)$	$\rightarrow$	$O_2(g)$	+	$4e^-$

The oxygen reacts with the carbon anodes to form carbon dioxide. The rods constantly need to be replaced because of this.

Using electrolysis to purify copper

Copper is extracted from its ore by reduction with carbon, but the copper produced is not pure enough for some of its uses, such as making electrical wiring. It can be purified using electrolysis.

The impure copper is made the anode in a cell with copper(II) sulphate as an electrolyte. The cathode is made from a thin piece of pure copper.

At the anode the copper atoms dissolve, forming copper ions:

copper atoms	$\rightarrow$	copper ions	+	electrons
$Cu(s)$	$\rightarrow$	$Cu^{2+}(aq)$	+	$2e^-$

At the cathode the copper ions are deposited to form copper atoms:

copper ions	+	electrons	$\rightarrow$	copper atoms
$Cu^{2+}(aq)$	+	$2e^-$	$\rightarrow$	$Cu(s)$

Copper is purified by electrolysis.

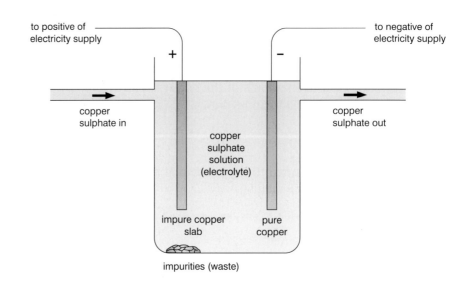

Predicting the products of electrolysis

Substances that undergo electrolysis are made of ions. The ions need to be able to move to the electrode so solids do not conduct electricity. The ionic solid must be **molten** or dissolved in water, i.e. as a solution.

Molten ionic compounds produce two ions which go to the oppositely charged electrode:

> **+ IONS (CATIONS) TO THE CATHODE (–)**
> **– IONS (ANIONS) TO THE ANODE (+)**

Some examples are given below:

molten ionic compound	ions	cathode (-)	anode (+)
NaCl	Na+ Cl⁻	2Na	Cl_2
$CuBr_2$	Cu^{2+} Br⁻	Cu	Br_2
ZnI_2	Zn^{2+} I⁻	Zn	I_2

Aqueous solutions are more complex because they contain the ions from the compound and the ions from water.

e.g. NaCl (aq)

$NaCl \rightarrow Na^+ + Cl^-$
$H_2O \rightarrow H^+ + OH^-$

Both positive ions will go to the cathode but only the H^+ ion is discharged as H_2.

Both negative ions go to the anode but only the Cl^- is discharged as Cl_2.

The general principle of electrolysis

The general rule is:
Cathode (-) - metals and hydrogen discharged
Anode (+) - non-metals discharged.

Extracting aluminium

Aluminium is extracted from the ore **bauxite** (aluminium oxide) by electrolysis. The aluminium oxide is insoluble, so it is **melted** to allow the ions to move when an electric current is passed through it. The anodes are made from carbon and the cathode is the carbon-lined steel case.

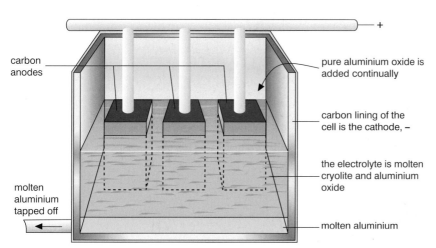

carbon anodes

pure aluminium oxide is added continually

carbon lining of the cell is the cathode, –

the electrolyte is molten cryolite and aluminium oxide

molten aluminium tapped off

molten aluminium

The extraction of aluminium is expensive. A mineral called cryolite is added to the aluminum oxide to lower the melting point and save energy costs.

At the cathode **aluminium** is formed:

aluminium ions	+	electrons	$\rightarrow$	aluminium
$Al^{3+}(l)$	+	$3e^-$	$\rightarrow$	$Al(l)$

At the anode **oxygen** is formed:

oxide ions	$\rightarrow$	oxygen molecules	+	electrons
$2O^{2-}(l)$	$\rightarrow$	$O_2(g)$	+	$4e^-$

The oxygen reacts with the carbon anodes to form carbon dioxide. The rods constantly need to be replaced because of this.

The chlor-alkali industry

The large-scale manufacture of chlorine, hydrogen and sodium hydroxide by the electrolysis of brine involves collecting the three substances and ensuring *they do not mix together* as they are produced in the electrolytic cell.

The two main electrolytic cells used in industry are:

1 The **mercury cell**

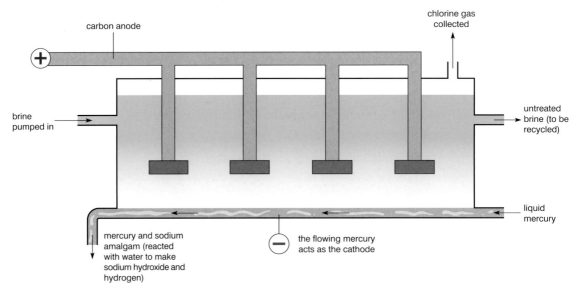

2 The **membrane cell**

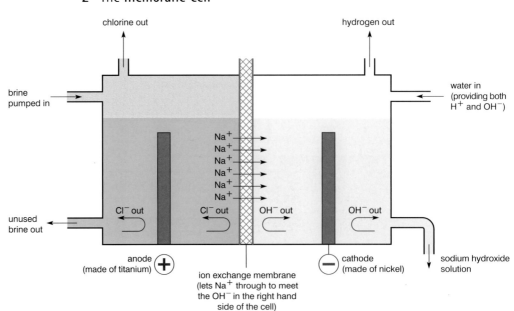

Both processes are very **efficient**, since there is little waste produced (the unused brine and mercury are recycled). The major **cost** is the electricity used.

Both the mercury cell and the membrane cell produce chlorine, hydrogen and sodium hydroxide.

The *major difference* between the two cells is that the membrane cell produces the three substances from the cell, while the mercury cell extracts the sodium as an amalgam. The amalgam of sodium and mercury is then reacted with water:

sodium + water → sodium hydroxide + hydrogen gas

This means the mercury cell is a more indirect method than the membrane cell.

What are the uses of the products of the chlor-alkali industry?

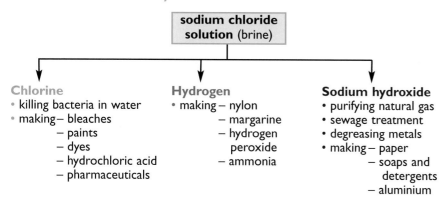

Typical products of the chlor-alkali industry

Chlorine
- killing bacteria in water
- making – bleaches
  - paints
  - dyes
  - hydrochloric acid
  - pharmaceuticals

Hydrogen
- making – nylon
  - margarine
  - hydrogen peroxide
  - ammonia

Sodium hydroxide
- purifying natural gas
- sewage treatment
- degreasing metals
- making – paper
  - soaps and detergents
  - aluminium

Electroplating of metals

Metals that are coated with a layer of another metal using electricity are described as being **electroplated**.

Chromium plating is probably the commonest example, for example taps, car bumpers, towel rails.

The diagram shows how a tap is chromium plated.

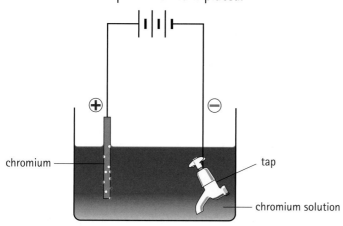

The object to be plated is made the cathode (to attract the positive chromium ions from solution), and the anode the pure chromium.

The chromium dissolves as the process proceeds, as it migrates across to the tap.

Conductors and insulators of electricity

Materials can be classified in a number of ways, e.g.
- metals and non-metals.
- ceramic and glasses.
- plastics.

Some physical properties of the different groups are the same, e.g. not conducting electricity, and some materials fit equally well into other classes, e.g. ceramics are non-metals.

Metals and non-metals

The table shows differences between these materials. In the home, copper is used for electrical cables because it is an excellent conductor of electricity. Copper cables are covered in plastic which is an insulator. Plastic also has the advantage of being flexible so cables can bend.

Metals	Non-metals
usually have high melting and boiling points	most have low melting and boiling points
have a shiny surface	have a dull surface
can be hammered, bent or stretched into shape	are brittle when solid
good conductors of heat and electricity	poor conductors of heat and electricity

Transmission of electricity on a national grid system uses aluminium for the cabling. The aluminium is wrapped around a central core of steel (for strength). Aluminium is a good conductor and is also light, i.e. low density solid.

The aluminium cables are fastened to pylons across the country. Ceramic holders join the cables to the pylons. Ceramics are made of clay, which is an insulator, so the pylons are not 'live' themselves.

Ceramics and glasses

A ceramic material is usually made from clay which has been heated to high temperatures in a kiln (oven) .This changes the structure of the clay and gives it a new set of properties as shown in the table.

good electrical insulators
high melting points
resistance to heat (they are 'refractory')
opaque
brittle and hard
strong under compression but weak under tension
chemically unreactive

Glass has the same properties as ceramics, except that it is transparent.

Electricity transmission in Finland. The ceramic discs are insulators and isolate the power lines from the rest of the pylon

Plastics

Plastics are synthetic materials made from large molecules. They have many useful properties.

- They are flexible
- Thermoplastics are easily melted and moulded
- Colourings are easily added.
- Plastics do not degrade easily
- Most burn quite easily

Plastics are generally non-biodegradable and so cause problems when it comes to disposing of them.

Ceramics are also non-biodegradable but the recycling of glass is an important environmental issue.

REVIEW QUESTIONS

Q1 Zinc bromide ($ZnBr_2$) is an ionic solid. Why does the solid not conduct electricity?

Q2 Sodium chloride (NaCl) is ionic. What are the products at the anode and cathode of (a) solid sodium chloride, (b) aqueous sodium chloride.

Q3 An iron fork is to be silver plated. Which metal would be the anode and which the cathode?

Q4 Write the half-equations for the reactions at the anode and cathode when molten silver iodide is electrolysed.

More questions on the CD ROM

Examination questions are on page 96.

6 CHEMICAL CHANGES

Measuring energy transfers

In most reactions, energy is transferred to the surroundings and the temperature goes up. These reactions are **exothermic**. In a minority of cases, energy is absorbed from the surroundings as a reaction takes place and the temperature goes down. These reactions are **endothermic**.

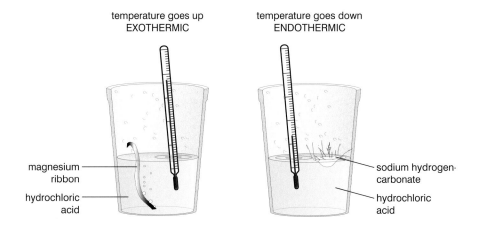

Energy transfers in a wide range of chemical reactions can be measured using a polystyrene cup as a calorimeter. If a lid is put on the cup, very little energy is transferred to the air and quite accurate results can be obtained.

All reactions involving the combustion of fuels are exothermic. The energy transferred when a fuel burns can be measured using a **calorimetric technique**, as shown in the diagram on the left.

The rise in temperature of the water is a measure of the energy transferred to the water. This technique will not give a very accurate answer because much of the energy will be transferred to the surrounding air. Nevertheless, the technique can be used to compare the energy released by the same amounts of different fuels.

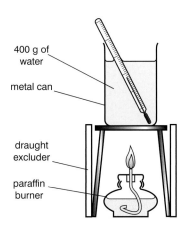

Measuring the energy produced on burning a liquid fuel.

The energy change can be calculated using the equation:

ΔH to the water	=	mass of water	×	specific heat capacity of water	×	rise in temperature of water
units in J or kJ		g or kg		4.2J g^{-1} °C^{-1} or 4.2 kJ kg^{-1} °C^{-1}		°C

Remembered as: $\Delta H = m \times \text{SHC} \times \Delta t$

Units are important in this equation, that is, when you use g for mass of water, then ΔH is in J, but using kg for the mass gives ΔH in kJ.

Since 1 cm^3 of water weighs 1 g, the mass of water in the beaker is the same as the volume of water in cm^3.

WORKED EXAMPLE

2.0 g of paraffin were burned in a spirit burner under a metal can containing 400 cm^3 of water. The temperature of the water rose from 20 °C to 70 °C. Calculate the energy produced by the paraffin in J g^{-1} and kJ g^{-1}.

Equation:	ΔH	=	mass of water × 4.2 × temperature change
Substitute values:	ΔH	=	400 × 4.2 × 50
Calculate:	ΔH	=	84000 J per 2 g of paraffin
		=	42000 J g^{-1}
		=	42 kJ g^{-1}

Energy level diagrams and ΔH

Here is a basic energy level diagram (right):

These (below) are the more advanced form of basic **energy level diagrams**:

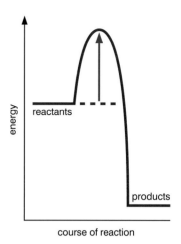

Activation energy

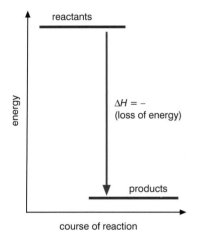

ΔH with a negative value

ΔH with a positive value

An **exothermic** reaction. Energy is being lost to the surroundings. ΔH is **negative**.

An **endothermic** reaction. Energy is being absorbed from the surroundings. ΔH is **positive**.

All ΔH values should have a − or + sign in front of them to show if they are exothermic or endothermic.

The activation energy diagram can now be completed as shown right. The reaction for this diagram is exothermic, with ΔH negative.

Production of energy

When a fuel is burnt the reaction can be considered to take place in two stages. In the first stage the **covalent bonds** between the atoms in the fuel molecules and the oxygen molecules are **broken**. In the second stage the atoms combine and **new covalent bonds are formed**. For example, in the combustion of propane:

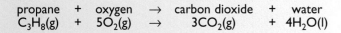

propane	+	oxygen	→	carbon dioxide	+	water
$C_3H_8(g)$	+	$5O_2(g)$	→	$3CO_2(g)$	+	$4H_2O(l)$

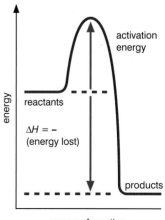

A full version of an energy level diagram

The two stages of the chemical reaction between propane and oxygen. Existing bonds are broken and new bonds are formed.

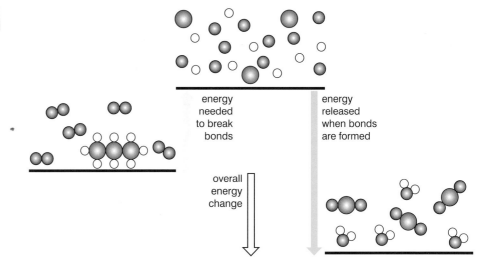

Stage 1: Energy is needed (absorbed from the surroundings) to break the bonds. This process is endothermic.

Stage 2: Energy is released (transferred to the surroundings) as the bonds form. This process is exothermic.

The overall reaction is exothermic because more energy is released when bonds are formed than is needed initially to break the bonds. A simplified **energy level diagram** showing the exothermic nature of the reaction is shown on the left.

The larger the alkane molecule, the more the energy that is released on combustion. This is because, although more bonds have to be broken in the first stage of the reaction, more bonds are formed in the second stage.

The increase in energy from one alkane to the next is almost constant, due to the extra CH_2 unit in the molecule.

In the table the energy released on combustion has been worked out per mole of alkane. In this way a comparison can be made when the same number of molecules of each alkane is burnt.

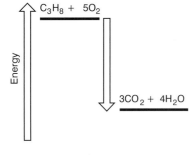

Alkane		Energy of combustion (kJ mol⁻¹)
methane	CH_4	882
ethane	C_2H_6	1542
propane	C_3H_8	2202
butane	C_4H_{10}	2877
pentane	C_5H_{12}	3487
hexane	C_6H_{14}	4141

Hydrogen as a fuel

The reaction between hydrogen and oxygen is very exothermic and produces a lot of heat energy.

$$2H_2(g) + O_2(g) \rightarrow 2H_2O(l)$$

Burning 2g of hydrogen makes 485J of energy.

The reaction is used for powering space rockets using the hydrogen as a rocket fuel.

Hydrogen is used as a fuel in space travel

Energy and radioactive isotopes

Nuclear power stations use the heat produced by the decay of radioactive isotopes.

The heat generated is used to boil water to make steam which then turns turbines, producing electricity.

Uranium – 235, ^{235}U is the radioactive isotope used as a fuel in nuclear reactions. The radioactive reaction produces heat.

Simple cells

Metals and solutions of their own salts can be used to generate electricity.

If the following experiment is set up the bulb glows showing that electricity has been produced by the zinc and copper half-cells.

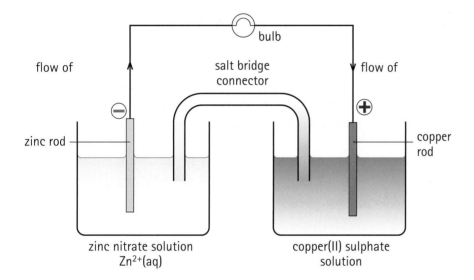

A simple cell

Zinc is higher than copper in the reactivity series, so is the producer of electrons (the cathode) and the copper takes the electrons (the anode, (+)).

The reactions are: Cathode $Zn(s) \rightarrow Zn^{2+}(aq) + 2e^-$ – OXIDATION(-)

Anode $Cu^{2+}(aq) + 2e^- \rightarrow Cu$ – REDUCTION(+)

See the section on **Redox** in Chapter 7. (You need to refer to the section on REDOX and see "OIL-RIG").

Although zinc/copper is used here as the example you can generate electricity from any pair of metals set up as shown in the diagram.

The amount of electricity produced depends on the position of the metals in the reactivity series. The rule is:

> **THE FURTHER APART THE METALS ARE IN THE REACTIVITY SERIES THE MORE ELECTRICITY IS PRODUCED.**

A battery-powered bus in Sweden.

Batteries

The words "battery" and "cell" are often used to mean the same thing. Battery really means a set of cells working together.

Batteries in the modern world range from the large lead acid battery used in cars and lorries to the tiny lithium/cadium batteries used in hearing aids, with cylinder type batteries used for torches, etc. in between in size.

The development of batteries as "mobile providers of electricity" and their impact on society is a fascinating study. Without batteries (of whatever type) there would be no mobile (cell) phones or laptop computers that are now taken for granted.

REVIEW QUESTIONS

Q1 A 0.2 g strip of magnesium ribbon is added to 40 cm^3 of hydrochloric acid in a polystyrene beaker. The temperature rises by 32°C. (The specific heat capacity of the hydrochloric acid can be assumed to be the same as that of water, i.e. 4.2 J g^{-1} °C^{-1}.) Calculate
   a   the energy released in the reaction
   b   the energy released per gram of magnesium.

Q2 Calcium oxide reacts with water as shown in the equation:
$$CaO(s) + H_2O(l) \rightarrow Ca(OH)_2(s)$$
An energy level diagram for this reaction is shown below.

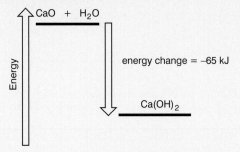

   a   What does the energy level diagram tell us about the type of energy change that takes place in this reaction?
   b   What does the energy level diagram indicate about the amounts of energy required to break bonds and form new bonds in this reaction?

Q3 Chlorine (Cl$_2$) and hydrogen (H$_2$) react together to make hydrogen chloride (HCl). The equation can be written as:
$$H–H + Cl–Cl \rightarrow H–Cl + H–Cl$$
When this reaction occurs, energy is transferred to the surroundings. Explain this in terms of the energy transfer processes taking place when bonds are broken and when bonds are made.

Q4 Why is a mixture of hydrogen and oxygen used as a fuel for rockets?

Q5 What is the fuel used in nuclear power stations?

More questions on the CD ROM

Examination questions are on page 96.

7 CHEMICAL REACTIONS

Videos & questions on the CD ROM

Fireworks. Explosives such as fireworks are very fast chemical reactions.

Speed of reaction

A chemical change, or **chemical reaction**, is quite different from the physical changes that occur, for example, when sugar dissolves in water.

FEATURES OF A CHEMICAL REACTION

One or more **new substances** are produced.

In many cases an **observable change** is apparent, for example the colour changes or a gas is produced.

An **apparent change in mass** can occur. This change is often quite small and difficult to detect unless accurate balances are used. Mass is conserved in a chemical reaction – the apparent change in mass usually occurs because one of the reactants or products is a gas.

An **energy change** is almost always involved. In most cases energy is released and the surroundings become warmer. In some cases energy is absorbed from the surroundings and so the surroundings become colder. Note: Some physical changes, such as evaporation, also produce energy changes.

Collision theory

For a chemical reaction to occur, the reacting particles (atoms, molecules or ions) must **collide**. The energy involved in the collision must be enough to break the chemical bonds in the reacting particles – or the particles will just bounce off one another.

A collision that has enough energy to result in a chemical reaction is an **effective collision**.

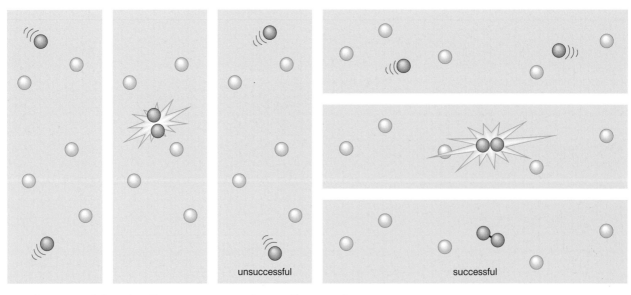

unsuccessful   successful

Particles must collide with sufficient energy to make an effective collision.

What can change the rate of a reaction?

There are six key factors that can change the rate of a reaction:
- **concentration** (of a solution)
- **temperature**
- **surface area** (of a solid)
- a **catalyst**
- **pressure** (of a gas)
- **light**.

A simple **collision theory** can be used to explain how these factors affect the rate of a reaction. Two important parts of the theory are:

1   The reacting particles must collide with each other.

2   There must be sufficient energy in the collision to overcome the activation energy.

Concentration

Increasing the concentration of a reactant will **increase the rate** of a reaction. When a piece of magnesium ribbon is added to a solution of hydrochloric acid, the following reaction occurs:

magnesium	+	hydrochloric acid	→	magnesium chloride	+	hydrogen
$Mg(s)$	+	$2HCl(aq)$	→	$MgCl_2(aq)$	+	$H_2(g)$

As the magnesium and acid come into contact, there is effervescence – 'fizzing', and hydrogen gas is given off. Two experiments were performed using the same length of magnesium ribbon, but different concentrations of acid. In experiment 1 the hydrochloric acid used was 2.0 mol dm^{-3}, in experiment 2 the acid was 0.5 mol dm^{-3}. The graph below shows the results of the two experiments.

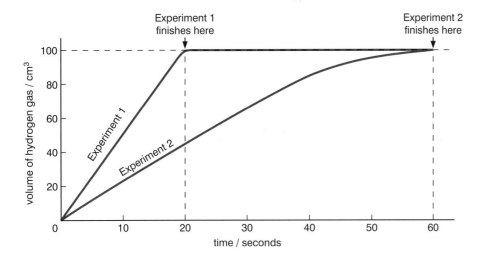

In experiment 1 the curve is steeper (has a greater gradient) than in experiment 2. In experiment 1 the reaction is complete after 20 seconds, whereas in experiment 2 it takes 60 seconds. The rate of the reaction is higher with 2.0 mol dm^{-3} hydrochloric acid than with 0.5 mol dm^{-3} hydrochloric acid. In the 2.0 mol dm^{-3} hydrochloric acid solution the hydrogen ions are more likely to collide with the surface of the magnesium ribbon than in the 0.5 mol dm^{-3} hydrochloric acid.

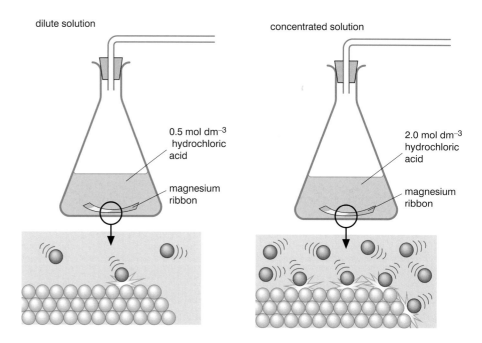

Temperature

Increasing the temperature will **increase the rate** of reaction. Warming a chemical transfers kinetic energy to the chemical's particles. More kinetic energy means that the particles move faster. As they are moving faster there will be more collisions each second. The increased energy of the collisions also means that the proportion of collisions that are effective will increase.

Increasing the temperature of a reaction such as that between calcium carbonate and hydrochloric acid will not increase the final amount of carbon dioxide produced. The **same amount** of gas will be produced in a **shorter time**.

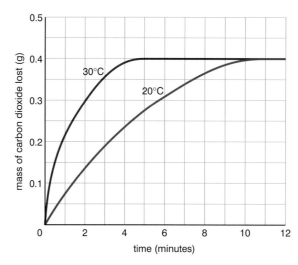

The rates of the two reactions are different but the final loss in mass is the same.

Surface area

Increasing the surface area of a solid reactant will **increase the rate** of a reaction. The reaction can only take place if the reacting particles collide. This means that the reaction takes place at the surface of the solid. The particles within the solid cannot react until those on the surface have reacted and moved away.

Powdered calcium carbonate has a much larger surface area than the same mass of marble chips. A lump of coal will burn slowly in the air whereas coal dust can react explosively.

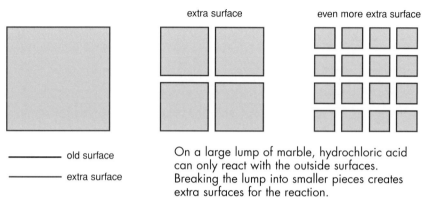

extra surface   even more extra surface

———— old surface

———— extra surface

On a large lump of marble, hydrochloric acid can only react with the outside surfaces. Breaking the lump into smaller pieces creates extra surfaces for the reaction.

Catalysts

A **catalyst** is a substance that alters the rate of a chemical reaction without being used up itself. The mass of the catalyst remains unchanged throughout the reaction.

Hydrogen peroxide decomposes slowly at room temperature into water and oxygen. This reaction is catalysed by manganese(IV) oxide.

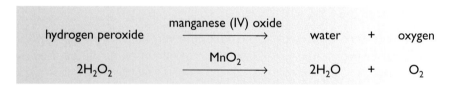

$$\text{hydrogen peroxide} \xrightarrow{\text{manganese (IV) oxide}} \text{water} + \text{oxygen}$$

$$2H_2O_2 \xrightarrow{MnO_2} 2H_2O + O_2$$

Most catalysts work by providing an alternative 'route' for the reaction, lowering the activation energy 'barrier'. This increases the number of effective collisions each second.

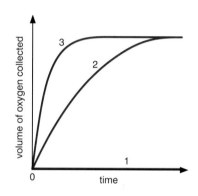

The manganese(IV) oxide has a dramatic effect on the rate of decomposition of hydrogen peroxide. The catalyst doesn't produce any extra oxygen but gives the same amount at a higher rate.
1 = no catalyst
2 = one spatula measure
3 = two spatula measures

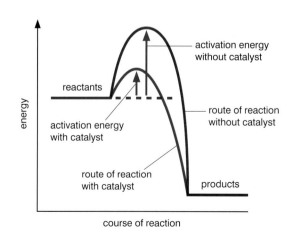

The catalyst provides a lower energy route from reactants to products.

Pressure

Increasing the pressure on a reaction between gases will **increase the rate** of the reaction. Increasing the pressure reduces the volume of the gas, moving the particles closer together. If the particles are closer together there will be more collisions and therefore more effective collisions.

The same number of particles are closer together in a smaller volume. There will be more effective collisions each second.

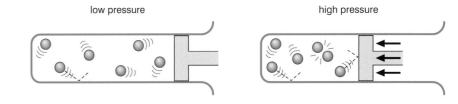

low pressure   high pressure

Effect of light on speed of reactions

Light energy (visible or ultra-violet radiation) can start or speed up some chemical reactions.

In photography, the film in a camera is coated in a film consisting of silver salts. These salts are silver chloride ($AgCl$), silver bromide ($AgBr$) and silver iodine (AgI). All three are sensitive to light but have different sensitivity.

When light hits the film the silver ions in the salts are reduced by gaining electrons:

$$Ag^+ + e^- \rightarrow Ag$$

Light energy speeds up this reduction process.

When the film is developed to produce negatives these show the dark and light patches of the pictures taken. The darker areas contain most silver, the lighter areas least from the silver salts.

The silver salts need to be kept in the dark but even then they very slowly change to silver over time. This is why photographic film has to be used by a certain date.

Photosynthesis in plants is also initiated by the light absorbed by the chlorophyll molecules:

$$6CO_2(g) + 6H_2O(l) \rightarrow C_6H_{12}O_6(aq) + O_2(g)$$
Carbon dioxide + water → glucose + oxygen

The negative image

Consequences

When reactions become faster and faster there is the risk of an explosion. For example, powders have a very large surface area so reactions with powders can be explosive. There have been explosions and fires in flour mills and mines (caused by coal dust) because of this.

Reversible reactions

Carbon burns in oxygen to form carbon dioxide.

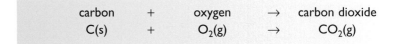

carbon	+	oxygen	→	carbon dioxide
C(s)	+	$O_2(g)$	→	$CO_2(g)$

The positive image

Carbon dioxide cannot be changed back into carbon and oxygen. The reaction cannot be reversed.

When blue copper(II) sulphate crystals are heated, a white powder is formed (anhydrous copper(II) sulphate) and water is lost as steam. If water is added to this white powder, blue copper(II) sulphate is re-formed. The reaction is **reversible**:

$$\text{copper(II) sulphate crystals} \rightleftharpoons \text{anhydrous copper(II) sulphate} + \text{water}$$
$$CuSO_4.5H_2O(s) \rightleftharpoons CuSO_4(s) + 5H_2O(l)$$

A reversible reaction can go from left to right or from right to left – notice the double-headed '$\rightleftharpoons$' arrow used when writing these equations.

Another reversible reaction is the reaction between ethene and water to make ethanol. This is one of the reactions used industrially to make ethanol:

$$\text{ethene} + \text{water} \rightleftharpoons \text{ethanol}$$
$$C_2H_4(g) + H_2O(g) \rightleftharpoons C_2H_5OH(g)$$

When ethene and water are heated in the presence of a catalyst in a sealed container, ethanol is produced.

As the ethene and water are used up, the rate of the forward reaction decreases. As the amount of ethanol increases the rate of the back reaction (the decomposition of ethanol) increases. Eventually the rate of formation of ethanol will exactly equal the rate of decomposition of ethanol. The amounts of ethene, water and ethanol will be constant. The reaction is said to be in **equilibrium**.

Changing the position of equilibrium

Reversible reactions can be a nuisance to an industrial chemist. You want to make a particular product but as soon as it forms it starts to change back into the reactants! Fortunately scientists have found ways of increasing the amount of product that can be obtained (the **yield**) in a reversible reaction by moving the position of balance to favour the products rather than the reactants.

The position of equilibrium or yield can be changed in the following ways:
* changing **concentrations**
* changing **pressure** (but only for reactions involving gases).
* changing **temperature** (but only for reactions involving gases).

In the following example:

$$A(g) + 2B(g) \rightleftharpoons 2C(g) \qquad \Delta H = +$$

The yield of C is *increased* by:

1 adding more A and B $\left.\right\}$ concentration
   removing C

2 increasing the **pressure** because there are 3 molecules on the left (high pressure) but only 2 molecules on the right (low pressure)

3 increasing the **temperature** because the reaction is endothermic (ΔH is +).

A **catalyst** increases the rate at which the equilibrium is achieved. It does not change the yield because it does not affect the position of the equilibrium.

Redox

When oxygen is added to an element or a compound the process is called **oxidation**:

$$2Cu(s)+O_2(g) \rightarrow 2CuO(s)$$

The copper has been oxidised.

Removing oxygen from a compound is called **reduction**:

$$CuO(s) + Zn(s) \rightarrow ZnO(s) + Cu(s)$$

The copper oxide has been *reduced*.

If we look more carefully at the last reaction we see the zinc has changed to zinc oxide, i.e. it has been oxidised at the same time as the copper oxide has been reduced.

This is one example of reduction and oxidation taking place at the same time, in the same reaction. These are called **redox** reactions.

There is another way of look at oxidation/reduction if we look at the equation in a different way:

$$CuO \quad + \quad Zn \quad \rightarrow \quad ZnO \quad + \quad Cu$$

CuO	Zn	ZnO	Cu
ionic compound	element	ionic compound	element

Rewrite it,

$$Cu^{2+} + O^{2-} + Zn \rightarrow Zn^{2+} + O^{2-} + Cu$$

Remove the oxygen because it is on both sides (it is unchanged and so a spectator ion),

$$Cu^{2+} + Zn \rightarrow Zn^{2+} + Cu$$

Split the equation into half- equations and add electrons to balance them:

$$Cu^{2+} + 2e^- \rightarrow Cu, \text{ i.e. CuO to Cu} \quad \textbf{Reduction}$$

$$Zn \rightarrow Zn^{2+} + 2e^-, \text{ i.e. Zn to ZnO} \quad \textbf{Oxidation}$$

We now have a new definition using electrons not oxygen:

OXIDATION IS LOSS OF ELECTRONS
REDUCTION IS GAIN OF ELECTRONS

REMEMBER THIS AS "OILRIG",
"OXIDATION IS LOSS – REDUCTION IS GAIN"

Oxidation numbers/states

When you learnt to write chemical formulae you were introduced to the use of roman numerals for metals that had more than one ion, e.g. iron as Fe^{2+} or Fe^{3+},

e.g. iron(II) oxide = FeO
e.g. iron(III)oxide = Fe_2O_3

The (II) and (III) are called **oxidation states**.
Fe^{2+}, i.e. (II) in formulae, has an oxidation number of +2.
Fe^{3+} has an oxidation number of +3.
O^{2-} has an oxidation number of –2.
You take the ion charge and reverse it, i.e. ion of 3- becomes oxidation number –3.
The oxidation state of elements is always 0 (zero).

If we look at the equation between Cu^{2+} and Zn again we can use oxidation states:

$Cu^{2+} + 2e^- \rightarrow Cu$ **Reduction**
+2   0

$Zn \rightarrow Zn^{2+} + 2e^-$ **Oxidation**

This gives another definition for oxidation/reduction:

> OXIDATION IS WHEN OXIDATION STATES **INCREASE**.
>
> REDUCTION IS WHEN OXIDATION STATES **DECREASE**.

Changes in oxidation state

Solid **potassium manganate(VII)** comes in the form of dark purple crystals.

Manganese is in the oxidation state +7 (the VII in the formula) and is the cause of the purple colour.

Potassium manganate(VII) crystals dissolve in water to produce a dark purple solution, which is a powerful oxidising agent and used in titrations. When used in titrations, the manganate(VII) ion is reduced to manganese(II) which is almost colourless:

MnO_4^{2-} $\rightarrow$ Mn^{2+}
+7   +2
purple   very pale pink

Another example of colour changes linked to changes in oxidation states is **potassium iodide**, KI, which is a white solid dissolving in water to form a colourless solution.

In some reactions, the iodide ion, I^-, is oxidised to iodine, which shows a dark orange colour:

$2I^-$ (aq) $\rightarrow$ I_2 (aq)
colourless   dark orange

Fumes of iodine produced when sodium iodide is oxidised by concentrated sulphuric acid

REVIEW QUESTIONS

Q1 For a chemical reaction to occur the reacting particles must collide. Why don't all collisions between the particles of the reactants lead to a chemical reaction?

Q2 The diagrams below show the activation energies of two different reactions A and B. Which reaction is likely to have the greater rate of reaction at a particular temperature?

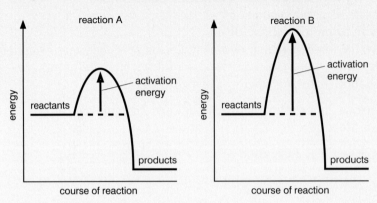

Q3 Look at the table of results obtained when dilute hydrochloric acid is added to marble chips.

Time (seconds)	0	10	20	30	40	50	60	70	80	90
Volume of gas (cm^3)	0	20	36	49	58	65	69	70	70	70

a What is the name of the gas produced in this reaction?
b Use the results to calculate the volume of gas produced:
  i   in the first 10 seconds
  ii between 10 and 20 seconds
  iii between 20 and 30 seconds
  iv between 80 and 90 seconds.
c Explain how your answers to part b show that the rate of reaction decreases as the reaction proceeds.
d Use collision theory to explain why the rate of reaction decreases as the reaction proceeds.
e In this experiment the rate of the reaction was followed by measuring the volume of gas produced every 10 seconds. What alternative measurement could have been used?

Q4 Why does increasing the temperature increase the rate of a reaction?

Q5 The graph shows the results obtained in three different experiments. In each experiment marble chips were added to 50 cm^3 of 1 mol dm^{-3} hydrochloric acid (in excess) at room temperature. The same mass of marble was used each time but different sized chips were used in each experiment.

a i In which experiment was the reaction the fastest?
   ii Give a reason for your answer.
b i Which experiment used the largest marble chips?
   ii Give a reason for your answer.
c i How long did it take for the reaction in experiment 2 to finish?
   ii Why did the reaction finish?
d Why was the same mass of carbon dioxide lost in each experiment?

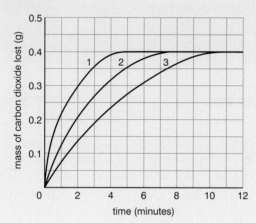

e Experiment 3 was repeated at 50 °C rather than room temperature. How would the results be different from those shown for experiment 3?

Q6 a What is a catalyst?
b How does the catalyst affect the rate of a reaction?

Q7 Explain how an image forms on the film in a camera.

Q8 When a chemical reaction is in equilibrium what does this mean?

Q9 What effect does a catalyst have on:
a the rate of reaction
b the yield of a reaction?

Q10 The following is a redox reaction:
Mg + ZnO → MgO + Zn

What is oxidised?
What is reduced?
What is the oxidising agent?
What is the reducing agent?
Give the change in oxidation number of (a) magnesium, (b) zinc.

More questions on the CD ROM

Examination questions are on page 96.

8 ACIDS, BASES AND SALTS

Videos & questions on the CD ROM

Testing hydrochloric acid, note the red colour indicating a strong acid.

Using Universal indicator to test sodium hydroxide, note the deep maroon colour indicating a strong alkali.

The characteristic properties of acids and bases

When any substance dissolves in water, it forms an **aqueous solution** shown by the state symbol (aq). Aqueous solutions can be acidic, alkaline or neutral.

Indicators are used to tell if a solution is acidic, alkaline or basic, or neutral. Indicators can be used either as liquids or in paper form, and they become different colours with **different solutions**.

The commonest indicator is **litmus** and its colours are shown in the table below:

Colour of litmus	Type of solution
red	acidic
purple	neutral
blue	alkaline

Universal Indicator – or **UI** – can show the **strengths** of solutions of the acids and alkalis because it has more colours. Each colour is linked to a number on a scale called the **pH scale**. The range of numbers is from 1 to 14.

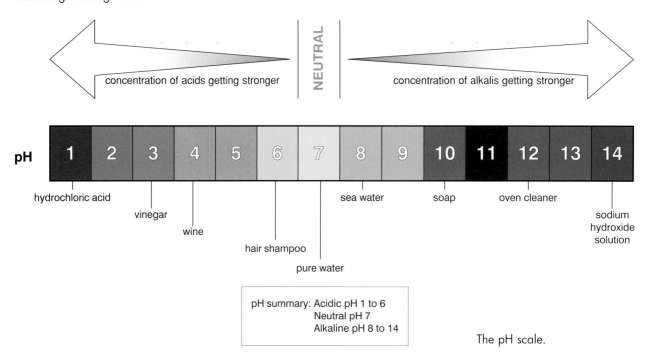

The pH scale.

pH summary: Acidic pH 1 to 6
Neutral pH 7
Alkaline pH 8 to 14

What are acids?

Acids are substances that contain **replaceable hydrogen atoms**. These hydrogen atoms are replaced in chemical reactions by metal atoms, and the compound formed is a **salt**.

Acids only show their acidic properties when **water** is present. This is because, in water, acids form hydrogen ions, H⁺ (which are also **protons**) and it is these ions that are responsible for acidic properties. For example:

$$HCl(aq) \rightarrow H^+(aq) + Cl^-(aq)$$

Basicity is the term used to describe how many hydrogen ions an acid molecule can have replaced. The table shows the basicity of some common acids.

Acid	Basicity of acid
hydrochloric acid, HCl	monobasic (one H^+)
nitric acid, HNO_3	monobasic (one H^+)
sulphuric acid, H_2SO_4	dibasic (two H^+'s)
phosphoric acid, H_3PO_4	tribasic (three H^+'s)

What are bases?

Bases are substances that accept an H⁺ ion from an acid in aqueous solution. If a base is soluble in water it is called an alkali, e.g. sodium hydroxide, NaOH, and potassium hydroxide, KOH.

Alkalis produce the hydroxide ion, OH⁻, in aqueous solutions, e.g.

$$NaOH(aq) \rightarrow Na^+(aq) + OH^-(aq)$$

Remember the following definitions :
• Acids are proton (H^+) donors in water
• Bases are proton (H^+) acceptors in water

The strengths of acids and bases

Acids and bases are described as being 'strong' or 'weak' depending on the 'degree of dissociation' (sometimes called 'ionisation') in water.

'Strong' acids and bases undergo 100% dissociation in water, e.g.

$$HCl(aq) \rightarrow H^+(aq) + Cl^-(aq)$$

$$NaOH(aq) \rightarrow Na^+(aq) + OH^-(aq)$$

This is why the arrow sign is used in these chemical equations.

'Weak' acids and bases only partially dissociate in water, e.g. ethanoic acid, CH_3COOH,

$$CH_3COOH(aq) \rightleftharpoons CH_3COO^-(aq) + H^+(aq)$$

E.g. ammonia solution (ammonium hydroxide)

$$NH_4OH(aq) \rightleftharpoons NH_4^+(aq) + OH^-(aq)$$

The partial dissociation is the reason why the equilibrium sign is used in these chemical equations .

'Weak' acids (pH 4 to 6) and 'weak' bases (pH 8 to 10) produce fewer ions in solution than 'strong' acids and bases at the same concentration. This is why their electrical conductivity is lower than 'strong' acids and bases, and also explains their slower rates of reactions.

A* EXTRA

• You need to be able to explain why a hydrogen ion, H⁺, is also a proton. The hydrogen atom is the simplest of all the atoms – it has a nucleus of only one proton (+) with one electron (–) in the energy shell (orbit) around it. When the electron is removed, it leaves just the proton, the positive hydrogen ion, H⁺.

The importance of controlling acidity in soil

If the soil is too acidic then the soil acidity can be neutralised using **quicklime**. Quicklime is made from limestone. Limestone is quarried from limestone rocks. It is heated in lime kilns to make calcium oxide or quicklime:

$$CaCO_3(s) \xrightarrow{1200\ °C} CaO(s) \ + \ CO_2(g)$$

limestone → quicklime

When quicklime is added to water, it makes calcium hydroxide, which is an alkali and so can neutralise the acidic soil.

$$CaO(s) \ + \ H_2O(l) \rightarrow Ca(OH)_2(s)$$

quicklime → slaked lime

Different plants grow better in different types of soil. The pH of a soil is an important factor in the growth of different plants ie. some plants prefer slightly acidic conditions and others slightly alkaline conditions.

Adding fertilisers to soil can also affect the pH and may have to be treated by adding acids or alkalis. The pH of soil can be measured by taking a small sample of soil, drying it carefully, putting it in a test-tube with distilled water and adding indicator solution or using indicator paper. The pH can be found from a pH chart.

Types of oxides

The **oxides** of elements can often be made by heating the element in air or oxygen. For example, the metal magnesium burns in oxygen to form magnesium oxide:

magnesium + oxygen → magnesium oxide
$$2Mg(s) \ + \ O_2(g) \rightarrow 2MgO(s)$$

Magnesium oxide forms as a white ash. When distilled water is added to the ash and the mixture is tested with universal indicator, the pH is greater than 7 – the oxide has formed an **alkaline** solution.

When sulphur is burnt in oxygen, sulphur dioxide gas is formed:

sulphur + oxygen → sulphur dioxide
$$S(s) \ + \ O_2(g) \rightarrow SO_2(g)$$

Magnesium burning in oxygen

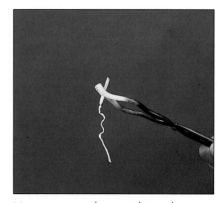

Magnesium oxide is a white ash

When this is dissolved in water and then tested with universal indicator solution, the pH is less than 7 – the oxide has formed an **acidic** solution.

The oxides of most elements can be classified as **basic oxides** or **acidic oxides**. Some elements form **neutral oxides**. For example, water is a neutral oxide. Basic oxides that dissolve in water are called **alkalis**.

Oxides that do not dissolve in water cannot be identified using the pH of their solutions. For the insoluble oxides the test is seeing if they will react with hydrochloric acid, HCl (these would be basic oxides) or sodium hydroxide solution, NaOH (these would be acidic oxides). Oxides that do not react with hydrochloric acid or sodium hydroxide are neutral oxides. **Basic oxides** are the oxides of metals. They contain the oxide ion, O^{2-}, e.g.

$$2Mg(s) + O_2(g) \rightarrow 2MgO(s).$$

These oxides have giant ionic structures. Basic oxides react with acids (neutralisation):

$$\text{acid + base} \quad \rightarrow \quad \text{a salt + water}$$
$$2HCl(aq) + MgO\ (s) \rightarrow MgCl_2(aq) + H_2O\ (l)$$

Acidic oxides are usually from non-metallic elements, e.g.

$$2S(s) + 3O_2(g) \rightarrow 2SO_3(g)$$

Acidic oxides usually have simple molecular structures and are usually gases. Acidic oxides react with bases (neutralisation), and dissolve in water to form acids, e.g.

$$SO_3(g) + H_2O\ (l) \rightarrow H_2SO_4\ (aq)$$
$$\text{sulphuric acid}$$

Oxide	Type of oxide	pH of solution	Other reactions of the oxide
Metal oxide	basic	more than 7 (alkaline)	reacts with an acid to form a salt + water
Non-metal oxide	acidic	less than 7 (acidic)	reacts with a base to form a salt + water

Amphoteric oxides are formed by less reactive metals like zinc, aluminium and lead. They can behave as both acidic oxides and basic oxides, so react with both bases and acids.

Neutral oxides do not react with acids or alkalis. One example of a neutral oxide is nitrogen monoxide, NO.

Preparation of salts

In the last session, it was explained that acids contain **replaceable hydrogen atoms**, and that when **metal atoms** take their place, a compound called a **salt** is formed. The names of salts have two parts, as shown:

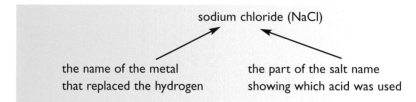

sodium chloride (NaCl)

the name of the metal that replaced the hydrogen

the part of the salt name showing which acid was used

The table shows the four commonest acids and their salt names.

Acid	Salt name
hydrochloric (HCl)	chloride (Cl^-)
nitric (HNO_3)	nitrate (NO_3^-)
sulphuric (H_2SO_4)	sulphate (SO_4^{2-})
phosphoric (H_3PO_4)	phosphate (PO_4^{3-})

Salts are **ionic compounds** where the first part of the name is of the metal ion which is a positive ion (cation), and the second part of the name is from the acid and is a negative ion (anion). For example:

copper(II) sulphate: Cu^{2+} and $SO_4^{2-} \rightarrow CuSO_4$

Sodium chloride crystals.

Copper(II) sulphate crystals.

Salts are often found in the form of **crystals**. Most salt crystals contain **water of crystallisation** which is responsible for their crystal shapes. Water of crystallisation is shown in the chemical formula of a salt. For example:

copper(II) sulphate crystals $CuSO_4.5H_2O$
iron(II) sulphate crystals $FeSO_4.7H_2O$

Name	Formula	Solubility in water
ammonium sulphate	$(NH_4)_2SO_4$	soluble
barium carbonate	$BaCO_3$	insoluble
barium chloride	$BaCl_2$	soluble
barium sulphate	$BaSO_4$	insoluble
lead chloride	$PbCl_2$	insoluble (in cold)
lead nitrate	$Pb(NO_3)_2$	soluble
magnesium carbonate	$MgCO_3$	insoluble
magnesium nitrate	$Mg(NO_3)_2$	soluble
potassium bromide	KBr	soluble
silver bromide	$AgBr$	insoluble
silver nitrate	$AgNO_3$	soluble
silver sulphate	Ag_2SO_4	insoluble
sodium carbonate	Na_2CO_3	soluble
sodium chloride	$NaCl$	soluble

Solubility of various salts in water.

Methods for making salts

There are five methods for making salts: four make **soluble salts** and one makes **insoluble salts**.

A. MAKING SOLUBLE SALTS

1. Acid + alkali → a salt + water
   e.g. $HCl(aq) + NaOH(aq) \rightarrow NaCl(aq) + H_2O(l)$

2. Acid + base → a salt + water
   e.g. $H_2SO_4(aq) + CuO(s) \rightarrow CuSO_4(aq) + H_2O(l)$

3. Acid + carbonate → a salt + water + carbon dioxide
   e.g. $2HNO_3(aq) + CuCO_3(s) \rightarrow Cu(NO_3)_2(aq) + H_2O(l) + CO_2(g)$

4. Acid + metal → a salt + hydrogen
   e.g. $2HCl(aq) + Mg(s) \rightarrow MgCl_2(aq) + H_2(g)$

The four general equations above are best remembered by the initials of the reactants:

A (acid) + A (alkali)
A (acid) + B (base)
A (acid) + C (carbonate)
A (acid) + M (metal)

The symbol '(aq)' after the formula of the salt shows that it is a **soluble salt**.

Neutralisation is the specific term used for the reactions of **acids** with **alkalis** and **bases**. When acids react with alkalis, the reaction is between H^+ ions and OH^- ions to make water, as:

$H^+(aq) + OH^-(aq) \rightarrow H_2O(l)$

Water is a weak electrolyte because it only partially dissociates back to the ions.

Reactions of acids with alkalis are used in the experimental procedure of **titration**, in which solutions react together to give the end-point shown by an indicator. Calculations are then performed to find the concentration of the acid or the alkali.

Apparatus for a titration.

Adding copper carbonate to hydrochloric acid.

B. MAKING INSOLUBLE SALTS

If two solutions of **soluble salts** are mixed together forming two new salts and one of the products is **insoluble**, the **insoluble salt** forms a **precipitate** – a 'solid made in solution'.
The general equation is:

> soluble + soluble → insoluble + soluble
> salt salt salt salt
> (precipitate)
>
> For example:
>
> $Na_2CO_3(aq) + CuSO_4(aq) \rightarrow CuCO_3(s) + Na_2SO_4(aq)$

The **state symbols** show the salts in solution as (aq) and the precipitate – the insoluble salt – as (s).

Making salts in the laboratory

A. SOLUBLE SALTS

Of the *four* methods for making soluble salts, symbol (aq), only *one* uses solution A(aq) + solution B(aq).

> *Method 1 (neutralisation):*
>
> acid(aq) + alkali(aq) → a salt(aq) + water(l)

The other three methods involve adding a solid(s) to a solution(aq).

> *Method 2:*
>
> acid(aq) + base(s) → a salt(aq) + water(l)
>
> *Method 3:*
>
> acid(aq) + carbonate(s) → a salt(aq) + water(l) + carbon dioxide(g)
>
> *Method 4:*
>
> acid(aq) + metal(s) → a salt(aq) + hydrogen(g)

The flow diagram shows how to make soluble salts from solids, namely in Methods 2, 3 and 4.

Making soluble salts

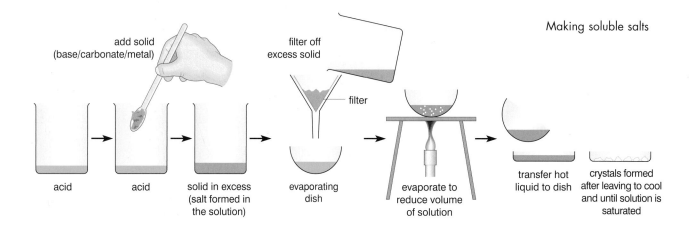

B. INSOLUBLE SALTS

Method 5 involves making a precipitate of an insoluble salt by mixing solutions of two soluble salts:

soluble + soluble → insoluble + soluble
salt(aq)   salt(aq)   salt(s)   salt(aq)

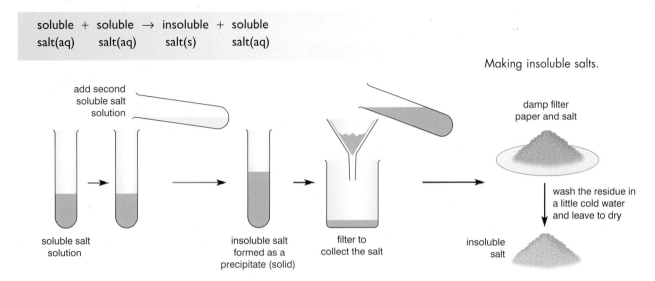

Making insoluble salts.

Identification of ions and gases

It is of the **highest importance** that you **work safely** when performing experiments in a chemistry laboratory. These are precautions you should follow:

- Wear **suitable clothing**, e.g. a laboratory coat or other protective clothing.
- Wear **safety goggles** to protect eyes.
- Wear **gloves** to protect hands.
- Perform experiments in a **fume cupboard** when hazardous gases are involved.

To work safely with chemicals, it is important to know what dangers they pose. Containers for chemical substances have hazard symbols to show what the dangers are. A substance may have more than one symbol.

Hazard symbol	Hazard	Explanation
	corrosive	Attacks and destroys living tissue, e.g. skin, eyes
	toxic	Can cause death when swallowed, breathed in or absorbed through the skin
	oxidising	Provides oxygen which allows other substances to burn far more fiercely
	harmful	Similar to toxic substances but less dangerous
	irritant	Not corrosive but can cause reddening or blistering of the skin
	highly flammable	Catches fire easily

Careful handling of hazardous substances.

Identifying gases

Many chemical reactions produce a **gas** as one of the products. Identifying the gas is often a step in identifying the **compound** that produced it in the reaction (see 'Testing for anions' on pages 86 and 87).

Gas	Formula	Test	Result of test
hydrogen	H_2	Put in a lighted splint (a flame)	'Pop' or 'squeaky pop' heard (flame usually goes out)
oxygen	O_2	Put in a glowing splint	Splint relights, producing a flame
carbon dioxide	CO_2	Pass gas through limewater	Limewater goes cloudy/milky
chlorine	Cl_2	Put in a piece of damp blue litmus paper	Paper goes red then white (decolourised)
ammonia	NH_3	Put in a piece of damp red litmus or UI paper	Paper goes blue

Identifying metal ions (cations)

Ions of metals are **cations – positive ions –** and are found in ionic compounds. There are two ways of identifying metal cations:

* *either* from **solids** of the compound

* *or* from **solutions** of the compound.

Metal ions in solids

A. FLAME TESTS

In a flame test, a piece of nichrome wire is dipped into concentrated hydrochloric acid, then into the solid compound, and then into a **blue** Bunsen flame. A colour is seen in the flame which identifies the metal ion in the compound (see flame tests, page 113).

Name of ion	Formula of ion	Colour seen in flame
lithium	Li^+	bright red
sodium	Na^+	golden yellow/orange
potassium	K^+	lilac (purple)
calcium	Ca^{2+}	brick red
barium	Ba^{2+}	apple green

B. TESTS ON SOLUTIONS IN WATER

Metal ions are found in **ionic compounds**, so most will dissolve in water to form solutions. These **solutions** can be tested with other substances to identify the aqueous cation:

Name of ion in solution	Formula	Test	Result
aluminium	$Al^{3+}(aq)$	Add sodium hydroxide solution in drops. Keep adding until in excess	White precipitate formed which dissolves in excess sodium hydroxide solution
calcium	$Ca^{2+}(aq)$	Add sodium hydroxide solution in drops. Keep adding until in excess	White precipitate formed which remains even when excess sodium hydroxide solution added
copper(II)	$Cu^{2+}(aq)$	Add sodium hydroxide solution in drops	Light blue precipitate formed
iron(II)	$Fe^{2+}(aq)$	Add sodium hydroxide solution in drops	Green precipitate formed. On standing, changes to reddish brown colour
iron(III)	$Fe^{3+}(aq)$	Add sodium hydroxide solution in drops	Reddish brown precipitate formed
magnesium	$Mg^{2+}(aq)$	Add sodium hydroxide solution in drops. Keep adding until in excess	White precipitate formed which remains, even when excess sodium hydroxide solution is added

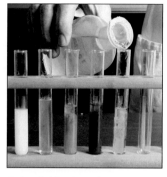

Colourful hydroxide precipitates of magnesium, barium, calcium, etc.

Identifying ammonium ions, NH_4^+

Ammonia gas is **very soluble** in water where it forms the ammonium ion and the hydroxide ion:

ammonia	+	water	→ ammonium ion	+	hydroxide ion
$NH_3(g)$	+	H_2O	→ $NH_4^+(aq)$	+	$OH^-(aq)$

This solution is alkaline, so when UI paper or red litmus paper is added to it, they both change to blue. This is not the test for ammonium ions – any alkaline solution will give this result.

The test for the **ammonium** ion is as in the diagram.

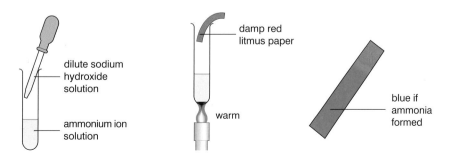

dilute sodium hydroxide solution

ammonium ion solution

damp red litmus paper

warm

blue if ammonia formed

Test for the ammonium ion, NH_4^+.

Identifying anions

As with metal cations, negative ions (anions) are tested as **solids** or as **solutions**.

A. TESTING FOR ANIONS IN SOLIDS

The following test for anions in solids applies only to **carbonates**.

Dilute hydrochloric or sulphuric acid is added to the solid, and any gas produced is passed through limewater. If the limewater goes cloudy/milky, the solid contains a carbonate.

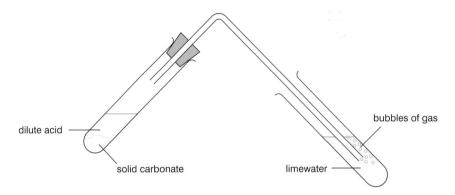

This reaction has been met before:

acid + carbonate → a salt + water + carbon dioxide

There are two solid carbonates which have colour changes that can be used to identify them:

1 **Copper(II) carbonate** is a **green** solid which when heated goes **black** and gives off carbon dioxide:

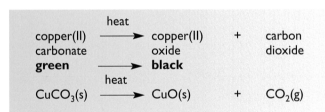

2 **Zinc carbonate** is a **white** solid which when heated goes yellow and gives off carbon dioxide.

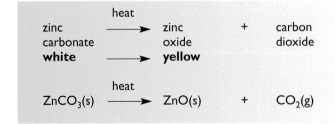

When cold, the zinc oxide changes from **yellow** back to **white**.

B. TESTING FOR ANIONS IN SOLUTION

Ionic compounds are soluble in water, and so they form solutions that contain anions.

Name of ion	Formula	Test	Result
chloride	Cl^-(aq)	To a solution of the halide ions add: 1. dilute nitric acid 2. silver nitrate solution	white precipitate (of AgCl)
bromide	Br^- (aq)		cream/off-white precipitate (of AgBr)
iodide	I^- (aq)		yellow precipitate (of AgI)
sulphate	SO_4^{2-}	Add: 1. dilute hydrochloric acid 2. barium chloride solution	white precipitate (of $BaSO_4$)
nitrate	NO_3^-	1. Add sodium hydroxide solution and warm 2. Add aluminium powder 3. Test any gas produced with damp red litmus paper	red litmus paper goes blue (ammonia gas is produced)

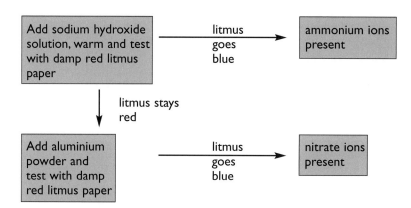

If the silver halides – AgCl, AgBr and AgI – formed as in the table above, are left to stand in daylight for a while, they go dark grey or black. This is because the light reduces them to silver. This darkening in light is the basis of photographic processes which use silver salts on camera film.

REVIEW QUESTIONS

Q1 Explain the difference between neutral and amphoteric oxides.

Q2 a What is an indicator?
     b What is the pH scale?
     c How are Universal Indicator and the pH scale linked?

Q3 Sulphuric acid, H_2SO_4, is a strong acid.
     a What is meant by a 'strong acid'?
     b Write the balanced chemical equation (including state symbols) for sulphuric acid producing ions when dissolved in water.
     c What would be the pH of sulphuric acid?

Q4 When lithium hydroxide, LiOH, dissolves in water, an alkaline solution is formed. Give the balanced chemical equation (including state symbols) for this reaction.

Q5 Methanoic acid, HCOOH, is a weak acid.
a What is meant by 'weak acid'?
b Write the balanced chemical equation for methanoic acid dissolving in water to produce ions.

Q6 Look at the table of experimental results at the end of the question.
a Which of the oxides is/are acidic? Explain how you decided.
b Which of the oxides is/are basic? Explain how you decided.
c Copper(II) oxide reacts with sulphuric acid (H_2SO_4).
  i What is the name given to this type of reaction?
  ii Write a word equation for the reaction.
  iii Write a symbol equation for the reaction.
  iv Which oxide A to D is most likely to be copper(II) oxide?

Oxide of element	pH of solution	Does it react with an acid?	Does it react with an alkali?
A	8	✓	✗
B	3	✗	✓
C	7	✗	✗
D	10	✓	✗

Q7 Complete the following equations and include state symbols:

a $2KOH(aq) + H_2SO_4(aq) \rightarrow$ _____ + _____

b $2HCl(aq) + MgO(s) \rightarrow$ _____ + _____

c $2HNO_3(aq) + BaCO_3(s) \rightarrow$ _____ + _____ + _____

d $2HCl(aq) + Zn(s)$ _____ + _____

e $ZnCl_2(aq) + K_2CO_3(aq) \rightarrow$ _____ + _____

Q8 Describe how you would make a sample of copper(II) sulphate crystals in the laboratory starting with copper(II) oxide powder and dilute sulphuric acid.
Your answer should include any pieces of apparatus used.

Q9 Write the balanced chemical equations (including state symbols) for the preparation of the following salts:
a zinc sulphate from solid zinc
b potassium chloride from potassium hydroxide solution
c copper(II) nitrate from copper(II) carbonate
d magnesium carbonate from magnesium chloride solution and potassium carbonate solution

Q10 A jar containing a chemical substance has two hazard labels on it showing it is both corrosive and highly flammable. What safety precautions should be taken when using this substance?

Q11 Describe the test for chlorine gas.

Q12 A solution is thought to contain the one of the cations aluminium, calcium or magnesium. Describe how you would identify which cation is present in the solution.

Q13 When a white powder is heated it changes in colour to yellow and gives off a gas. When cold, it becomes white again. Identify the white solid that is heated and the gas it gives off.

More questions on the CD ROM

Examination questions are on page 96.

EXAMINATION QUESTIONS

Q1 Ammonia is a gas which forms an alkaline
solution when dissolved in water.

a   Complete the diagram on the right to show the
arrangement of the molecules in ammonia gas.

O represents a single molecule of ammonia.

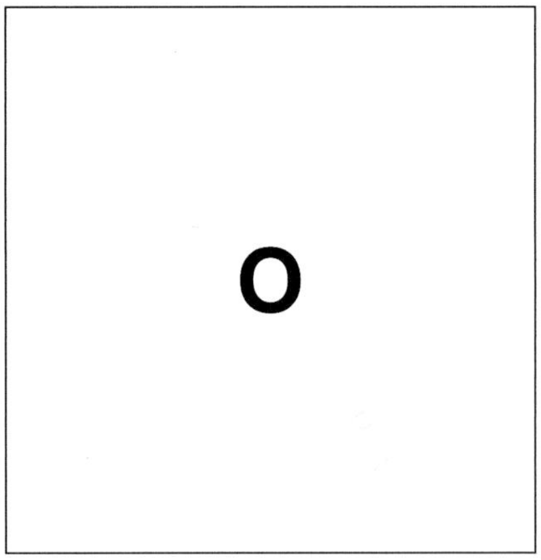

[2]

b   Which one of the following values is most likely to represent the pH of a dilute
solution of ammonia? Put a ring around the correct answer.

pH2   pH6   pH7   pH9   [1]

c   The structure of the ammonia molecule is shown here.

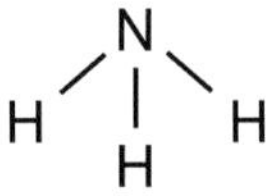

i   Write the simplest formula for ammonia.
_____ [1]

ii   Describe the type of bonding in a molecule of ammonia.
_____ [1]

iii   Ammonia is a gas at room temperature. Suggest why ammonia has a low
boiling point.
_____ [1]

d   Many fertilisers contain ammonium sulphate.
i   Which acid must be added to ammonia solution to make ammonium sulphate?
Put a ring around the correct answer.

HCl HNO_3 H_3PO_4 H_2SO_4 [1]

ii   Fill in the missing words in the following sentence using two of the words from
the list.

air   hydrogen   nitrogen   soil   sodium   water

Fertilisers are needed in agriculture to replace the _____ ,
phosphorus and other elements which are removed from the _____
when crops are grown.   [2]

e   A solution of ammonia has a strong smell.
A beaker of ammonia solution is put
in the corner of a room which
is free of draughts.

At first, the girl by the closed window cannot smell the ammonia.
After 30 seconds she smells the ammonia.
Use the kinetic particle theory to explain these facts.

_____

_____

_____

_____ [3]

f   The diagram shows the apparatus used
    for oxidising ammonia in the laboratory.
    First, nitrogen(II) oxide, NO, is produced.
    This then reacts with oxygen to form
    nitrogen(IV) oxide, NO_2.

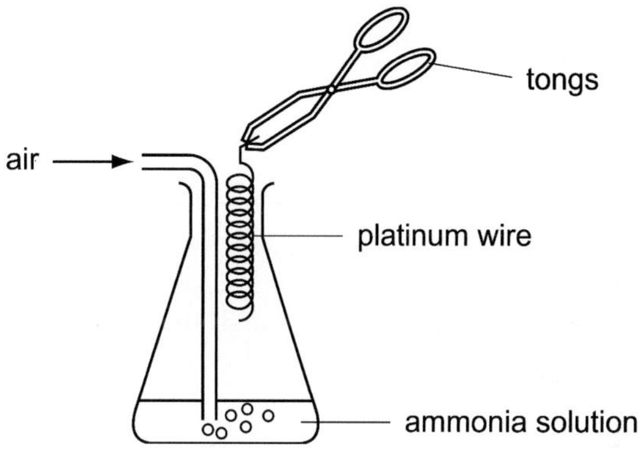

air →

tongs

platinum wire

ammonia solution

   i   Where does the oxygen come
       from in this reaction?

_____ [1]

   ii Balance the equation for the reaction of nitrogen(II) oxide with oxygen.

$$2NO + O_2 \rightleftharpoons .....NO_2$$ [1]

_____ [1]

   iii What is the meaning of the symbol $\rightleftharpoons$? [1]
   iv The platinum wire acts as a catalyst in the reaction. As the reaction takes place,
       the wire begins to glow red hot. What does this show about the reaction?

_____ [1]

Q2 The electroplating of iron with chromium involves four stages.
   1 The iron object is cleaned with sulphuric acid, then washed with water.
   2 The iron is plated with copper.
   3 It is then plated with nickel to prevent corrosion.
   4 It is then plated with chromium.
   a   The equation for stage 1 is

$$Fe + H_2SO_4 \rightarrow FeSO4 + H_2$$

   i   Write a word equation for this reaction.

_____ [2]

   ii Describe a test for the gas given off in this reaction.
       test _____

       result _____ [2]

   b   The diagram shows how iron is electroplated with copper.

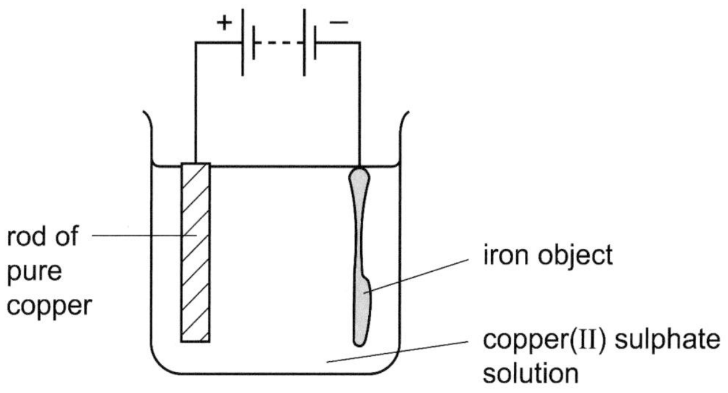

rod of
pure
copper

iron object

copper(II) sulphate
solution

    i   Choose a word from the list below which describes the iron object. Put a ring around the correct answer.

        anion   anode   cathode   cation   [1]

    ii   What is the purpose of the copper(II) sulphate solution?

        _____ [1]

    iii Describe what happens during the electroplating to

        the iron object, _____

        the rod of pure copper. _____ [2]

    iv Describe a test for copper(II) ions.

        test _____

        result _____

        _____ [3]

c   Suggest why chromium is used to electroplate articles.

    _____ [1]

d   The information below shows the reactivity of chromium, copper and iron with warm hydrochloric acid.

    chromium – few bubbles of gas produced every second
    copper – no bubbles of gas produced
    iron – many bubbles of gas produced every second

    Put these three metals in order of their reactivity with hydrochloric acid.

    Most reactive →

    Least reactive →   [1]

Q3 A South Korean chemist has discovered a cure for smelly socks. Small particles of silver are attached to a polymer, poly(propene), and this is woven into the socks.

a   i   Give the structural formula of the monomer.

                                            [1]

    ii   Draw the structural formula of the polymer.

                                            [2]

    iii Suggest which one, monomer or polymer, will react with aqueous bromine and why?

        _____

        _____ [2]

b   To show that the polymer contains silver the following test was carried out.

    The polymer fibres were chopped into small pieces and warmed with nitric acid. The silver atoms were oxidised to silver(I) ions. The mixture was filtered. Aqueous sodium chloride was added to the filtrate and a white precipitate formed.

    i   Why was the mixture filtered?

        _____ [2]

ii   Explain why the change of silver atoms to silver ions is oxidation.

_____ [1]

iii Give the name of the white precipitate.

_____ [1]

c   The unpleasant smell is caused by carboxylic acids. Bacteria cause the fats on the
skin to be hydrolysed to these acids. Silver kills the bacteria and prevents the
hydrolysis of the fats.
   i   Fats are esters. Give the name and structural formula of an ester.
   name _____ [1]
   structural formula

   ┌───┐
   │   │
   │   │
   └───┘
                                                           [1]

   ii   Complete the word equation.
   Ester + water → carboxylic acid   +   _____   [1]

d   Propanoic acid is a weak acid.
   i   The following equation represents its reaction with ammonia.

   $CH_3 CH_2 COOH + NH_3 \rightarrow CH_3 CH_2 COO^- + NH_4^+$

   Explain why propanoic acid behaves as an acid and ammonia as a base.

   _____

   _____ [3]

   ii   Explain the expression weak acid.

   _____ [1]

Q4 The diagram shows the apparatus used to find out the effect of an electric current on a
concentrated aqueous solution of sodium chloride.

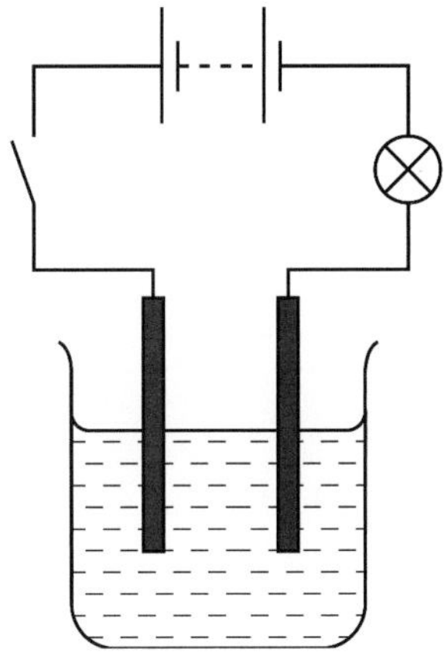

a   On the diagram label the electrodes [1]
b   Give three observations when the circuit is switched on.
   1 _____
   2 _____
   3 _____ [3]
c   i   Name the product at the positive electrode (anode).

   _____ [1]

   ii   State a test for this product and the result of the test.
   test _____
   result _____ [2]

Q5 In a set of experiments zinc was reacted with sulphuric acid to form hydrogen. The apparatus below was used.

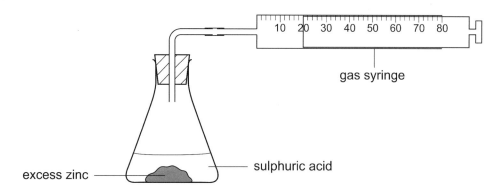

gas syringe

excess zinc — sulphuric acid

The same mass of zinc was used each time. The volume of acid used was different each time.
Use the syringe diagrams to record the volume of hydrogen produced each time in the table.

Table of results

volume of sulphuric acid/cm^3	syringe diagram	volume of hydrogen/cm^3
0	10 20 30 40 50 60 70 80	
5	10 20 30 40 50 60 70 80	
15	10 20 30 40 50 60 70 80	
20	10 20 30 40 50 60 70 80	
25	10 20 30 40 50 60 70 80	
30	10 20 30 40 50 60 70 80	
35	10 20 30 40 50 60 70 80	
40	10 20 30 40 50 60 70 80	

[4]

a   Plot the results on the grid below. Draw a smooth line graph.

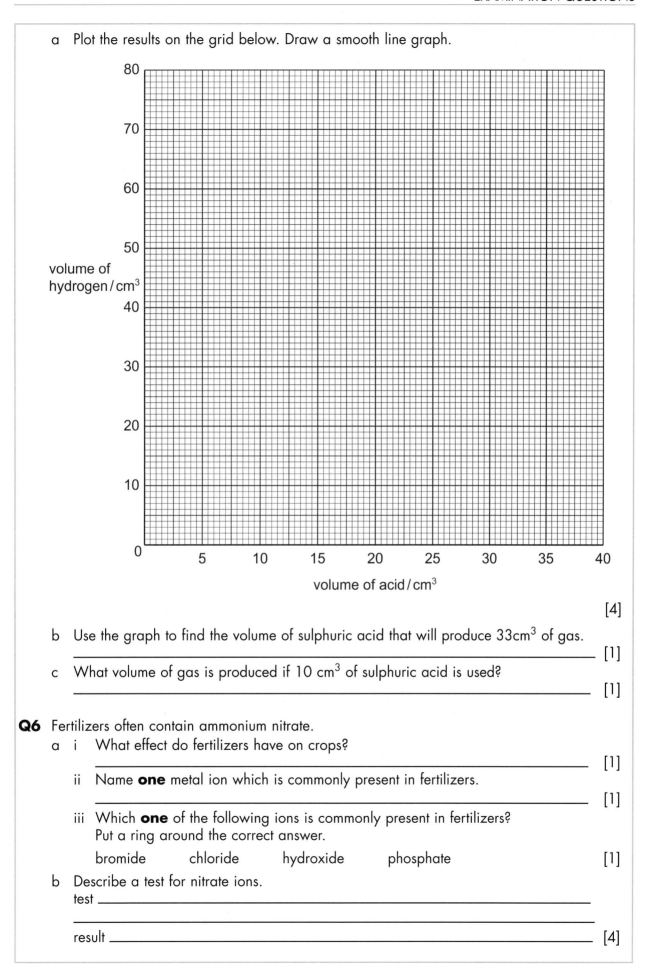

volume of hydrogen / cm³

volume of acid / cm³

[4]

b   Use the graph to find the volume of sulphuric acid that will produce 33cm³ of gas.

_____ [1]

c   What volume of gas is produced if 10 cm³ of sulphuric acid is used?

_____ [1]

Q6 Fertilizers often contain ammonium nitrate.

a   i   What effect do fertilizers have on crops?

_____ [1]

ii   Name **one** metal ion which is commonly present in fertilizers.

_____ [1]

iii Which **one** of the following ions is commonly present in fertilizers?
     Put a ring around the correct answer.

bromide   chloride   hydroxide   phosphate   [1]

b   Describe a test for nitrate ions.

test _____

_____

result _____ [4]

c Ammonium nitrate can be made by adding nitric acid to a solution of ammonia.
  i What type of reaction is this?

  _____ [1]

  ii Complete the symbol equation for this reaction.

  _____ + $HNO_3(aq)$ → $NH_4NO_3(aq)$

d Which two of the following statements about ammonia are true?
  Tick two boxes.

  ammonia is insoluble in water ☐

  ammonia turns red litmus blue ☐

  a solution of ammonia in water has a pH of 7 ☐

  ammonia has a molecular structure ☐ [2]

Q7 The electrolysis of a concentrated solution of sodium chloride, provides us with chemicals.
  a Sodium chloride has an ionic giant structure.
    Which one of the following is a correct description of a property of sodium chloride.
    Tick one box.

    sodium chloride has a low melting point ☐

    sodium chloride conducts electricity when it is solid ☐

    sodium chloride has a high boiling point ☐

    sodium chloride is insoluble in water ☐ [1]

  b i Explain what is meant by the term electrolysis.

    _____

    _____ [1]

    ii At which electrode is hydrogen produced during the electrolysis of aqueous
       sodium chloride?

    _____ [1]

    iii Name a suitable substance that can be used for the electrodes.

    _____ [1]

  c i State the name of the particle which is added to a chlorine atom to make
      a chloride ion.

    _____ [1]

    ii Describe a test for chloride ions.
       test _____

       result _____ [2]

  d If chlorine is allowed to mix with sodium hydroxide, sodium chlorate(I),
    NaOCl is formed.
    Balance the equation for this reaction.

    Cl_2 + _____ NaOH → NaCl + NaOCl + H_2O [1]

  e One tonne (1 000 kg) of a commercial solution of sodium hydroxide produced by
    electrolysis contains the following masses of compounds.

compound	mass of compound kg/ tonne
sodium hydroxide	510
sodium chloride	10
sodium chlorate(V)	9
water	471
total	1000

    i   How many kilograms of sodium hydroxide will be present in 5 tonnes of the solution?

_____ [1]

    ii All the water from one tonne of impure sodium hydroxide is evaporated. What would the approximate percentage of the remaining impurities be? Put a ring around the correct answer.

    0.036%   3.6%   36%   96%   [1]

f   The hydrogen obtained by electrolysis can be used in the manufacture of margarine.

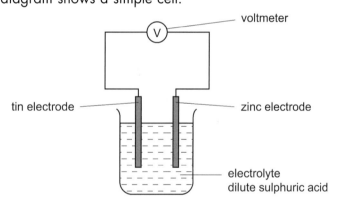

    i   Complete the following sentences about this reaction using words from the list.

    catalyst   **inhibitor**   **monomeric**   **saturated**   **unsaturated**

    Hydrogen gas is bubbled through _____ carbon compounds using a nickel _____ which speeds up the reaction.
The margarines produced are _____ compounds.   [3]

    ii State one other use of hydrogen.

_____ [1]

Q8 The following diagram shows a simple cell.

    i   Predict how the voltage of the cell would change if the tin electrode was replaced with a silver one.

                                                            [1]

    ii Which electrode would go into the solution as positive ions? Give a reason for your choice.

                                                            [1]

    ii State how you can predict the direction of the electron flow in cells of this type.

                                                            [1]

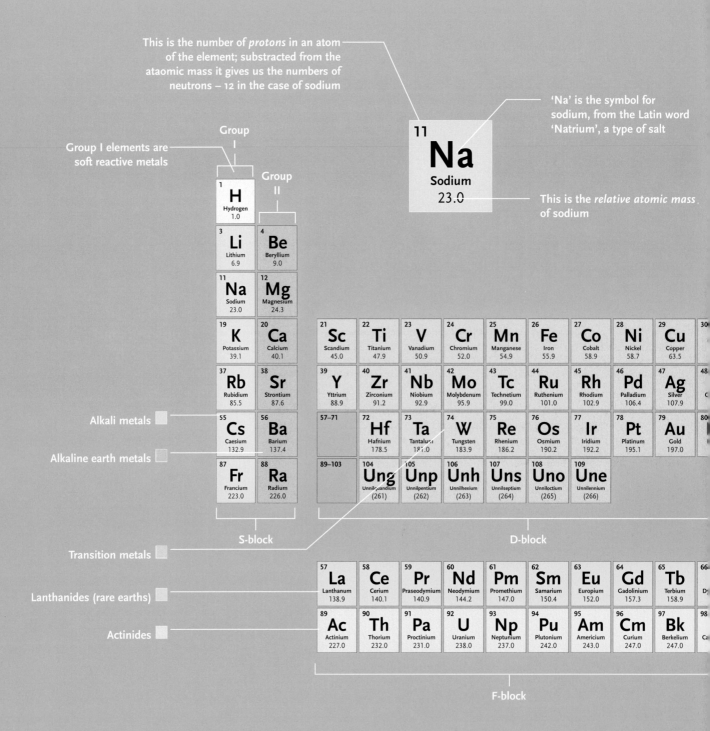

This is the number of *protons* in an atom of the element; substracted from the ataomic mass it gives us the numbers of neutrons – 12 in the case of sodium

‘Na’ is the symbol for sodium, from the Latin word ‘Natrium’, a type of salt

This is the *relative atomic mass* of sodium

Group I elements are soft reactive metals

Group I

Group II

11		
Na		
Sodium		
23.0		

Alkali metals

Alkaline earth metals

S-block

D-block

Transition metals

Lanthanides (rare earths)

Actinides

F-block

1	
H	
Hydrogen	
1.0	

3	4
Li	**Be**
Lithium	Beryllium
6.9	9.0

11	12
Na	**Mg**
Sodium	Magnesium
23.0	24.3

19	20
K	**Ca**
Potassium	Calcium
39.1	40.1

37	38
Rb	**Sr**
Rubidium	Strontium
85.5	87.6

55	56
Cs	**Ba**
Caesium	Barium
132.9	137.4

87	88
Fr	**Ra**
Francium	Radium
223.0	226.0

21	22	23	24	25	26	27	28	29	30
Sc	**Ti**	**V**	**Cr**	**Mn**	**Fe**	**Co**	**Ni**	**Cu**	
Scandium	Titanium	Vanadium	Chromium	Manganese	Iron	Cobalt	Nickel	Copper	
45.0	47.9	50.9	52.0	54.9	55.9	58.9	58.7	63.5	

39	40	41	42	43	44	45	46	47	48
Y	**Zr**	**Nb**	**Mo**	**Tc**	**Ru**	**Rh**	**Pd**	**Ag**	
Yttrium	Zirconium	Niobium	Molybdenum	Technetium	Ruthenium	Rhodium	Palladium	Silver	
88.9	91.2	92.9	95.9	99.0	101.0	102.9	106.4	107.9	

57–71	72	73	74	75	76	77	78	79	80
	Hf	**Ta**	**W**	**Re**	**Os**	**Ir**	**Pt**	**Au**	
	Hafnium	Tantalum	Tungsten	Rhenium	Osmium	Iridium	Platinum	Gold	
	178.5	181.0	183.9	186.2	190.2	192.2	195.1	197.0	

89–103	104	105	106	107	108	109
	Ung	**Unp**	**Unh**	**Uns**	**Uno**	**Une**
	Unnilquandium	Unnilpentium	Unnilhexium	Unnilseptium	Unniloctium	Unnilennium
	(261)	(262)	(263)	(264)	(265)	(266)

57	58	59	60	61	62	63	64	65	66
La	**Ce**	**Pr**	**Nd**	**Pm**	**Sm**	**Eu**	**Gd**	**Tb**	
Lanthanum	Cerium	Praseodymium	Neodymium	Promethium	Samarium	Europium	Gadolinium	Terbium	
138.9	140.1	140.9	144.2	147.0	150.4	152.0	157.3	158.9	

89	90	91	92	93	94	95	96	97	98
Ac	**Th**	**Pa**	**U**	**Np**	**Pu**	**Am**	**Cm**	**Bk**	
Actinium	Thorium	Proctinium	Uranium	Neptunium	Plutonium	Americium	Curium	Berkelium	
227.0	232.0	231.0	238.0	237.0	242.0	243.0	247.0	247.0	

A map of the chemical world

The first maps of the world were made by Greek and Arab scholars, and have always told us more than simply how to get to where we are going. How far must we travel, how long will it take, and what will we find when we get there? For visitors to a new country or town, a map is the first place to turn to. Chemistry has its own map – the periodic table. All known elements are listed there. From the information given, we can determine their atomic structure, predict which are solid, liquid or gas, and learn much about their properties. In the world of inorganic chemistry, the periodic table is an indispensable guide.

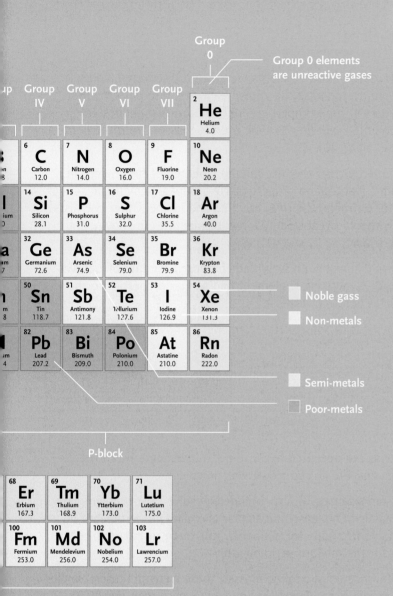

Group
0

Group 0 elements
are unreactive gases

Group IV	Group V	Group VI	Group VII	Group 0

Noble gas

Non-metals

Semi-metals

Poor-metals

P-block

9 THE PERIODIC TABLE

Organising the elements

In the nineteenth century, new elements were being discovered, and chemists were trying to organise the known elements into patterns that related to similarities in their properties. **John Dalton** first suggested arranging the elements according to their **atomic masses**, from the lightest to the heaviest (see page 20).

Starting in 1817, the German chemist **Johann Dobereiner** first made the link between atomic masses and properties. He grouped elements in sets of three – **triads** – for example, chlorine, bromine and iodine. Other chemists did not accept his theory because only a few elements were known, and not all fitted into triads.

In 1864, the British chemist **John Newlands** proposed the **law of octaves** – an idea from music – where every element had similar properties to the element eight places before or after it.

Newlands' arrangement of some of the elements is shown below.

1	2	3	4	5	6	7
H	Li	Be	B	C	N	O
F	Na	Mg	Al	Si	P	S
Cl	K	Ca	Cr	Ti	Mn	Fe

Newlands' table was not accepted because not all elements fitted the pattern of octaves and the link to music was ridiculed.

In 1869, the Russian scientist **Dimitri Mendeleev** solved the problem. Like others, he grouped elements based on similar chemical properties but, importantly, his table left **gaps for elements still to be discovered**. His work is the basis for the modern periodic table.

Because Mendeleev was using atomic masses, there were still discrepancies in the table. For example, he placed the unreactive gas argon (M_r 39.9) after potassium (M_r 39.1) and in with the reactive metals sodium and lithium.

When the structure of the atom was better known, the elements were arranged in order of **increasing atomic number**, and then the patterns worked. (Atomic number is the number of protons in the atom.) Mendeleev had been very close with his original table.

How are elements classified in the modern periodic table?

Elements are the building blocks from which all materials are made. Over 100 elements have now been identified, and each element has its own properties and reactions. In the **periodic table**, elements with similar properties and reactions are put close together.

The periodic table arranges the elements in order of increasing atomic number. As atoms are neutral, the atomic number gives the number of electrons. The elements are then arranged in **periods** and **groups**.

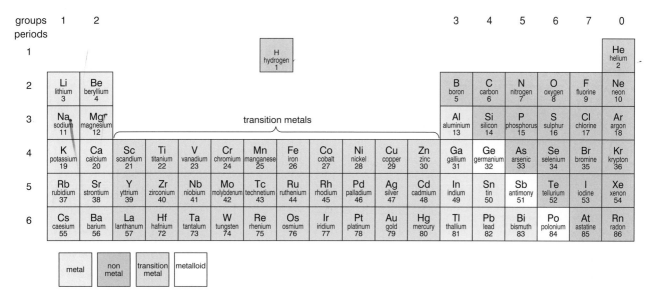

Periods

Rows of elements are arranged in increasing atomic number from left to right. Rows correspond to periods which are numbered from 1 to 7.

As we go across a period each successive atom of the elements gains one proton, one electron (in the same outer shell/orbit) and variable numbers of neutrons.

You can see how this works in the diagram below :

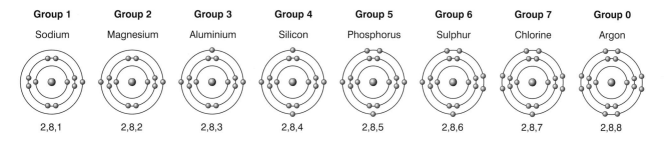

Group 1	Group 2	Group 3	Group 4	Group 5	Group 6	Group 7	Group 0
Sodium	Magnesium	Aluminium	Silicon	Phosphorus	Sulphur	Chlorine	Argon
2,8,1	2,8,2	2,8,3	2,8,4	2,8,5	2,8,6	2,8,7	2,8,8

As we go across a period like period 3 (sodium to argon) the following trends take place

1. Metals on the left going to non-metals on the right

2. Group 1 elements are the most reactive metal group, and as you go to the left the reactivity of the groups decreases. Group 4 elements are the least reactive.

Continuing left from Group 4 the reactivity increases until Group 7 the most reactve of the non-metal groups.

The first period contains only two elements, hydrogen and helium.

The elements in the middle block of the periodic table in periods 4, 5 and 6 are called the **transition metals**. One of the typical properties of transition metals and their compounds is their ability to act as catalysts and speed up the rate of a chemical reaction by providing an alternative pathway with a lower activation energy, e.g. vanadium (V) oxide in the Contact process and iron in the Haber process.

Groups

Columns contain elements with the atomic number increasing down the column. They are numbered from 1 to 7 and 0.

Elements in a group have similar properties – they are a 'chemical family'.

Some groups have family names – the **alkali metals** (group 1), the **halogens** (group 7) and the **noble gases** (group 0).

We can explain why elements in the same group have similar reactions in terms of the electron structures of their atoms. Elements with the same number of electrons in their outer shells have similar chemical properties.

Metals and non-metals

Most elements can be classified as either **metals** or **non-metals**. In the periodic table, the metals are arranged on the left and in the middle, and the non-metals are on the right.

Metalloid elements are between metals and non-metals. They have some properties of metals and some of non-metals. Examples of metalloids are silicon and germanium.

Metals and non-metals have quite different physical and chemical properties.

Group properties

Most elements are metals. Some metals are highly reactive whilst others are almost completely unreactive. The two types of metals are found in different parts of the periodic table.

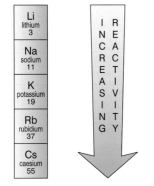

Group 1 elements become more reactive as you go further down the group.

Group 1 – the alkali metals

These very reactive metals all have only **one electron** in their outer electron shell. This electron is readily given away when the metal reacts with non-metals. The more electrons a metal atom has to lose in a reaction, the more energy is needed to start the reaction. This is why the group 2 elements are less reactive – they have to lose two electrons when they react (see ionic bonding, page 22).

Reactivity increases down the group because, as the atom gets bigger, the outer electron is further away from the nucleus and so can be removed more easily, as the atoms react and form **cations**.

Properties of group 1 metals

Soft and easy to cut.

Shiny when cut, but quickly tarnish in the air.

Very low melting points compared with most metals.

Very low densities compared with most metals (lithium, sodium and potassium will float on water).

React very easily with air, water and elements such as chlorine. The alkali metals are so reactive that they are stored in oil to prevent reaction with air and water.

Reaction	Observations	Equations
Air or oxygen	The metals burn easily and their compounds colour flames: • lithium – red • sodium – yellow/orange • potassium – lilac A white solid oxide is formed.	lithium + oxygen → lithium oxide $4Li(s) + O_2(g) \rightarrow 2Li_2O(s)$ sodium + oxygen → sodium oxide $4Na(s) + O_2(g) \rightarrow 2Na_2O(s)$ potassium + oxygen → potassium oxide $4K(s) + O_2(g) \rightarrow 2K_2O(s)$

Reaction	Observations	Equations
Water	The metals react vigorously. They float on the surface, moving around rapidly. The heat of the reaction melts the metal so it forms a sphere. Bubbles of gas are given off, and the metal 'disappears'. With the more reactive metals (e.g. potassium) the hydrogen gas produced burns. The resulting solution is alkaline.	lithium + water → lithium hydroxide + hydrogen $2Li(s) + 2H_2O(l) \rightarrow 2LiOH(aq) + H_2(g)$ sodium + water → sodium hydroxide + hydrogen $2Na(s) + 2H_2O(l) \rightarrow 2NaOH(aq) + H_2(g)$ potassium + water → potassium hydroxide + hydrogen $2K(s) + 2H_2O(l) \rightarrow 2KOH(aq) + H_2(g)$
Chlorine	The metals react easily, burning in the chlorine to form a white solid.	lithium + chlorine → lithium chloride $2Li(s) + Cl_2(g) \rightarrow 2LiCl(s)$ sodium + chlorine → sodium chloride $2Na(s) + Cl_2(g) \rightarrow 2NaCl(s)$ potassium + chlorine → potassium chloride $2K(s) + Cl_2(g) \rightarrow 2KCl(s)$

Uses for group 1 metals

The compounds of the alkali metals are widely used:

- lithium carbonate – in light sensitive lenses for glasses
- lithium hydroxide – removes carbon dioxide in air-conditioning systems
- sodium chloride – table salt
- sodium carbonate – a water softener
- sodium hydroxide – used in paper manufacture
- monosodium glutamate – a flavour enhancer
- sodium sulphite – a preservative
- potassium nitrate – a fertiliser; also used in explosives.

The non-metals

There are only about 20 non-metal elements. There is a wide range of reactivity between different groups of non-metals. The most reactive non-metals are found in group 7, the least reactive are found in the next group, group 0.

F	
fluorine	
9	
Cl	
chlorine	
17	
Br	
bromine	
35	
I	
iodine	
53	
At	
astatine	
85	

INCREASING REACTIVITY

The elements become more reactive as you go further up the group.

At room temperature and atomospheric pressure, chlorine is a pale green gas, bromine an orange liquid and iodine is a grey/black solid.

Group 7 – The halogens

The term 'halogen' means 'salt-maker' and the halogens react with most metals to make salts.

The halogen elements have seven electrons in their outermost electron shell, so they only need to gain one electron to obtain a full outer electron shell, which makes them very reactive. The halogens react with metals, gaining an electron and forming a singly charged negative ion (see ionic bonding, page 22.)

The reactivity of the elements decreases down the group because, as the atom gets bigger, an eighth electron will be further from the attractive force of the nucleus. This means it is harder for the atom to gain this electron.

Differences between the group 7 elements

Appearance: fluorine is a pale yellow gas; chlorine is a yellow-green gas; bromine is a brown liquid; iodine is a grey/black solid.

Similarities between the group 7 elements

All have 7 electrons in their outermost electron shell.

All exist as diatomic molecules (molecules containing two atoms – e.g. F_2, Cl_2, Br_2, I_2).

Reaction	Observations	Equations
Water	The halogens dissolve in water and also react with it, forming solutions that behave as bleaches. Chlorine solution is pale yellow. Bromine solution is brown. Iodine solution is brown.	chlorine + water → hydrochloric acid + chloric(I) acid $Cl_2(g) + H_2O(l) \rightarrow HCl(aq) + HClO(aq)$
Metals	The halogens will form salts with all metals. For example, gold leaf will catch fire in chlorine without heating. With a metal such as iron, brown fumes of iron(III) chloride form.	iron + chlorine → iron(III) chloride $2Fe(s) + 3Cl_2(g) \rightarrow 2FeCl_3(s)$ Fluorine forms salts called fluorides. Chlorine forms salts called chlorides. Bromine forms salts called bromides. Iodine forms salts called iodides.

Reaction	Observations	Equations
Displacement chlorine gas → potassium iodide solution iodine being formed	A more reactive halogen will displace a less reactive halogen from a solution of a salt. Chlorine displaces bromine from sodium bromide solution. The colourless solution (sodium bromide) will turn brown as the chlorine is added due to the formation of bromine. Chlorine displaces iodine from sodium iodide solution. The colourless solution (sodium iodide) will turn brown as the chlorine is added due to the formation of iodine.	chlorine + sodium bromide → sodium chloride + bromine $Cl_2(g) + 2NaBr(aq) \rightarrow 2NaCl(aq) + Br_2(aq)$ chlorine + sodium iodide → sodium chloride + iodine $Cl_2(g) + 2NaI(aq) \rightarrow 2NaCl(aq) + I_2(aq)$

The displacement reactions between halogens and halide ions in water are examples of REDOX reactions, i.e. oxidation and reduction processes taking place together, e.g.

$$Cl_2(g) + 2Br^-(aq) \rightarrow 2Cl^-(aq) + Br_2(l)$$

This equation can be rewritten as two separate half-equations showing the involvement of the electrons:

(a) $Cl_2 + 2e^- \rightarrow 2Cl^-$

i.e. the chlorine is **reduced** by gaining electrons from the bromide ions.

(b) $2Br^- \rightarrow Br_2 + 2e^-$

i.e. the bromide ions are **oxidised** by losing electrons to chlorine.

Uses of halogens

The halogens and their compounds have a wide range of uses:

- fluorides – in toothpaste help to prevent tooth decay
- fluorine compounds – make plastics like Teflon (the non-stick surface on pans)
- chlorofluorocarbons – propellants in aerosols and refrigerants (now being phased out due to their effect on the ozone layer)
- chlorine – a bleach
- chlorine compounds – kill bacteria in drinking water and are used in antiseptics
- hydrochloric acid – widely used in industry
- bromine compounds – make pesticides
- silver bromide – the light sensitive film coating on photographic film
- iodine solution – an antiseptic.

The Dead Sea is very high in bromides which give it great buoyancy

Predicting properties of elements

Metallic elements are on the left of the Periodic Table, and non-metallic elements are on the right. In the middle of the Table, Group 4 is the best example, as it is where metals meet non-metals.

As you go down any group in the Periodic Table, the properties change as the atoms become larger, i.e. more electron orbits and greater numbers of protons and neutrons in the nucleus. The size of an atom is described in a term called **atomic radius**.

There are general rules that need to be learned so that you can predict the properties of other elements in the same Group.

1   As you go down a metallic element group, e.g. Group 1, the elements become more reactive as the atoms get larger. In Group 1, lithium (Li) is the least reactive element.

Metallic elements lose electrons when they react, and the larger atoms lose electrons more easily than small atoms because the outer electrons are closer to the positive attraction of the protons in the nucleus. The easier it is for a metallic atom to lose its outer electrons the more reactive it is.

2   As you go down a non-metallic element group, e.g. Group 7, the elements become less reactive as the atoms get larger.

In Group 7, fluorine (F) is the most reactive element.

Non-metallic elements gain electrons when they react. The smaller atoms near the top of the group do not have the attractive pull of the protons reduced by larger numbers of electron orbits around them.

Trends in other groups

The trend in **increasing reactivity** down a metallic group, like Group 1, is the same for Groups 2 and 3, which are also mainly metallic.

The trend in decreasing reactivity down a non-metallic group, like Group 7, is the same for Groups 5 and 7, which are mainly non-metallic.

Group 4 shows best of all the change from metallic properties to non-metallic properties.

Group 4
C   non-metal
Si   non-metal
Ge   metalloid
Sn   metal
Pb   metal

'Metalloid' means that germanium behaves sometimes like a metal and sometimes like a non-metal.

The rules for predicting trends are:

1   AS YOU GO **UP** A GROUP THE **NON–METALLIC** CHARACTER INCREASES

2   AS YOU GO **DOWN** A GROUP THE **METALLIC** CHARACTER INCREASES.

Transition elements

The transition metals are listed in the centre of the periodic table.

All the transition metals have **more than one electron in their outer electron shell**. They are much less reactive than Group 1 and Group 2 metals and so are more 'everyday' metals. They have much higher melting points and densities. They react much more slowly with water and with oxygen.

They are widely used as construction metals (particularly iron), and they are frequently used as **catalysts** in the chemical industry.

One of the typical properties of transition metals and their compounds is their ability to act as catalysts and speed up the rate of a chemical reaction by providing an alternative pathway with a lower activation energy, e.g. vanadium (V) oxide in the Contact process and iron in the Haber process.

Property	Group 1 metal	Transition metal
Melting point	low	high
Density	low	high
Colours of compounds	white	coloured
Reactions with water/air	vigorous	slow or no reaction
Reactions with acid	violent (dangerous)	slow or no reaction

Transition metals have more than one oxidation state. For example, copper forms Cu^+ ions and Cu^{2+} ions as shown in its compounds copper (I) oxide, Cu_2O, and copper (II) oxide, CuO.

Also, iron forms Fe^{2+} ions and Fe^{3+} ions as shown in iron (II) hydroxide , $Fe(OH)_2$, and iron (III) hydroxide, $Fe(OH)_3$.

The **compounds** of the transition metals are usually **coloured**. Copper compounds are usually blue or green; iron compounds tend to be either green or brown. When sodium hydroxide solution is added to the solution of a transition metal compound, a precipitate of the metal hydroxide is formed. The colour of the precipitate will help to identify the metal. For example:

copper sulphate	+	sodium hydroxide	→	copper(II) hydroxide	+	sodium sulphate
$CuSO_4(aq)$	+	$2NaOH(aq)$	→	$Cu(OH)_2(s)$	+	$Na_2SO_4(aq)$

This can be written as an ionic equation (see page 34):

$$Cu^{2+}(aq) + 2OH^-(aq) \rightarrow Cu(OH)_2(s)$$

Colour of metal hydroxide	Likely metal present
blue	copper (II) Cu^{2+}
green	nickel (II) Ni^{2+}
green turning to brown	iron (II) Fe^{2+}
orange/brown	iron (III) Fe^{3+}

Transition metal compounds and other metal compounds produce characteristic colours in **flame tests**.

Metal ion	Flame colour
lithium	red
sodium	orange/yellow
potassium	lilac
copper	blue/green
calcium	brick red
strontium	crimson
barium	green

The colour of the flame can be used to identify the metal ions present.

Name	Symbol
Helium	He
Neon	Ne
Argon	Ar
Krypton	Kr
Xenon	Xe
Radon	Rn

The noble gases

This is a group of **very unreactive** non-metals. They used to be called the inert gases as it was thought that they didn't react with anything! But scientists later managed to produce fluorine compounds of some of the noble gases. As far as your school laboratory work is concerned, however, they are completely unreactive

This can be explained in terms of their electronic structures. The atoms all have **complete outer electron shells**. They don't need to lose electrons (as metals do), or gain electrons (as most non-metals do).

Similarities of the noble gases

Full outer electron shells.

Very unreactive.

Gases.

Exist as single atoms – they are **monatomic** (He, Ne, Ar, Kr, Xe, Rn).

How are the noble gases used?

Helium – in balloons.

Neon – in red tube lights.

Argon – in light bulbs.

Neon lighting in Hong Kong

REVIEW QUESTIONS

Q1 Look at the diagram representing the periodic table. The letters stand for elements.

a Which element is in group 4?
b Which element is in the second period?
c Which element is a noble gas?
d Which element is a transition metal?
e Which element is a metalloid?
f Which elements are non-metals?
g Which element is most likely to be a gas?

Q2 Why do elements in the same group react in similar ways?

Q3 This question is about the group 1 elements.
 a Which is the most reactive of the elements?
 b Why are the elements stored in oil?
 c Which element is the easiest to cut?
 d Why do the elements tarnish quickly when they are cut?
 e Why is the group known as the alkali metals?
 f Why does sodium float when added to water?
 g Write word equations and symbol equations for the
  following reactions:
  i rubidium and oxygen
  ii caesium and water
  iii potassium and chlorine.

Q4 This question is about the group 7 elements.
 a Which is the most reactive of the elements?
 b Which of the elements exists as a liquid at room temperature
 and pressure?
 c Which of the elements exists as a solid at room temperature
 and pressure?
 d Why are halogens such reactive elements?
 e Write word and symbol equations for the following reactions:
 i sodium and chlorine
 ii magnesium and bromine
 iii hydrogen and fluorine.

Q5 The table below records the results of some reactions.

	sodium chloride	sodium bromide	sodium iodide
chlorine	✗		✓
bromine		✗	✓
iodine			✗

A ✓ indicates a reaction occurred, a ✗ indicates no reaction
occurred.
 a Give the colours of the following solutions:
  i aqueous chlorine (chlorine water)
  ii aqueous bromine
  iii aqueous iodine
  iv aqueous sodium bromide
 b What would be observed in the reaction between aqueous
  chlorine and sodium bromide solution?
 c Complete the table of results. Use a 3 or 7 as appropriate.
 d Write a word equation and symbol equation for the reaction
  between bromine and sodium iodide.

Q6 This question is about the transition metals.
    a Give two differences in the physical properties of the transition metals compared with the alkali metals.
    b Transition metals are used as catalysts. What is a catalyst?
    c Suggest why the alkali metals are more reactive than the transition metals.

Q7 Look at the table of observations below.

Compound tested	Colour of compound	Colour produced in a flame test	Effect of adding sodium hydroxide solution to a solution of the compound
A	white	orange	no change
B	green	blue/green	blue precipitate formed
C	white	brick red	white precipitate formed

    a Identify the metal present in each of the three compounds.
    b Explain why C could not contain a metal from group 1 of the periodic table.
    c Write an ionic equation for the reaction of a solution of B with sodium hydroxide solution.

Q8 Explain why the noble gases are so unreactive.

Q9 In the periodic table what is the trend in reactivity
    a down a metallic element group?
    b down a non-metallic element group?

Q10 In terms of electron transfer in bonding, what is the difference between metallic and non-metallic elements?

Videos & questions on the CD ROM

Q11 Why are large metal atoms more reactive than smaller atoms in the same group?

Examination questions are on page 139.

10 METALS

Properties of metals

Most elements are metals. Some metals are highly reactive whilst others are almost completely unreactive. Refer back to the section on metals within the Periodic table (page 102) for the general properties of metals.

The use of alloys

An alloy is a metal with two or more other elements added to it.

The reason for producing alloys is to improve the property of the metal. The table below shows some examples.

alloy	property improved
steel	hardness
bronze	hardness
solder	lower the melting point
cupro-nickel	cheaper than silver (used for coins)
stainless steel	resistance to corrosion
brass	easier to shape and stamp into shape

Alloys are used for coins

The structure of alloys

The structure of pure metallic elements is usually shown as a solid structure.

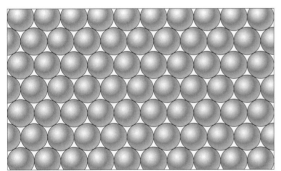
Particles in a solid.

This is a simplified picture, but surprisingly, such a structure is very weak. If there is the slightest difference between the planes of atoms, the metal will break at the point.

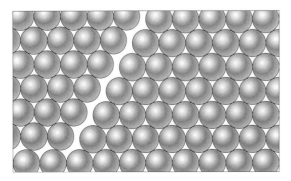

The more irregular (jumbled-up) the metal atoms are, the stronger the metal is. This is why alloy structures are stronger: because of the elements added.

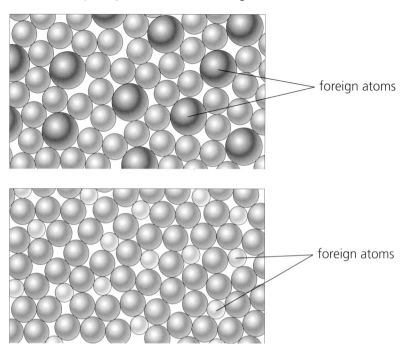

foreign atoms

foreign atoms

This process of 'jumbling up' the metal atoms is why steel that is heated to red hot, and then plunged into cold water is made stronger. The heat jumbles up the atoms and the sudden cold sets the atoms in their jumbled positions.

Reactivity series

Elements can be arranged in order of their reactivity. The more reactive a metal is, the easier it is to form their compounds and the harder it is to break down their compounds. By looking at the reactivity we can predict how metals might react.

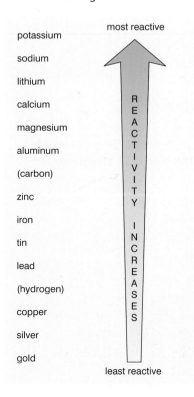

most reactive

potassium
sodium
lithium
calcium
magnesium
aluminum
(carbon)
zinc
iron
tin
lead
(hydrogen)
copper
silver
gold

REACTIVITY INCREASES

least reactive

Here is the reactivity series. It shows elements, mainly metals, in order of decreasing reactivity

Chemical reactions and a reactivity series

The pattern in the reactions of an element can be related to the reactivity series.

For example, in the reactions to extract metals from their ores (page 115) the elements that are below carbon in the reactivity series can be obtained by heating their oxides with carbon.

This is called a **displacement reaction**. The more reactive element, carbon, pushes the less reactive metal, such as iron, out of its compound.

In fact, any element higher up the reactivity series can displace an element lower down the series.

For example, magnesium is higher up the reactivity series than copper. So if magnesium powder is heated with copper oxide then copper and magnesium oxide are produced.

magnesium	+	copper(II) oxide	$\rightarrow$	magnesium oxide	+	copper
$Mg(s)$	+	$CuO(s)$	$\rightarrow$	$MgO(s)$	+	$Cu(s)$

Your teacher may show you this experiment.

What will happen if copper is heated with magnesium oxide? Nothing happens because copper is lower in the reactivity series than magnesium.

This coin is eroding. Copper is produced by the action of more reactive metals

Many such experiments could be carried out to establish the reactivity series. The changes in reactivity down the series of metals can be shown by their reactions with oxygen, water and acids. The reactions of some of the metals in the series are given below.

	Metal	Symbol	Reaction with oxygen
Most reactive	potassium	K	burns brightly in air with a purple flame: $4K(s)+O_2(g) \rightarrow 2K_2O(s)$
	sodium	Na	burns in air with an orange flame: $4Na(s)+O_2(g) \rightarrow 2Na_2O(s)$
	calcium	Ca	burns in air with brick-red flame: $2Ca(s)+O_2(g) \rightarrow 2CaO(s)$
	magnesium	Mg	burns in air with bright white flame: $2Mg(s)+O_2(g) \rightarrow 2MgO(s)$
least reactive	copper	Cu	does not burn, but slowly forms a black oxide layer: $2Cu(s)+O_2(g) \rightarrow 2CuO(s)$

Metal	Symbol	Reaction with water	Reaction with acid
potassium	K	violent reaction in cold water, forming hydrogen which then burns: $2K(s)+2H_2O(l) \rightarrow 2KOH(aq)+H_2(g)$	very violent and dangerous reaction, which should never be tried in the laboratory: $2K(s)+2HCl(aq) \rightarrow 2KCl(aq)+H_2(g)$
sodium	Na	vigorous reaction in cold water $2Na(s)+2H_2O(l) \rightarrow 2NaOH(aq)+H_2(g)$	dangerously violent reaction: $2Na(s)+H_2SO_4(aq) \rightarrow Na_2SO_4(aq)+H_2(g)$
calcium	Ca	reacts well with cold water forming a precipitate of calcium hydroxide: $Ca(s)+2H_2O(l) \rightarrow Ca(OH)_2(s)+H_2(g)$	very vigorous reaction: $Ca(s)+2HNO_3(aq) \rightarrow Ca(NO_3)_2(aq)+H_2(g)$
magnesium	Mg	little or no reaction with water, but burns readily in steam: $Mg(s)+H_2O(g) \rightarrow MgO(s)+H_2(g)$	vigorous reaction: $Mg(s)+2HCl(aq) \rightarrow MgCl_2(aq)+H_2(g)$
copper	Cu	no reaction	little reaction with sulphuric or hydrochloric acid, but will react with nitric acid: $3Cu(s)+8HNO_3(aq) \rightarrow 3Cu(NO_3)_2(aq)+4H_2O(l)+2NO(g)$

Using displacement reactions to establish a reactivity series

Displacement reactions of metals and their compounds in aqueous solution can be used to work out the reactivity series.

In the same way that a more reactive element can push a less reactive element out of a compound, a more reactive metal ion in aqueous solution can displace a less reactive one.

For example, if you add zinc to copper(II) sulphate solution the zinc will displace the copper because zinc is a more reactive metal than copper. When the experiment is carried out the blue colour of the copper ion will fade as copper is produced and zinc ions are made.

> zinc + copper sulphate solution → zinc sulphate solution + copper
>
> $Zn(s) + Cu^{2+} + (aq) + SO_4^{2-}(aq) → Zn^{2+}(aq) + SO_4^{2-}(aq) + Cu(s)$

To build up a whole reactivity series, a set of reactions can be tried to see whether metals can displace metal ions, following the general rule that a more reactive metal can displace a less reactive metal.

For example, you may have seem the reaction of copper wire with silver nitrate solution. As the reaction proceeds a grey precipitate appears (this is silver) and the solution begins to turn blue as Cu(II) ions are produced from the copper.

> copper + silver nitrate → copper nitrate + silver
>
> $Cu(s) + 2AgNO_3(aq) → Cu(NO_3)_2(aq) + 2Ag(s)$

This shows that silver can be displaced by copper and so silver is below copper in the reactivity series

Heating hydroxides

Sodium hydroxide, NaOH, and potassium hydroxide, KOH, are not changed by heating them. Calcium hydroxide, $Ca(OH)_2$, and magnesium hydroxide, $Mg(OH)_2$, behave in the same way:

> hydroxide + heat → oxide + water
>
> $Ca(OH)_2(s) → CaO(s) + H_2O(l)$
>
> $Mg(OH)_2(s) → MgO(s) + H_2O(l)$

Iron(III) hydroxide, $Fe(OH)_3$, also decomposes to oxide and water:

> $2Fe(OH)_3(s) → Fe_2O_3(s) + 3H_2O(l)$

Copper(II) hydroxide, $Cu(OH)_2$, and zinc hydroxide, $Zn(OH)_2$, are also decomposed by heating.

HEATING NITRATES

Sodium nitrate, $NaNO_3$, and potassium nitrate, KNO_3, behaves the same when heated:

nitrate + heat + nitrite + oxygen

$2NaNO_3$ (s) $\rightarrow$ $2NaNO_2$ (s) + O_2 (g)

$2KNO_3$ (s) $\rightarrow$ $2KNO_2$ (s) + O_2 (g)

All other nitrates behave in the same way when heated:

$2Ca(NO_3)_2$ (s) $\rightarrow$ $2CaO$(s) + $4NO_2$ (g) + O_2(g)

$2Mg(NO_3)_2$ (s) $\rightarrow$ $2MgO$(s) + $4NO_2$ (g) + O_2(g)

$2Fe(NO_3)_2$ (s) $\rightarrow$ $2FeO$(s) + $4NO_2$ (g) + O_2(g)

$2Cu(NO_3)_2$ (s) $\rightarrow$ $2CuO$(s) + $4NO_2$ (g) + O_2(g)

$2Zn(NO_3)_2$ (s) $\rightarrow$ $2ZnO$(s) + $4NO_2$ (g) + O_2(g)

THE UNREACTIVITY OF ALUMINIUM

Aluminium's position in the reactivity series means that it should be quite reactive. However, it does not react with acids and is resistant to corrosion. This is because, although it may look shiny, it has a thin coating of aluminium oxide, Al_2O_3, all over its surface. Aluminium oxide is very unreactive and protects the aluminium below its surface.

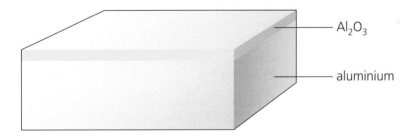

Al₂O₃

aluminium

Extraction of metals

Metals are found in the form of **ores** containing **minerals** mixed with unwanted rock. In almost all cases, the mineral is a compound of the metal, not the pure metal. One exception is gold, which exists naturally in a pure state.

Extracting a metal from its ore usually involves two steps:
1   The mineral is physically separated from unwanted rock
2   The mineral is chemically broken down to obtain the metal.

Reactivity of metals

The chemical method chosen to break down a mineral depends on the reactivity of the metal. The **more reactive** a metal is, the **harder** it is to break down its compounds. The more reactive metals are obtained from their minerals by the process of **electrolysis**.

The less reactive metals can be obtained by heating their oxides with carbon. This method will only work for metals below carbon in the **reactivity series**. It involves the **reduction** of a metal oxide to the metal.

Metal	Extraction method
potassium sodium calcium magnesium aluminium	The most reactive metals are obtained using electrolysis.
(carbon)	
zinc iron tin lead copper	These metals are below carbon in the reactivity series and so can be obtained by heating their oxides with carbon.
silver gold	The least reactive metals are found as pure elements.

Using carbon to extract copper

Copper is extracted by heating the mineral **malachite** (copper(II) carbonate) with carbon. The reaction takes place in two stages:

Stage 1 – The malachite decomposes:

copper(II) carbonate → copper(II) oxide + carbon dioxide

$$CuCO_3(s) \rightarrow CuO(s) + CO_2(g)$$

Stage 2 – The copper(II) oxide is reduced by the carbon:

copper(II) oxide + carbon → copper + carbon dioxide

$$2CuO(s) + C(s) \rightarrow 2Cu(s) + CO_2(g)$$

The copper produced by this process is purified by electrolysis.

The blast furnace

Iron is produced on a very large scale by reduction using carbon. The reaction takes place in a huge furnace called a **blast furnace**. The main ore of iron is haematite, iron(III) oxide (Fe_2O_3)

Three important raw materials are put in the top of the furnace: **iron ore** (iron(III) oxide), **coke** (the source of carbon needed for the reduction) and **limestone**, needed to remove the impurities as a 'slag'.

Coke

Limestone

Iron ore

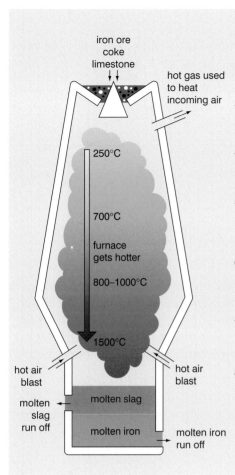

iron ore
coke
limestone

hot gas used
to heat
incoming air

250°C

700°C

furnace
gets hotter

800–1000°C

1500°C

hot air
blast

hot air
blast

molten
slag
run off

molten slag

molten iron

molten iron
run off

1 Iron ore, coke and limestone are fed into the top of the blast furnace

2 Hot air is blasted up the furnace from the bottom

3 Oxygen from the air reacts with coke to form carbon dioxide:
$C(s) + O_2(g) \longrightarrow CO_2(g)$

4 Carbon dioxide reacts with more coke to form carbon monoxide:
$CO_2(g) + C(s) \longrightarrow 2CO(g)$

5 Carbon monoxide is a reducing agent. Iron(III) oxide is reduced to iron:
reduction = loss of oxygen
$Fe_2O_3(s) + 3CO(g) \longrightarrow 2Fe(l) + 3CO_2(g)$

6 Dense molten iron runs to the bottom of the furnace and is run off. There are many impurities in iron ore. The limestone helps to remove these as shown in 7 and 8.

7 Limestone is broken down by heat to calcium oxide:
$CaCO_3(s) \longrightarrow CaO(s) + CO_2(g)$

8 Calcium oxide reacts with impurities like sand (silicon dioxide) to form a liquid called 'slag':
$CaO(s) + SiO_2(s) \longrightarrow CaSiO_3(l)$
impurity   slag
The liquid slag falls to the bottom of the furnace and is tapped off.

Molten iron

Slag

A blast furnace is used to reduce iron(III) oxide to iron.

The overall reaction is:

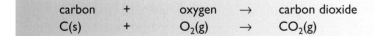

| iron oxide | + | carbon | → | iron | + | carbon dioxide |
| $2Fe_2O_3(s)$ | + | $3C$ | → | $4Fe$ | + | $3CO_2$ |

The reduction happens in three stages.

Stage 1 – The coke (carbon) reacts with oxygen 'blasted' into the furnace:

| carbon | + | oxygen | → | carbon dioxide |
| $C(s)$ | + | $O_2(g)$ | → | $CO_2(g)$ |

Stage 2 – The carbon dioxide is reduced by unreacted coke to form carbon monoxide:

| carbon dioxide | + | carbon | → | carbon monoxide |
| $CO_2(g)$ | + | $C(s)$ | → | $2CO(g)$ |

Stage 3 – The iron(III) oxide is reduced by the carbon monoxide to iron:

| iron(III) oxide | + | carbon monoxide | → | iron | + | carbon dioxide |
| $Fe_2O_3(s)$ | + | $3CO(g)$ | → | $2Fe(s)$ | + | $3CO_2(g)$ |

Extraction of zinc

Zinc is extracted from its ore **zinc blende**. Zinc blende is the original name for zinc sulphide, ZnS.

The zinc blende is first heated in air to convert it to the oxide:

$$2ZnS(s) + 3O_2(g) \rightarrow 2SO_2(g) + 2ZnO(s)$$

The oxide is then reduced using carbon monoxide:

$$ZnO(s) + CO(g) \rightarrow Zn(s) + CO_2(g)$$

and zinc metal is produced.

Uses of metal

USES OF ALUMINIUM

The uses of aluminium are based on its properties of having a low density but being a strong metal as well as being unreactive (because of its oxide coating). These properties make it useful in the manufacture of aircraft (because it is light and strong) and food containers (because it does not corrode).

USES OF ZINC

Zinc is used to make the alloy brass by mixing it with copper. Covering iron with zinc is called 'galvanising', and zinc stops the iron from rusting (corroding).

USES OF COPPER

Copper is an excellent conductor of electricity and this is why it is used for electrical cables.

Copper is also an excellent conductor of heat with a high melting point. These properties make it ideal for cooking utensils.

Making steel from iron

Iron from the blast furnace is **brittle** and **corrodes** very easily because it contains a large percentage of carbon (from the coke).

The corrosion of iron is called **rusting** and it is a chemical reaction between iron, water and oxygen. Common ways of protecting iron from rusting are:

- **Galvanising** – covering iron in zinc. The zinc corrodes instead of the iron if the coating is damaged. This is called **sacrificial protection**.

- **Alloying** – mixing iron with other metals to make steel.

In **steel making**, molten pig iron (from the blast furnace) is mixed with smaller amounts of scrap iron and steel. Limestone, $CaCO_3$, is also added and the whole mixture melted. Oxygen is blasted through the molten mixture which reacts with the carbon in the pig iron to make carbon monoxide so removing some of the carbon content.

$$2C(s) + O_2(g) \rightarrow 2CO(g)$$

The limestone is changed by the heat into calcium oxide,

$$CaCO_3 \rightarrow CaO + CO_2$$

The oxygen blown through the mixture also converts any impurities into their oxides. The calcium oxide reacts with these oxides to form slag and so are removed from the iron / steel mixture.

Steel is iron with 0.1-1.5% carbon content. Steel is more resistant to corrosion and is less brittle than iron. It has a wide range of uses, depending on its carbon content. For example:

> mild steel (<0.3%) – car bodies, machinery
> medium carbon (0.3 – 0.9%) – rail tracks
> high carbon (0.9 – 1.5%) – knives

Stainless steels are made by adding a wide range of metals to steel such as chromium, nickel, vanadium and cobalt. Each one gives the steel particular properties for specific uses. For example, vanadium steel is used to make high precision, hard-wearing industrial tools. They are also used for making cutlery and in equipment in chemical plants.

REVIEW QUESTIONS

Q1 Iron is made from iron ore (iron oxide) in a blast furnace by heating with carbon.
  a Write a word equation for the overall reaction.
  b Is the iron oxide oxidised or reduced in this reaction? Explain your answer.
  c Why is limestone also added to the blast furnace?

Q2 Why are alloys often used instead of pure metals?

Q3 In terms of structure, what do 'foreign' atoms do to the structure of a pure metal?

Q4 Write the equation for the action of heat on:
  a potassium nitrate
  b magnesium hydroxide
  c copper nitrate

Q5 Why is aluminium not as reactive as might be expected from its position in the reactivity series?

Q6 What is the chemical formula of the ore of zinc called 'zinc blende'?

Q7 Why is copper used for cooking pans?

Videos & questions on the CD ROM

Examination questions are on page 139.

11 AIR AND WATER

A chemical test for water

The test for water is to add it to anhydrous copper sulphate solid. if the liquid is water the powder will turn from white to blue.

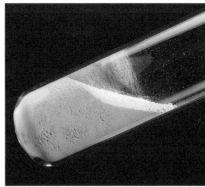

When copper(II) sulphate crystals are heated they turn from blue to white.

The reaction can then be reversed by adding water.

The water cycle

The recirculation of water that takes place all over the Earth is called the **water cycle**.

Water cycle.

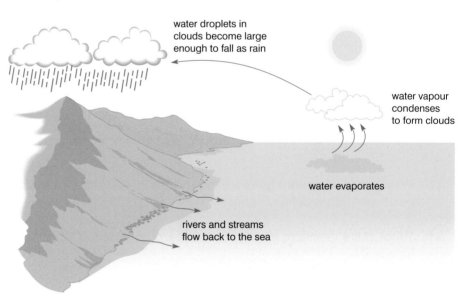

water droplets in clouds become large enough to fall as rain

water vapour condenses to form clouds

water evaporates

rivers and streams flow back to the sea

The rainfall pattern over the planet determines where there will be desert regions, rainforests, and areas of land that can or cannot be used for growing plants. Ultimately, rainfall decides the **economics** of the countries of the world.

Global warming is thought to be responsible for **climate changes** that are affecting both where there is rainfall and how much there is of it. This could be causing both increased risks of **flooding** in some regions and **droughts** in others.

Water is essential for life on Earth, and the **demand for drinking water** is increasing as the world's population grows. Most **industrial processes** use water either as a raw material or for cooling processes. Two-thirds of the water used is used in the home. The rest is used by industry, for example, it takes 200 000 litres of water to make 1 tonne of steel.

Water stored in reservoirs needs to be purified to produce drinkable **tap water**.

| Water from reservoirs goes to water treatment plant. | ▶ | Water filtered through coarse gravel to remove larger pieces of dirt. | ▶ | Water filtered through beds of fine gravel and sand to remove small particles. | ▶ | Chlorine passed through to kill bacteria. | ▶ | Water supply to homes and industry. |

Water pipes discharging in Thailand.

The treatment of water to purify it for safe drinking.

In addition, tap water in certain areas is treated with sodium fluoride (NaF) to reduce tooth decay.

The composition of clean air

Air is a **mixture** of gases that has remained fairly constant for the last 200 million years. The amount of **water vapour** varies, depending where on the Earth you are. For example, a desert area has low water vapour.

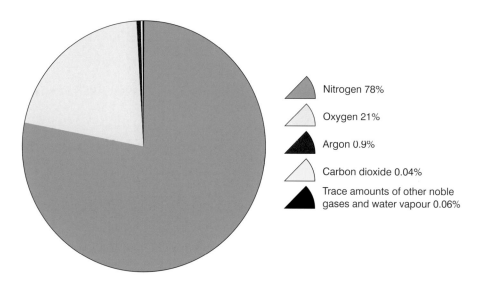

- Nitrogen 78%
- Oxygen 21%
- Argon 0.9%
- Carbon dioxide 0.04%
- Trace amounts of other noble gases and water vapour 0.06%

The composition of air today.

The composition of the air is kept fairly constant by two cycles – the **nitrogen** and **carbon cycles**.

The nitrogen cycle

Living things need nitrogen to make proteins, which are required, for example, to make new cells for growth.

The air is 79% nitrogen gas (N_2), but nitrogen gas is very unreactive and cannot be used by plants or animals. Instead, plants use nitrogen in the form of **nitrates** (NO_3^- ions).

The process of getting nitrogen into this useful form is called **nitrogen fixation**.

In the **nitrogen cycle**:

- Nitrogen-fixing bacteria take nitrogen from the air (don't forget there is air in soil) to form nitrogen-containing compounds such as nitrates. Some of these bacteria are free-living in the soil, but some live in swellings, called root nodules, on the roots of leguminous plants, e.g. beans, peas and clover.

- Nitrifying bacteria convert ammonia from the decayed remains and waste of animals and plants into nitrates.

- Denitrifying bacteria convert nitrates back into nitrogen.

- Animals gain nitrogen when they take in protein by eating meat or plant material.

Pollutants in the air

The pollutants in the air come from a variety of sources.
Some come from burning waste, some from power stations burning coal and gas, industry produces pollutants as well.

The commonest pollutants in the air are:
- Carbon monoxide: incomplete combustion of hydrocarbons (petrol / coal / gas / diesel)
- Sulphur dioxide: burning petrol and coal
- Oxides of nitrogen: burning fossil fuels (petrol / diesel / coal)
- Lead compounds: burning leaded petrol.

How is the atmosphere changing, and why?

There are two major impacts caused by the **burning of fossil fuels** – the **greenhouse effect** and **acid rain**.

The greenhouse effect

Carbon dioxide, methane and CFCs are known as **greenhouse gases**. The levels of these gases in the atmosphere are increasing due to the burning of fossil fuels, pollution from farm animals and the use of CFCs in aerosols and refrigerators.

Short-wave radiation from the Sun warms the ground, and the warm Earth gives off heat as long-wave radiation. Much of this radiation is stopped from escaping from the Earth by the greenhouse gases. This is known as the **greenhouse effect**.

The greenhouse effect is responsible for keeping the Earth warmer than it would otherwise be. The greenhouse effect is normal – and important for life on Earth. However, it is thought that increasing levels of greenhouse gases are stopping even more heat escaping and that the Earth is slowly warming up. This is known as **global warming**. If global warming continues, the Earth's climate may change and sea levels rise as polar ice melts.

The temperature of the Earth is gradually increasing, but we do not know for certain if the greenhouse effect is responsible. It may be that the observed rise in recent global temperatures is part of a natural cycle – there have been Ice Ages and intermediate warm periods before. Many people are concerned that it is not part of a cycle and say we should act now to reduce emissions of these greenhouse gases.

Cycling is encouraged in Amsterdam to cut down air. pollution

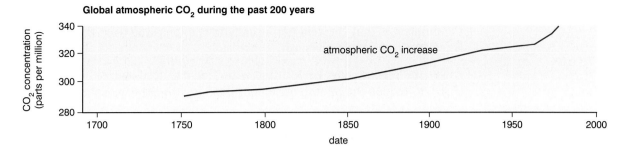

Global atmospheric CO₂ during the past 200 years

atmospheric CO_2 increase

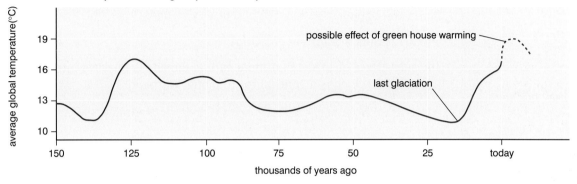

Global temperature during the past 150 000 years

possible effect of green house warming

last glaciation

thousands of years ago

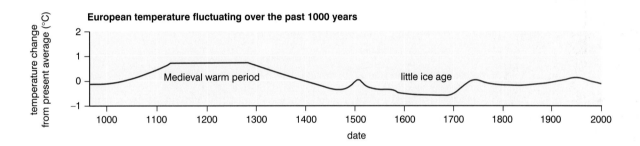

European temperature fluctuating over the past 1000 years

Medieval warm period

little ice age

date

Acid rain

Burning fossil fuels gives off many gases, including **sulphur dioxide** and various **nitrogen oxides**.

sulphur + oxygen → sulphur dioxide

$$S(s) + O_2(g) \rightarrow SO_2(g)$$

Sulphur dioxide combines with water to form sulphuric acid. Nitrogen oxide combines with water to form nitric acid. These substances can make the rain acidic (called **acid rain**).

sulphur dioxide + oxygen + water → sulphuric acid

$$2SO_2(g) + O_2(g) + 2H_2O(l) \rightarrow 2H_2SO_4(aq)$$

Buildings, particularly those made of limestone and marble (both are forms of calcium carbonate, $CaCO_3$), are damaged by acid rain. Metal structures are also attacked by sulphuric acid.

Acid rain **harms plants** that take in the acidic water and the **animals** that live in the affected rivers and lakes. Acid rain also washes ions such as calcium and magnesium out of the soil, **depleting the minerals available to plants**. It also washes **aluminium**, which is poisonous to fish, out of the soil and into rivers and lakes.

Most lakes in Scandinavia are highly acidic due to acid rain. The acid can be neutralised by spreading slaked lime.

129

Some of the reactions occuring in a catalytic converter:

carbon monoxide + oxygen → carbon dioxide

$$2CO(g) + O_2(g) \rightarrow 2\ CO_2(g)$$

nitrogen monoxide + carbon monoxide → nitrogen + carbon dioxide

$$2NO(g) + 2CO(g) \rightarrow N_2(g) + 2CO_2(g)$$

nitrogen monoxide → nitrogen + oxygen

$$2NO(g) \rightarrow N_2(g) + O_2(g)$$

hydrocarbons + oxygen → carbon dioxide + water

Reducing emission of the gases causing acid rain is expensive, and part of the problem is that the acid rain usually falls a long way from the places where the gases were given off.

Power stations are now being fitted with 'flue gas desulphurisation plants' (FGD), to reduce the release of sulphur dioxide into the atmosphere.

Catalytic converters are fitted to the exhaust systems of vehicles to reduce the level of pollutants being released into the atmosphere from burning petrol.

The catalytic converters change emissions such as carbon monoxide (CO) and nitrogen oxides (nitogen(II) oxide, NO) into nitrogen, carbon dioxide and water vapour,

e.g. $2CO(g) + O_2(g) \rightarrow 2\ CO_2(g)$

The side-effect of this is that more carbon dioxide is released into the atmosphere which is a contributor to global warming.

The problem of acid rain.

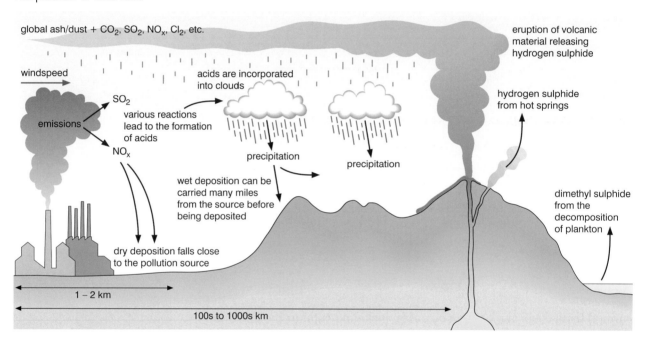

Uses of oxygen

In medicine, oxygen in its pure form is used to help patients with breathing difficulties e.g. in oxygen tents.

Oxygen is needed for burning / combustion and one of its uses is in welding. The oxygen is mixed with acetylene and burnt to produce a high-temperature flame.

The fractional distillation of air

Fractional distillation is a method of separating mixtures of liquids. It uses the difference in boiling points of the liquids in the mixture. When heated the liquid with the lowest boiling point turns to a gas first, leaves the mixture and is then cooled back to a liquid. The next lowest boiling point liquid then comes out, and so on (see page 16).

Fractional distillation is the method used to collect oxygen (and nitrogen) from the air. Air is a gas so it has to be liquefied first using low temperature and high pressure.

The liquid air is heated and nitrogen comes off first (boiling point = -196°C) then the oxygen (boiling point = -183°C).

In both cases the gaseous elements are cooled and put under pressure as they are collected to liquefy them again. The gases are stored in cylinders.

Methods of preventing rusting

Metals are affected over time by the oxygen and water in the atmosphere. If they react together the metal is corroded. The **corrosion** of iron is called **rusting**.

In rusting:

$$2Fe(s) + O_2(g) + 2H_2O(l) \rightarrow 2Fe(OH)_2(s)$$

the iron (II) hydroxide is further affected:

$$4Fe(OH)_2 (s) + air + water \rightarrow 2Fe_2O_3 \, xH_2O$$

$Fe_2O_3 \, xH_2O$ is the general formula for rust, and x varies depending upon conditions.

Overall, $Fe \rightarrow Fe^{3+} + 3e-$

so rusting is an oxidation process.

Methods preventing rusting fall into three main categories:

1   Stopping oxygen and water reaching the iron.

Oiling /greasing e.g. bicycle chains
Painting e.g. car bodies

2   Alloying

Iron is mixed with other metals to produce alloys e.g. stainless steel that do not rust.

3   Sacrificial protection

The iron is covered by, or in contact with, another metal which is higher in the reactivity series, i.e. more reactive than iron.

The more reactive metal will corrode instead of the iron, i.e. it is "sacrificed" to protect the iron.

In galvanising, iron is covered with a coating of zinc. Even if the zinc surface is scratched, exposing the iron, the zinc corrodes not the iron.

In the presence of the exposed iron and the zinc in contact with it, an electrochemical cell is set up when water comes into contact with the two metals. Zinc is the anode (+) and the iron the cathode (-) .

Zinc is more reactive than iron so forms ions in preference to the iron,

$$Zn \rightarrow Zn^{2+} + 2e^-$$

The zinc is oxidised by losing electrons to form the ions and so is 'sacrificed' instead of the iron rusting (and turning to ions). The electrons from the zinc anode move to the iron cathode. This prevents the rusting process shown below,

$$Fe \rightarrow Fe^{2+} + 2e^-$$

Ship's hulls made of iron have zinc bars attached to them. The zinc bars corrode, not the hull.

Compounds of nitrogen

Fertilisers contain minerals that plants need to grow in a fast and healthy way.

These are often called NPK fertilisers, because they contain compounds of nitrogen, phosphorus and potassium. Nitrogen compounds are needed to make proteins in the plant. Phosphorus compounds help root growth and function. Potassium compounds encourage flower and fruit formation.

The Haber process

Ammonia is used to make nitrogen-containing fertilisers.

It is manufactured in the **Haber process** from nitrogen and hydrogen. The conditions include an iron catalyst, a temperature of 450 °C and 200 times atmospheric pressure. The nitrogen for the process comes from the fractional distillation of liquid air and the hydrogen from reacting methane or other hydrocarbons with steam.

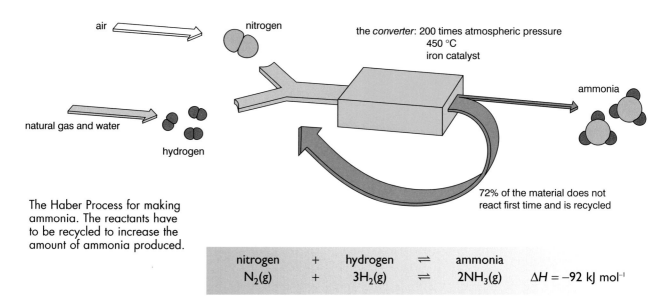

The Haber Process for making ammonia. The reactants have to be recycled to increase the amount of ammonia produced.

nitrogen	+	hydrogen	⇌	ammonia	
$N_2(g)$	+	$3H_2(g)$	⇌	$2NH_3(g)$	$\Delta H = -92$ kJ mol^{-1}

The greatest yield of ammonia would be made using a low temperature (it is exothermic) but this would be slow. The temperature used of 450 °C is a compromise since not so much is made, but it is produced faster. The iron catalyst is used to increase the rate also – it does not increase the yield. High pressure increases the yield and also the rate.

The graph shows the effect of temperature and pressure on the yield of ammonia.

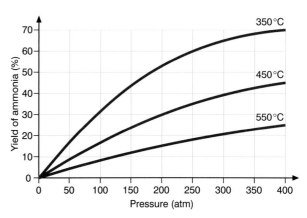

Effect of temperature and pressure on yield of ammonia.

Ammonium salts

Ammonium salts will react with a base to produce ammonia gas. An example is the reaction of ammonium chloride with calcium hydroxide to produce ammonia in the laboratory.

The gas evolved can be tested by putting in a piece of moist red litmus paper. The gas will turn the paper blue, showing that it is alkaline. Ammonia is the only common alkaline gas (see page 90).

Carbon dioxide

Carbon dioxide is formed from combustion.

Most of the common fuels used today are hydrocarbons – substances that contain **only** carbon and hydrogen atoms.

When a hydrocarbon is burnt in a plentiful supply of air it reacts with the oxygen in the air (it is **oxidised**) to form carbon dioxide and water. This reaction is an example of **combustion**.

| hydrocarbon | + | oxygen | → | carbon dioxide | + | water |

For example, when methane (natural gas) is burnt:

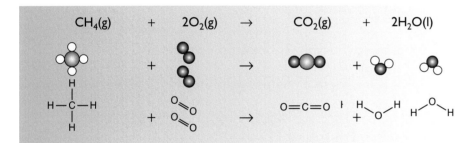

The complete combustion of methane in a plentiful supply of air.

The air contains only about 20% oxygen by volume. When a hydrocarbon fuel is burnt there is not always enough oxygen for complete combustion.

Carbon dioxide is also a product of respiration.

Plants take in carbon dioxide because they need the carbon (and oxygen) to use in **photosynthesis** to make carbohydrates and then other substances such as protein.

When animals eat plants, they use some of the carbon-containing compounds to grow and some to release energy in respiration.

As a waste product of respiration, animals breathe out carbon as carbon dioxide, which is then available for plants to use. (Don't forget that plants also respire, producing carbon dioxide.)

Carbon dioxide is also released when animal and plant remains decay (**decomposition**) and when wood, peat or fossil fuels are burnt (**combustion**).

It can be made in the laboratory by the reaction of an acid and a carbonate.

calcium carbonate + hydrochloric acid → carbon dioxide + water + calcium chloride

$$CaCO_3(s) + 2HCl(aq) \rightarrow CO_2(g) + H_2O(l) + CaCl_2(aq)$$

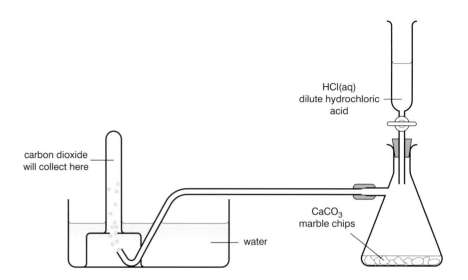

HCl(aq) dilute hydrochloric acid

carbon dioxide will collect here

$CaCO_3$ marble chips

water

REVIEW QUESTIONS

Q1 Describe how oxygen is obtained from the air.

Q2 What is the cause of the rusting of iron?

More questions on the CD ROM

Q3 An iron nail is coated with a layer of zinc to stop it rusting.
  a What is this called?
  b Explain how zinc protects the iron from rusting.

Examination questions are on page 139.

12 SULPHUR

Sulphur is found in many places in the world, and is often released by volcanoes. Many elements form compounds with sulphur, which are called sulphides.

Sulphur is mainly used for the manufacture of sulphuric acid. As sulphur dioxide it is used as a bleach in the manufacture of wood pulp for paper and as a food preservative (by killing bacteria).

The contact process

Sulphuric acid is a very important starting material in the chemical industry. It is used in the manufacture of many other chemicals, from fertilisers to plastics.

It is manufactured in a process known as the **contact process** – sulphur dioxide is oxidised to sulphur trioxide.

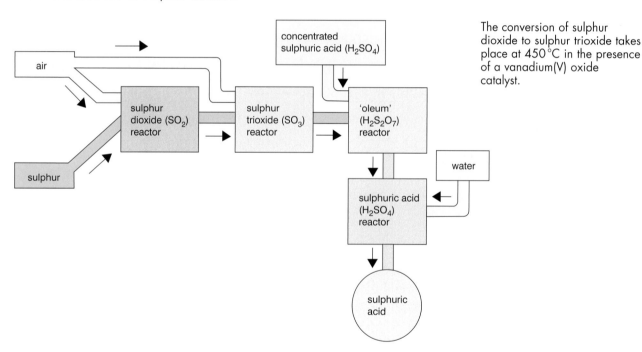

The conversion of sulphur dioxide to sulphur trioxide takes place at 450 °C in the presence of a vanadium(V) oxide catalyst.

The equations for the steps in making sulphuric acid are:

1   sulphur   +   oxygen $\rightarrow$ sulphur dioxide
       $S(s)$ + $O_2(g)$ $\rightarrow$ $SO_2(g)$

2 sulphur dioxide +   oxygen $\rightleftharpoons$ sulphur trioxide
    $2SO_2(g)$ + $O_2(g)$ $\rightleftharpoons$ $2SO_3(g)$ $\Delta H = -192 \text{ kJ mol}^{-1}$

3 sulphur trioxide + sulphuric acid $\rightarrow$ 'oleum'
                (concentrated)
     $SO_3(g)$ + $H_2SO_4(l)$ $\rightarrow$ $H_2S_2O_7(l)$

4   'oleum'   +   water $\rightarrow$ sulphuric acid
 $H_2S_2O_7(l)$ + $H_2O(l)$ $\rightarrow$ $2H_2SO_4(aq)$

It would seem simpler to make sulphuric acid by adding sulphur trioxide straight to water to avoid steps 3 and 4:

$$H_2O(l) + SO_3(g) \rightarrow H_2SO_4(l)$$

This is dangerous because the reaction is very exothermic and an 'acid mist' is made.

Step 2 above is the reaction of the contact process. The greatest yield of sulphur trioxide would be made at a low temperature (the reaction is exothermic), but this would be slow, so the compromise temperature of 450 °C is used – less is made but in a shorter time. High pressure would make more SO_3 but the equipment required would be costly. A catalyst increases the rate but not the yield.

Dilute sulphuric acid

Dilute sulphuric acid, H_2SO_4 is a typical acid.

1. It produces H^+ ions in aqueous solution,

    $$H_2SO_4(aq) \rightarrow 2H^+(aq) + SO_4^{2-}(aq)$$

2. It reacts with metals to form a salt and hydrogen gas,

    $$Mg(s) + H_2SO_4(aq) \rightarrow MgSO_4(aq) + H_2(g)$$

3. It reacts with alkalis to make salts (neutralisation)

    $$2NaOH(aq) + H_2SO_4(aq) \rightarrow Na_2SO_4(aq) + 2H_2O(l)$$

4. It reacts with bases to make salts (neutralisation)

    $$ZnO(s) + H_2SO_4(aq) \rightarrow ZnSO_4(aq) + H_2O(l)$$

5. It reacts with carbonates to make a salt, carbon dioxide and water,

    $$K_2CO_3(s) + H_2SO_4(aq) \rightarrow K_2SO_4(aq) + CO_2(g) + H_2O(l)$$

REVIEW QUESTION

Videos & questions on the CD ROM

Q1 In the production of sulphuric acid, why is the sulphur trioxide from the contact process not added straight to water to make sulphuric acid?

Examination questions are on page 139.

13 CARBONATES

What are the uses of limestone and its products?

Limestone is still used for buildings in some areas, but the major uses of calcium carbonate and its products are in a wide range of **industries**.

For centuries, limestone has been heated in lime kilns to make 'quicklime' or calcium oxide, CaO:

$$CaCO_3(s) \xrightarrow{1200\ °C} CaO(s) + CO_2(g)$$

limestone   quicklime

This is an example of **thermal decomposition**, namely the use of heat ('thermal') to break up a substance.

A modern rotary kiln is shown below.

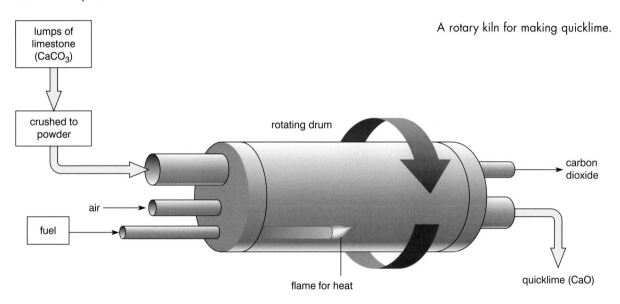

lumps of limestone ($CaCO_3$)

crushed to powder

air

fuel

rotating drum

flame for heat

carbon dioxide

quicklime (CaO)

A rotary kiln for making quicklime.

When **water** is added to calcium oxide (quicklime), a vigorous **exothermic** (heat-producing) reaction takes place, and **slaked lime** – calcium hydroxide, $Ca(OH)_2$, is formed.

$$CaO(s) + H_2O(l) \rightarrow Ca(OH)_2(s)$$

quicklime   slaked lime

Slaked lime is an **alkali**, which is the basis of many of its uses.

The **major uses** of limestone, quicklime and slaked lime are given below:

Limestone (CaCO$_3$)
- crushed and used as **aggregate** for road building
- added as a powder to lakes to **neutralise acidity**
- mixed with clay to make **cement**
- used to extract iron in the **blast furnace**
- heated with soda and sand to make **glass**
- used to **neutralise acid gases**, e.g. SO$_2$ produced by power stations

Quicklime (CaO)
- added to soil to **neutralise acidity**
- used in making **steel** from iron
- used as **drying agent** in industry

Slaked lime (Ca(OH)$_2$)
- added to soil to **neutralise acidity**
- used in **mortar** for building
- used to make **pottery**
- in solution, it is called **limewater**, used for tests for carbon dioxide, CO$_2$(g)

REVIEW QUESTIONS

Q1 Why are millions of tonnes of limestone quarried every year worldwide?

Q2 Write the balanced chemical equations, including state symbols, for the following:
a changing limestone into quicklime
b changing quicklime into slaked lime.

Q3 a Describe the limewater test for carbon dioxide.
b Write the word equation and the balanced chemical reaction (including state symbols) for the reaction occurring in the limewater test.

Videos & questions on the CD ROM

Q4 How is limestone used in power stations?

Examination questions are on page 139.

EXAMINATION QUESTIONS

Q1 The halogens are a group of diatomic non-metals showing a trend in colour, state and reactivity.

a In this description, what is the meaning of

    i   diatomic, _____ [1]

    ii state? _____ [1]

b The table gives some information about some of the halogens.

element	melting point /°C	boiling point /°C	colour	state at room temperature
chlorine	-101	-35	green	
bromine	-7	+59		
iodine	+114		grey-black	

    i   Complete the last column in the table to show the state of each of the halogens at room temperature. [2]

    ii State the colour of bromine.

    _____ [1]

    iii Suggest a value for the boiling point of iodine.

    _____ [1]

c Complete the word equation for the reaction of chlorine with potassium iodide.

    chlorine + potassium iodide → _____ + _____ [2]

d i Draw a diagram to show the electronic structure of a chlorine molecule. Show only the outer electrons.

[2]

    ii State a use of chlorine.

    _____ [1]

e The structures of some substances containing halogens are shown below.

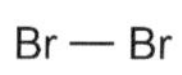

Br — Br

Na⁺ Cl⁻ Na⁺ Cl⁻
Cl⁻ Na⁺ Cl⁻ Na⁺
Na⁺ Cl⁻ Na⁺ Cl⁻

H — Cl

F — Br with F, F

A 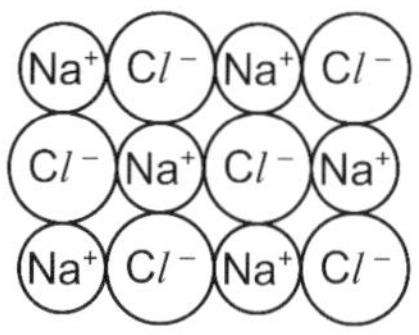   **B** 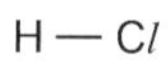   **C** 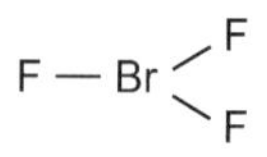   **D**

    i   Which one of these structures, **A**, **B**, **C** or **D**, shows an element?

    _____ [1]

ii Which one of these structures forms hydrochloric acid when dissolved in water?

_____ [1]

iii Complete the following sentence. Structure **B** conducts electricity when it is molten because

_____ [2]

f Astatine, At, is below iodine in Group VII of the Periodic Table.
i In which Period of the Periodic Table is astatine?

_____ [1]

ii How many protons does astatine have in its nucleus?

_____ [1]

iii Astatine has many isotopes. What do you understand by the term isotopes?

_____
_____ [1]

iv The most common isotope of astatine has a nucleon number (mass number) of 210. Calculate the number of neutrons in this isotope of astatine.

_____ [1]

Q2 Three of the halogens in Group VII are:
     chlorine
     bromine
     iodine

a i How does their colour change down the Group?

_____ [1]

ii How does their physical state (solid, liquid or gas) change down the Group?

_____ [1]

iii Predict the colour and physical state of fluorine.
colour _____
physical state _____ [2]

b Describe how you could distinguish between aqueous potassium bromide and aqueous potassium iodide.
test _____
result with bromide _____
result with iodide _____ [3]

c 0.015 moles of iodine react with 0.045 moles of chlorine to form 0.030 moles of a single product. Complete the equation.
I_2 + _____ Cl_2 → _____ [2]

d Traces of chlorine can be separated from bromine vapour by diffusion.
Which gas would diffuse the faster and why?

_____
_____ [2]

Q3 The Carlsbad caverns in New Mexico are very large underground caves. Although the walls of these caves are coated with gypsum (hydrated calcium sulphate), the caves have been formed in limestone.

a It is believed that the caves were formed by sulphuric acid reacting with the limestone.
i Complete the word equation.

calcium   sulphuric →   calcium
carbonate + acid   sulphate + _____ + _____ [1]

   ii Describe how you could test the water entering the cave to show that it
       contained sulphate ions.
       test _____
       result _____ [2]
   iii How could you show that the water entering the cave has a high concentration
       of hydrogen ions?
       _____ [1]

b Hydrogen sulphide gas which was escaping from nearby petroleum deposits was
   being oxidised to sulphuric acid.
   i Complete the equation for this reaction forming sulphuric acid.

      H_2S + _____ O_2 → _____ [2]

   ii Explain why all the hydrogen sulphide should be removed from the petroleum
       before it is used as a fuel.

       _____

       _____ [2]

   iii Draw a diagram to show the arrangement of the valency electrons in one
       molecule of the covalent compound hydrogen sulphide.
       Use o to represent an electron from a sulphur atom.
       Use x to represent an electron from a hydrogen atom.

       [2]

c Sulphuric acid is manufactured by the Contact Process. Sulphur dioxide is oxidised
   to sulphur trioxide by oxygen.

   $2SO_2 + O_2 → 2SO_3$

   i Name the catalyst used in this reaction.

       _____ [1]

   ii What temperature is used for this reaction?

       _____ [1]

   iii Describe how sulphur trioxide is changed into sulphuric acid.

       _____

       _____ [2]

d Gypsum is hydrated calcium sulphate, $CaSO_4.xH_2O$. It contains 20.9% water.
   by mass.
   Calculate x.
   M_r: $CaSO_4$, 136; H_2O, 18.
   79.1 g of $CaSO_4$ = _____ moles
   20.9 g of H_2O = _____ moles
   x = _____ [3]

Q4 The position of aluminium in the reactivity series of metals is shown below.

magnesium
aluminium
zinc
copper

a Aluminium is extracted by the electrolysis of its molten oxide.

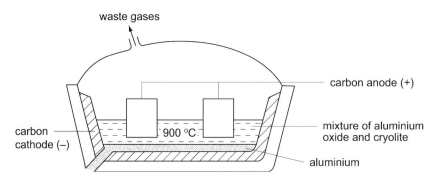

i Name the main ore of aluminium.

_____ [1]

ii Why does the molten electrolyte contain cryolite?

_____ [1]

iii Oxygen is produced at the positive electrode (anode). Name another gas which is given off at this electrode.

_____ [1]

b Aluminium reacts very slowly with aqueous copper(II) sulphate.

$$2Al(s) + 3CuSO_4(aq) \rightarrow Al_2(SO_4)_3(aq) + 3Cu(s)$$

i Which of the two metals has the greater tendency to form ions?

_____ [1]

ii Describe what you would see when this reaction occurs.

_____ [1]

iii Explain why aluminium reacts so slowly.

_____ [1]

c Complete the following table by writing "reaction" or "no reaction" in the spaces provided.

oxide	type of oxide	reaction with acid	reaction with alkali
magnesium	basic	....	....
aluminium	amphoteric	....	....

[2]

d Predict the equations for the decomposition of the following aluminium compounds.

i _____ $Al(OH)_3 \rightarrow$ _____ + _____ [2]

ii aluminium nitrate $\rightarrow$ _____ + _____ + _____ [2]

Q5 A small piece of limestone was heated strongly and left to cool. A few drops of cold water were added. The solid expanded and gave off steam.

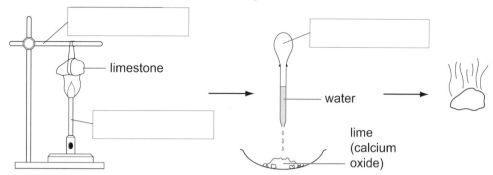

a   Complete the empty boxes to identify the pieces of apparatus labelled.   [3]
b   What type of chemical reaction takes place when water is added?   [1]
_____   [1]

Q6 The table below gives some information about the elements in Group I of the Periodic Table.

element	boiling point / °C	density / g cm^{-3}	radius of atom in the metal / nm	reactivity with water
lithium	1342	0.53	0.157	
sodium	883	0.97	0.191	rapid
potassium	760	0.86	0.235	very rapid
rubidium		1.53	0.250	extremely rapid
caesium	669	1.88		explosive

a   How does the density of the Group I elements change down the Group?
_____   [2]

b   Suggest a value for the boiling point of rubidium.
_____   [1]

c   Suggest a value for the radius of a caesium atom.
d   Use the information in the table to suggest how fast lithium reacts with water compared with the other Group I metals.
_____   [1]

e   State three properties shown by all metals.
1 _____
2 _____
3 _____   [3]

f) When sodium reacts with water, hydrogen is given off.
$$2Na(s) \ + \ 2H_2O(l) \ \rightarrow \ 2NaOH(aq) \ + \ H_2(g)$$
i   State the name of the other product formed in this reaction.
_____   [1]

ii Describe a test for hydrogen.
test _____
result _____   [2]

g   The diagrams below show three types of hydrogen atom.

   i   State the name of the positively charged particle in the nucleus.

   _____ [1]

   ii What is the name given to atoms with the same number of positive charges in the nucleus but different numbers of neutrons?

   _____ [1]

   iii State the number of nucleons in a single atom of tritium.

   _____ [1]

   iv Tritium is a radioactive form of hydrogen.
       State one medical use of radioactivity.

   _____ [1]

Q7   The table below shows the composition of the mixture of gases coming from a typical car exhaust.

gas	% of the gas in the exhaust fumes
carbon dioxide	9
carbon monoxide	5
oxygen	4
hydrogen	2
hydrocarbons	0.2
nitrogen oxides	0.2
sulphur dioxide	less than 0.003
gas X	79.6

a   State the name of the gas X.

   _____ [1]

b   The carbon dioxide comes from the burning of hydrocarbons, such as octane, in the petrol.
   i) Complete the word equation for the complete combustion of octane.
       octane + _____ → carbon dioxide + _____   [2]
   ii Which two chemical elements are present in hydrocarbons?

   _____ [1]

   iii To which homologous series of hydrocarbons does octane belong?

   _____ [1]

c   Suggest a reason for the presence of carbon monoxide in the exhaust fumes.

   _____ [1]

d   Nitrogen oxides are present in small quantities in the exhaust fumes.
   i   Complete the following equation for the formation of nitrogen dioxide.
       $N_2(g)$ + _____ $O_2(g)$ → + _____ $NO_2(g)$ [1]
   ii State one harmful effect of nitrogen dioxide on organisms.

   _____ [1]

e Sulphur dioxide is an atmospheric pollutant which is only found in small amounts in car exhausts.

   i What is the main source of sulphur dioxide pollution of the atmosphere?

_____ [1]

   ii Sulphur dioxide is oxidised in the air to sulphur trioxide. The sulphur trioxide may dissolve in rainwater to form a dilute solution of sulphuric acid, H_2SO_4. State the meaning of the term *oxidation*.

_____ [1]

   iii Calculate the relative molecular mass of sulphuric acid.

_____ [1]

   iv Sulphuric acid reacts with metals such as iron. Complete the following word equation for the reaction of sulphuric acid with iron.

sulphuric acid + iron → _____ + _____ [2]

   v What effect does acid rain have on buildings made of stone containing calcium carbonate?

_____ [1]

Q8 a Two of the gases in air are nitrogen and oxygen. Name two other gases present in unpolluted air.

[2]

b Two common pollutants present in air are sulphur dioxide and lead compounds. State the source and harmful effect of each.

sulphur dioxide

source	
harmful effect	

[3]

lead compounds

source	
harmful effect	

[3]

c Respiration and photosynthesis are two of the processes that determine the percentage of oxygen and of carbon dioxide in the air.

   i Name another process that changes the percentages of these two gases in air.

[1]

   ii The equation for photosynthesis is given below.

$6CO_2 + 6H_2O \rightarrow C_6H_{12}O_6 + 6O_2$

This is an endothermic reaction.

Complete the reaction for respiration.

$C_6H_{12}O_6 + 6O_2 \rightarrow$ [_____] + [_____]

This is an [_____] reaction. [2]

Q9 a i In the space at the top of the series, write an ionic equation that includes a more reactive metal. [1]

ii Define oxidation in terms of electron transfer.

[1]

iii Explain why the positive ions are likely to be oxidising agents.

[1]

iv Which positive ion(s) can oxidise mercury metal (Hg)? [1]

[1]

Q10 Two of the stages in water purification are filtration and chlorination. The diagram below shows a filter tank.

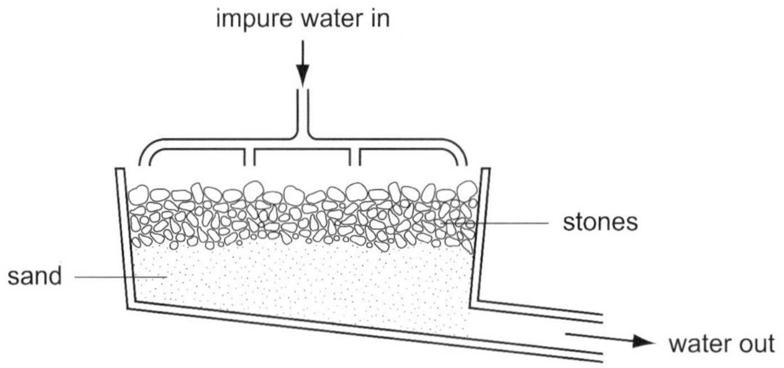

impure water in

stones

sand

water out

a Explain how this filter helps purify the water.

_____

_____

_____ [2]

b i Why is chlorine added during water purification?

_____

ii After chlorination, the water is acidic. A small amount of slaked lime is added to the acidic water. Explain why slaked lime is added.

_____

iii What is the chemical name for slaked lime?

_____

iv State one other use of slaked lime.

_____ [4]

c i State the boiling point of pure water.

_____ [2]

ii Describe a chemical test for water.

test _____ [1]

result _____ [1]

iii State one use of water in the home.

_____ [1]

d   The diagram shows the arrangement of particles in the three different states of water.

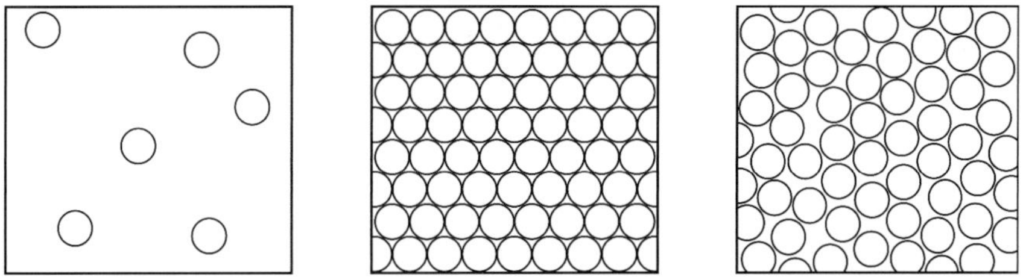

| A | B | C |

Which of these diagrams, A, B or C, shows water in a solid state?

_____ [1]

e   Steam reacts with ethene in the presence of a catalyst. Complete the word equation for this reaction.
    ethene + steam → _____ [1]

f   Potassium reacts violently with water. Complete the word equation for this reaction.
    potassium + water → _____ + _____ [2]

Q11 Look at the list of five elements below.
    argon
    bromine
    chlorine
    iodine
    potassium

a   Put these five elements in order of increasing proton number.

_____ [1]

b   Put these five elements in order of increasing relative atomic mass.

_____ [1]

c   The orders of proton number and relative atomic mass for these five elements are different. Which one of the following is the most likely explanation for this?
    Tick one box.

The proton number of a particular element may vary.   ☐

The presence of neutrons.   ☐

The atoms easily gain or lose electrons.   ☐

The number of protons must always equal the number of neutrons. ☐   [1]

d   Which of the five elements in the list are in the same group of the Periodic Table?

_____ [1]

e   i   From the list, choose one element which has one electron in its outer shell.

_____ [1]

    ii From the list, choose one element which has a full outer shell of electrons.

_____ [1]

f   Which two of the following statements about argon are correct?
    Tick two boxes.

Argon is a noble gas.   ☐

Argon reacts readily with potassium.   ☐

Argon is used to fill weather balloons.   ☐

Argon is used in light bulbs.   ☐   [2]

Living in the age of oil

Ancient alchemists tried to turn cheap metals into gold. They did
not succeed, but they gave us the science of chemistry. Today, we
extract 'liquid gold' – petroleum (crude oil) – from rocks deep
inside the earth, either on land, as in the oil fields of Kuwait and
Saudi Arabia, or under the sea, as in the Arabian Gulf and South
East Asia. We then turn it into fuel for transport, oil for heating
and bitumen for our roads. Petrochemicals made from petroleum
are everywhere. Our world depends on synthetic fertilizers,
pesticides, drugs, textiles and plastics, and all of these products
are based on carbon. Organic chemistry is the study of carbon
compounds, and is essential to our modern age.

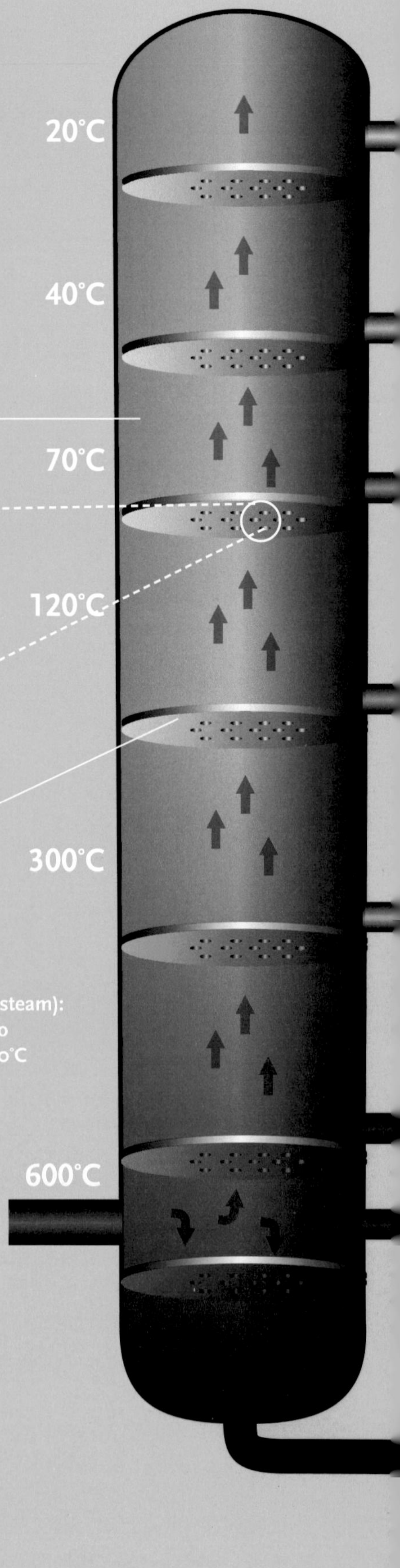

20°C

40°C

Distillation Column

70°C

Bubble cap:
the heated oil vapour rises
through the column

120°C

Crude oil:
is the unprocessed oil as it is
pumped out of the ground.
On average it contains 84%
carbon and 14% nitrogen

Trays with holes and bubble caps
collect the condensed liquids

300°C

Boiler (superheated steam):
heats the crude oil to
a temperature of 600°C

600°C

ORGANIC CHEMISTRY

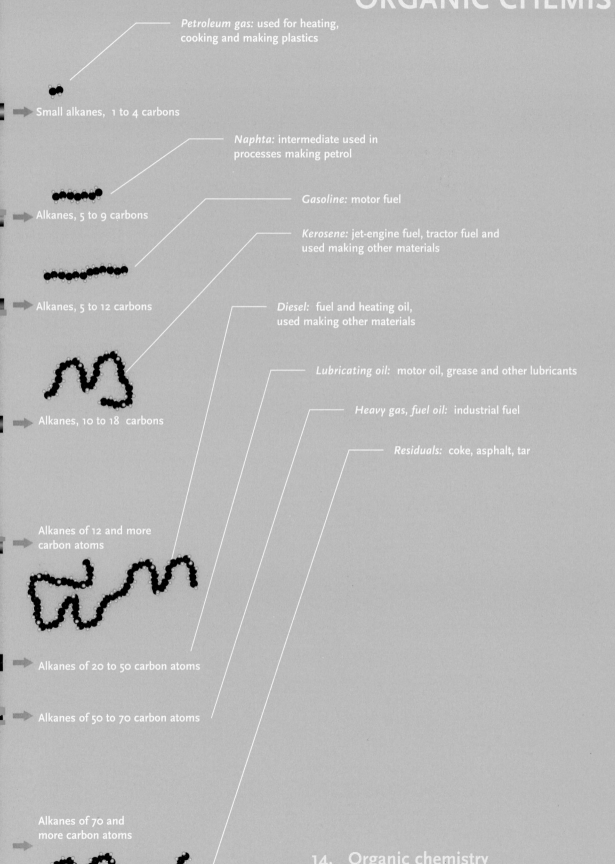

Petroleum gas: used for heating, cooking and making plastics

→ Small alkanes, 1 to 4 carbons

Naphta: intermediate used in processes making petrol

→ Alkanes, 5 to 9 carbons

Gasoline: motor fuel

Kerosene: jet-engine fuel, tractor fuel and used making other materials

→ Alkanes, 5 to 12 carbons

Diesel: fuel and heating oil, used making other materials

Lubricating oil: motor oil, grease and other lubricants

→ Alkanes, 10 to 18 carbons

Heavy gas, fuel oil: industrial fuel

Residuals: coke, asphalt, tar

→ Alkanes of 12 and more carbon atoms

→ Alkanes of 20 to 50 carbon atoms

→ Alkanes of 50 to 70 carbon atoms

→ Alkanes of 70 and more carbon atoms

14 ORGANIC CHEMISTRY

You should check with your tutor about the aspects of this topic that you will be covering in your studies, before studying this section.

Alkanes and alkenes

There are two common families of hydrocarbons, the **alkanes** and the **alkenes**. Members of a family have similar chemical properties, and physical properties that change gradually from one member to the next.

Many alkanes are obtained from **crude oil (petroleum)** by **fractional distillation**. The first members of the family are used extensively as fuels. Apart from burning, however, they are remarkably unreactive. Alkanes are made up of atoms joined by single covalent bonds, so they are known as **saturated** hydrocarbons.

		Molecular formula	Displayed formula	Boiling point (°C)	State at room temperature and pressure
Alkanes	methane	CH_4		−162	gas
	ethane	C_2H_6		−89	gas
	propane	C_3H_8		−42	gas
	butane	C_4H_{10}		0	gas
	pentane	C_5H_{12}		36	liquid
Alkenes	ethene	C_2H_4		−104	gas
	propene	C_3H_6		−48	gas
	butene	C_4H_8		−6	gas
	pentene	C_5H_{10}		30	liquid

The alkenes are often formed in the cracking process. They contain one or more carbon-carbon double bonds. This makes them unsaturated. They burn well and are reactive in other ways. Their reactivity is due to the carbon–carbon double bond.

What are alcohols?

Alcohols are molecules containing the **–OH functional group** which is responsible for their properties and reactions.

Alcohols have the general formula $C_nH_{2n+1}OH$ and belong to the same homologous series, part of which is shown below.

Alcohol	Formula	Structure	Boiling point/°C
Methanol	CH_3OH	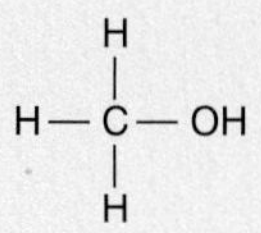	65
Ethanol	C_2H_5OH	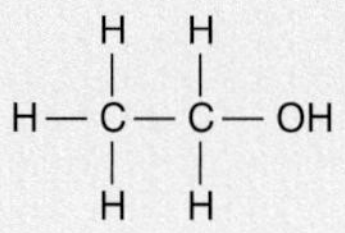	76
Propanol	C_3H_7OH	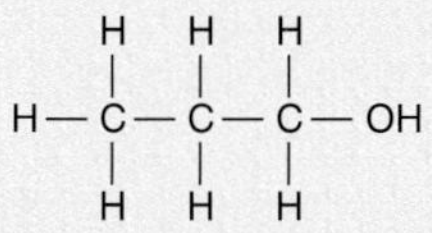	97
Butanol	C_4H_7OH	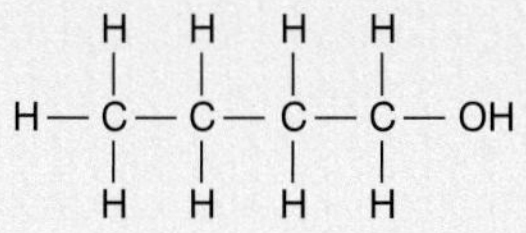	117

Alcohols form structural isomers depending on where the –OH group is placed on the carbon chain. For example:

propan-1-ol

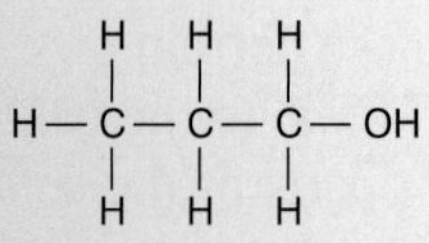

propan-2-ol

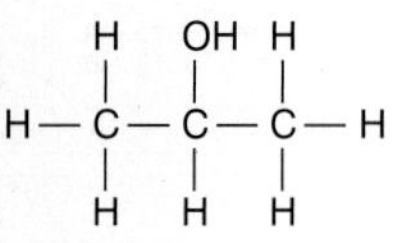

What are carboxylic acids?

Carboxylic acids make up a homologous series of compounds containing the functional group –COOH.

Acid	Formula	Structure
methanoic acid	HCOOH	
ethanoic acid	CH₃COOH	
propanoic acid	C₂H₅COOH	
butanoic acid	C₃H₇COOH	

Fuels

Crude oil, natural gas and coal are **fossil fuels**.

Crude oil was formed millions of years ago from the remains of animals and plants that were pressed together under layers of rock. It is usually found deep underground, trapped between layers of rock that it can't seep through (**impermeable** rock). Natural gas is often trapped in pockets above the crude oil.

The supply of fossil fuels is limited – they are called **'finite'** or **non-renewable** fuels. They are an extremely valuable resource which must be used efficiently.

A Kuwaiti oil field on fire after the retreat by Iraq in the Gulf War

Fossil fuels contain many useful chemicals, and we need to separate these chemicals so that they are not wasted. For example, coal is often converted into coke by removing some of the chemicals in the coal. When the coke is burnt as a fuel, these chemicals are not wasted.

Separating the fractions

The chemicals in crude oil are separated into useful **fractions** by a process known as **fractional distillation**.

The crude oil is heated in a furnace and passed into the bottom of a **fractionating column**. The vapour mixture given off rises up the column and the different fractions condense out at different parts of the column. The fractions that come off near the top of the column are light-coloured runny liquids. Those removed near the bottom of the column are dark and treacle-like. Thick liquids that are not runny, such as these bottom-most fractions, are described as 'viscous'.

A refinery in Malaysia

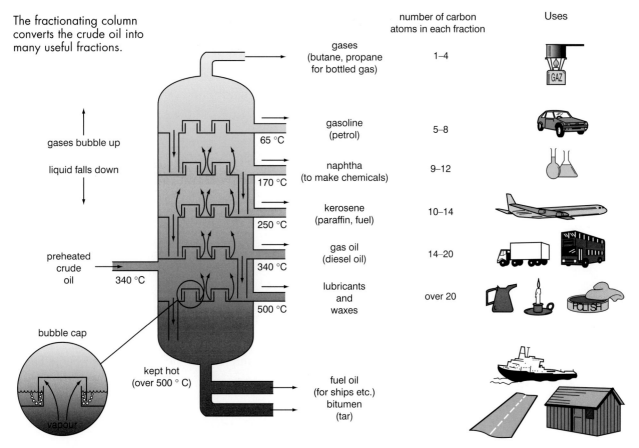

The fractionating column converts the crude oil into many useful fractions.

number of carbon atoms in each fraction

Uses

gases (butane, propane for bottled gas) — 1–4

gasoline (petrol) — 5–8

naphtha (to make chemicals) — 9–12

kerosene (paraffin, fuel) — 10–14

gas oil (diesel oil) — 14–20

lubricants and waxes — over 20

gases bubble up

liquid falls down

65 °C
170 °C
250 °C
340 °C
500 °C

preheated crude oil — 340 °C

bubble cap

kept hot (over 500 °C)

fuel oil (for ships etc.) bitumen (tar)

vapour

How does fractional distillation work?

The components present in crude oil separate because they have different boiling points. A simple particle model explains why their boiling points differ. Crude oil is a mixture of **hydrocarbon** molecules which contain only carbon and hydrogen. The molecules are chemically bonded in similar ways with strong covalent bonds, but contain different numbers of carbon atoms (see page 23).

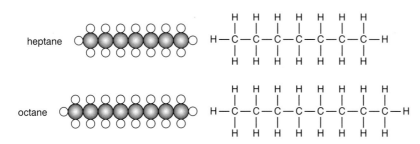

heptane

octane

Notice that octane has one more carbon atom and two more hydrogen atoms than heptane. Their formulae differ by CH_2.

The weak attractive forces between the molecules have to be broken if the hydrocarbon is to boil. The longer a hydrocarbon molecule is, the stronger the intermolecular forces are between the molecules. The stronger these forces, the higher the boiling point, since more energy is needed to overcome the larger forces.

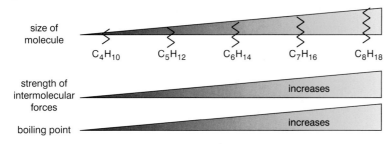

size of molecule

C_4H_{10} C_5H_{12} C_6H_{14} C_7H_{16} C_8H_{18}

strength of intermolecular forces — increases

boiling point — increases

The smaller-molecule hydrocarbons more readily form a vapour – they are more **volatile**. For example, we can smell petrol (with molecules containing between 5 and 10 carbon atoms) much more easily than engine oil (with molecules containing between 14 and 20 carbon atoms) because petrol is more volatile.

Another difference between the fractions is how easily they burn and how smoky their flames are.

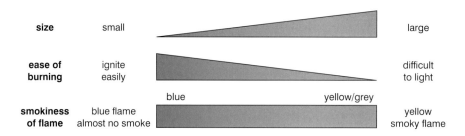

Cracking the oil fractions

The composition of crude oil varies in different parts of the world. The table shows the composition of a sample of crude oil from the Middle East after fractional distillation.

Fraction (in order of increasing boiling point)	Percentage produced by fractional distillation
liquefied petroleum gases (LPG)	3
petrol	13
naphtha	9
paraffin	12
diesel	14
heavy oils (and the residue bitumen)	49

The larger molecules can be broken down into smaller ones by **cracking**. Cracking requires a **high temperature** and a **catalyst**.

Hydrogen can be manufactured by extracting it from hydrocarbons in various ways.

For example if methane is heated with steam in a limited amount of oxygen over a nickel catalyst,

$$CH_4(g) \ + \ H_2O(g) \ \rightarrow \ CO(g) \ + \ 3H_2(g)$$

$$2CH_4(g) \ + \ O_2(g) \ \rightarrow \ 2CO(g) \ + \ 4H_2(g)$$

Hydrocarbons can be heated in the absence of air and 'cracked' to produce hydrogen and other hydrocarbons

$$e.g. \quad C_2H_6(g) \ \rightarrow \ CH_2{=}CH_2(g) \ + \ H_2(g)$$

Homologous series

The families of hydrocarbons called alkanes and alkenes form two **homologous series**.

Members of the same homologous series:
- Have the same general formula, e.g. alkanes are C_nH_{2n+2}.
- Have similar chemical properties.
- Differ from the one before in the series by one carbon atom, e.g. $-CH_2-$ is added to the carbon chain every time. This means that members of the same series behave chemically the same. Melting points and boiling points will be different because of the increasing length of the carbon chain.
- Show a gradual increase in physical properties, e.g. melting point and boiling point because of the increasing length of the carbon chain.
- Contain the same functional group, e.g. alkenes all contain the carbon-carbon double bond.

Alkanes and alkenes are all organic compounds. Their properties are summarised below:

	Alkanes	**Alkenes**
General formula	C_nH_{2n+2}	C_nH_{2n}
Description	saturated (no double C=C bond)	unsaturated (contains a double C=C bond)
Combustion	burn in oxygen to form CO_2 and H_2O (CO if low supply of oxygen)	burn in oxygen to form CO_2 and H_2O (CO if low supply of oxygen)
Reactivity	low	high (because of double C=C bond) undergo addition reactions
Chemical test	none	turn bromine water from brown to colourless (an addition reaction)
Uses	fuels and being cracked to make alkenes	fuels making polymers (addition reactions)

Isomerism

The names of hydrocarbons are based on the number of carbons in the longest chain of atoms within their molecules.

The carbon atoms in a hydrocarbon molecule can be arranged in different ways. For example, in butane, C_4H_{10}, the carbon atoms can be positioned in two ways, while retaining the same molecular formula:

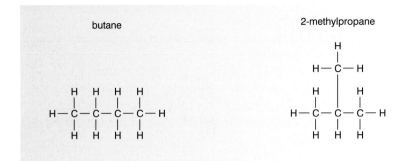

butane

2-methylpropane

2-Methylpropane is a **structural isomer** (same atoms but rearranged) of butane which has a longer chain of carbons. This feature of alkane structure is called **structural isomerism**.

Alkenes show the same property, depending on the position of the double C=C bond. For example, alternatives of butene (C_4H_8) structure are:

but-1-ene

but-2-ene

Each carbon atom has four bonds linked to either H atoms or other C atoms by single or double bonds.

The table shows isomers of the alkane C_5H_{12}.

Isomer	Pentane	2-Methylbutane	2,2-Dimethylpropane
Structure			
Boiling point (°C)	36	27	11

Alkanes

To summarise, alkanes are generally unreactive except in terms of combustion (burning).

Combustion

Most of the common fuels used today are hydrocarbons – substances that contain **only** carbon and hydrogen atoms.

When a hydrocarbon is burnt in a plentiful supply of air it reacts with the oxygen in the air (it is **oxidised**) to form carbon dioxide and water. This reaction is an example of **combustion**.

hydrocarbon   +   oxygen   →   carbon dioxide   +   water

For example, when methane (natural gas) is burnt:

$$CH_4(g) \quad + \quad 2O_2(g) \quad \rightarrow \quad CO_2(g) \quad + \quad 2H_2O(l)$$

The complete combustion of methane in a plentiful supply of air.

The air contains only about 20% oxygen by volume. When a hydrocarbon fuel is burnt there is not always enough oxygen for complete combustion. Instead, some **incomplete combustion** occurs, forming **carbon** or **carbon monoxide**:

methane	+	oxygen	→	carbon monoxide	+	water
$2CH_4(g)$	+	$3O_2(g)$	→	$2CO(g)$	+	$4H_2O(l)$
methane	+	oxygen	→	carbon	+	water
$CH_4(g)$	+	$O_2(g)$	→	$C(s)$	+	$2H_2O(l)$

Incomplete combustion is **costly** because the full energy content of the fuel is not being released and the formation of carbon or soot reduces the efficiency of the burner being used. It can be **dangerous** as carbon monoxide is extremely poisonous. Carbon monoxide molecules attach to the haemoglobin of the blood, preventing oxygen from doing so. Brain cells deprived of their supply of oxygen will quickly die.

The tell-tale sign that a fuel is burning incompletely is that the flame is **yellow**. When complete combustion occurs the flame will be **blue**.

The chlorination of methane

Alkanes can react with chlorine to form substituted alkanes in the presence of ultraviolet light, e.g. sunlight. For example, with methane, chlorine can substitute (replace) each of the four hydrogen atoms This reaction only takes place in the presence of ultraviolet (uv) light, which provides the energy to initiate the reaction.

Halogenation is the replacement of one or more hydrogens in an organic compound by halogen atoms.

When methane is reacted with chlorine the products of the reaction depend on whether there is an excess of methane or an excess of chlorine. If there is an excess of methane it forms chloromethane and hydrogen chloride.

$$\text{methane} + \text{chlorine} \xrightarrow{\text{uv}} \text{chloromethane} + \text{hydrogen chloride}$$
$$CH_4(g) + Cl_2(g) \rightarrow CH_3Cl(g) + HCl(g)$$

If there is an excess of chlorine then trichloromethane and tetrachloromethane are formed.

$$\text{methane} + \text{chlorine (in excess)} \xrightarrow{\text{uv}} \text{chloromethane} + \text{dichloromethane} + \text{trichloromethane}$$
$$CH_4 + Cl_2 \rightarrow CH_3Cl + CH_2Cl_2 + CHCl_3$$
$$+ \text{tetrachloromethane} + \text{hydrogen chloride}$$
$$+ CCl_4 + HCl$$

Another example of an alkane undergoing substitution by a halogen is ethane, C_2H_6, reacting with bromine in the presence of uv light.

As with methane and chlorine or bromine a large number of products are formed, e.g. C_2H_5Br, $C_2H_4Br_2$, $C_2H_3Br_3$, etc., as the hydrogen atoms in the ethane are replaced by bromine atoms.

Alkenes

The alkenes are often formed in the cracking process. They contain one or more carbon-carbon double bonds. Hydrocarbons with at least one double bond are known as **unsaturated** hydrocarbons. Alkenes burn well and are reactive in other ways also. Their reactivity is due to the carbon–carbon double bond.

Alkenes can be distinguished from alkanes by adding **bromine water** to the hydrocarbon. Alkanes do not react with bromine water, but an alkene will decolourise it. The type of reaction is known as an **addition** reaction:

ethene	+	bromine	→	1,2-dibromoethane
(colourless gas)		(brown liquid)		(colourless liquid)

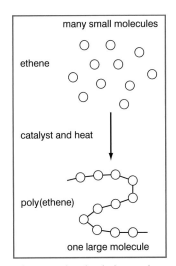

Ethene molecules link together to produce a long polymer chain of poly(ethene).

Polymers

Alkenes can be used to make **polymers** which are very large molecules made up of many identical smaller molecules called **monomers**. Alkenes are able to react with themselves. They join together into long chains like adding beads to a necklace. When the monomers add together like this the material produced is called an **addition polymer**. Poly(ethene) or polythene is made this way.

Another addition reaction of alkenes is adding hydrogen (in the presence of a catalyst) to make an alkane:

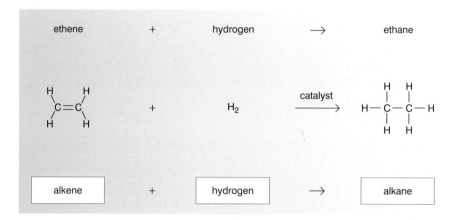

Margarine is made of olive oil whose unsaturated molecules have been saturated with hydrogen.

This reaction is used to make **margarine**. Vegetable oils contain unsaturated fats (i.e. fats with C=C double bonds). When hydrogen is added to these fats they become saturated and **harder**, so producing margarine.

Alcohols

Ethanol, commonly just called 'alcohol', is the most widely used of the alcohol family. The major uses of ethanol are given below:

Use of ethanol	Reason
Alcoholic drinks, e.g. wine, beer, spirits	Affects the brain. It is a depressant, so releases inhibitions. Poisonous in large quantities.
Solvent, e.g. perfumes	The −OH group allows it to dissolve in water, and it dissolves other organic compounds
Fuel, e.g. for cars	It only releases CO_2 and H_2O into the environment, not other pollutant gases as from petrol. It is a renewable resource because it comes from plants, e.g. sugar beet, sugar cane.

Ethanol is made by the process of **fermentation**.

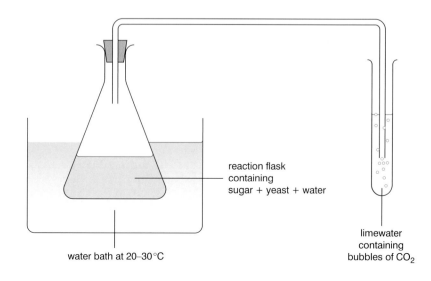

Fermentation apparatus.

Cutting sugar cane to be distilled into alcohol for fuel.

The chemical reaction for fermentation is:

$$\text{sugar} \xrightarrow{\text{yeast}} \text{ethanol} + \text{carbon dioxide}$$

$$C_6H_{12}O_6 \xrightarrow{\text{yeast}} 2C_2H_5OH + 2CO_2$$

Air needs to be kept out of the fermentation flask or its presence could oxidise the ethanol being formed to ethanoic acid ('vinegar' taste). The fermentation process stops when the sugar has all been converted to ethanol or insufficient yeast remains to carry on the sugar conversion.

The **source** of the sugar determines the type of alcoholic drink produced, for example, grapes for wine, hops for beer.

At the end of the fermentation process, which takes time because it is an enzymic reaction (yeast) and a batch process, pure alcohol is extracted by **fractional distillation**. The mixture is boiled and the alcohol vapour reaches the top of the fractionating column where it condenses back to a liquid.

Apparatus for fractional distillation of alcohol.

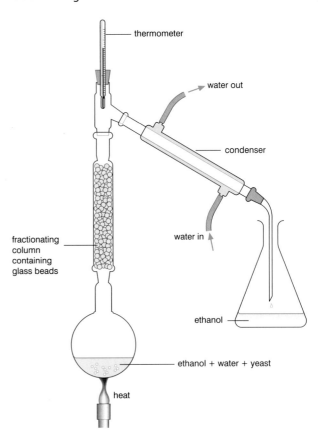

On an **industrial scale**, ethanol is made from alkenes produced by the refining of crude oil. The reaction is:

$$\text{ethene} + \text{steam} \xrightarrow[\substack{\text{phosphoric acid} \\ \text{as catalyst}}]{300\,°C,\ 70\ \text{atm}} \text{ethanol}$$

These are quite extreme conditions in terms of energy (300 °C) and specialist plant equipment (to generate 70 atmospheres), and so the cost is high.

This process has the advantages over fermentation of being a continuous process and of producing ethanol at a fast rate. The economic comparison between fermentation and hydration is a complex issue.

What are the reactions of ethanol (and other alcohols)?

The reason why ethanol is such an important chemical compound (as are other alcohols) is that it can be converted into other important compounds.

Ethanol reacts in the following ways because of the –OH functional group:

1   With sodium to give hydrogen gas:

sodium + ethanol   →   sodium ethanoate + hydrogen

$2Na(s) + 2C_2H_5OH(l)$ → $2C_2H_5ONa(s)$ + $H_2(g)$

2   With ethanoic acid (and concentrated sulphuric acid as a catalyst) to make ethyl ethanoate:

ethanoic acid   +   ethanol $\overset{\text{conc.}H_2SO_4}{\rightleftharpoons}$ ethyl ethanoate

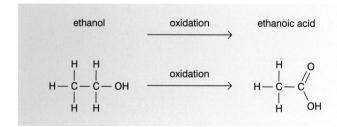

Oils from plants, such as olive oil, are esters of long-chain carboxylic acids and the alcohol propane –1, 2, 3–triol.

Ethyl ethanoate belongs to a family called esters which have pleasant smells and are used as fragrances.

3   Ethanol can be oxidised to make ethanoic acid (a carboxylic acid) by heating it with potassium dichromate (VI) solution and sulphuric acid as the oxidising agent:

ethanol $\xrightarrow{\text{oxidation}}$ ethanoic acid

Acids

Carboxylic acids are used in industry and found in nature:

methanoic acid	The acid that ants can make and use to attack other insects, or for defence.
ethanoic acid	The main constituent of vinegar which is used as a preservative and flavouring. It is also used to make the fibre called acetate rayon.
citric acid	Found in fruits like oranges, lemons and limes. It is added to soft drinks to give them their sharp taste.
ascorbic acid	Known as vitamin C. It is found in citrus fruits like oranges, lemons and limes, as well as some fresh fruits. It is essential for human health.
salicylic acid	This is aspirin and is used for pain relief and to prevent heart attacks.

What are the reactions of carboxylic acids?

Carboxylic acids can be made by the oxidation of alcohols. Oxygen from the air will oxidise the alcohols, but very slowly. In the laboratory alcohols are heated with acidified potassium chromate (VI) solution, as the oxidising agent. Examples are shown:

These are the reactions of carboxylic acids:

1   **Esters** are made by reaction with alcohols (with concentrated sulphuric acid as a catalyst):

2   **Salts** are made by reactions with alkalis, carbonates and hydrogencarbonates:

ethanoic acid + sodium carbonate $\longrightarrow$ sodium ethanoate + water + carbon dioxide

$$2 \; H\!-\!\overset{\displaystyle H}{\underset{\displaystyle H}{C}}\!-\!C\!\!\overset{\displaystyle O}{\underset{\displaystyle OH}{\diagup}} \;+\; Na_2CO_3 \;\longrightarrow\; 2 \; H\!-\!\overset{\displaystyle H}{\underset{\displaystyle H}{C}}\!-\!C\!\!\overset{\displaystyle O}{\underset{\displaystyle ONa}{\diagup}} \;+\; H_2O \;+\; CO_2$$

ethanoic acid + sodium hydrogen-carbonate $\longrightarrow$ sodium ethanoate + water + carbon dioxide

$$H\!-\!\overset{\displaystyle H}{\underset{\displaystyle H}{C}}\!-\!C\!\!\overset{\displaystyle O}{\underset{\displaystyle OH}{\diagup}} \;+\; NaHCO_3 \;\longrightarrow\; H\!-\!\overset{\displaystyle H}{\underset{\displaystyle H}{C}}\!-\!C\!\!\overset{\displaystyle O}{\underset{\displaystyle ONa}{\diagup}} \;+\; H_2O \;+\; CO_2$$

The reaction of carboxylic acids with carbonates and hydrogencarbonates to form carbon dioxide is used as a **chemical test** to identify the acids.

Carboxylic acids are **weak acids** because they only partially dissociate into ions (see page 77):

$$CH_3COOH \;\rightleftharpoons\; CH_3COO^- \;+\; H^+$$

Macromolecules

Macromolecule is the term used to describe very large molecules made up of smaller molecules joining up together.

The smaller molecules are called "monomers" (mono = one, mer = unit) and the larger molecules (macromolecules) "polymers" (poly = many).

Synthetic polymers

The changing of monomers to polymers is called "polymerisation".

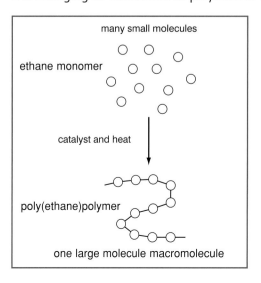

There are two ways of making macromolecules (polymers):

ADDITION POLYMERISATION

In this case the monomer molecules are the same as each other and contain a double carbon – carbon (alkene) bond. The double bond "opens up" and they join together (forming single carbon – carbon bonds), e.g. making poly(ethene) from ethene.

ethene $\rightarrow$ poly(ethene)

$$\left(\begin{array}{c} H \\ \diagdown \\ C = C \\ \diagup \quad \diagdown \\ H \qquad H \end{array}\right) \rightarrow \quad \text{vvv} \quad \begin{array}{cccccc} H & H & H & H & H & H \\ | & | & | & | & | & | \\ C{-}C{-}C{-}C{-}C{-}C \\ | & | & | & | & | & | \\ H & H & H & H & H & H \end{array} \text{vvv}$$

CONDENSATION POLYMERISATION

In this reaction two different molecules are joined together using reactions between the different reactive groups on the molecules. For example, nylon is made from a molecule with a carboxylic acid group (-COOH) and another molecule with an amine group (-NH$_2$).

They react to form an amide link:

Nylon is a polyamide.

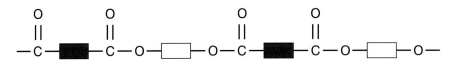

Another example is Terylene, which is made from two different monomer molecules, one with a carboxylic acid group (-COOH) and another with an alcohol group (-OH). They react to form an ester link:

Terylene is described as a polyester.

As a general rule, addition polymerisation is used to make plastics.

By changing the atoms or groups of atoms attached to the carbon–carbon double bond, a whole range of different polymers can be made:

Condensation polymerisation is used for man-made fibres for clothes, ropes, e.tc., such as nylon and terylene.

Problems with plastics

Plastics are very difficult to dispose of. Most of them are not **biodegradable** – they cannot be decomposed by bacteria in the soil. Currently, most waste plastic material is buried in landfill sites or is burnt, but burning plastics produces toxic fumes and landfill sites are filling up.

Some types of plastic can be melted down and used again. These are **thermoplastics.** Other types of plastic decompose when they are heated. These are **thermosetting** plastics. Recycling is difficult because the different types of plastic must be separated.

Name of monomer	Displayed formula of monomer	Name of polymer	Displayed formula of polymer	Uses of polymer
ethene	H H \ / C=C / \ H H	poly(ethene)	H H | | —C—C— | | H H /n	buckets, bowls, plastic bags
chloroethene (vinyl chloride)	H H \ / C=C / \ Cl H	poly(chloroethene) (polyvinylchloride)	H H | | —C—C— | | Cl H /n	plastic sheets, artificial leather
phenylethene (styrene)	H H \ / C==C / \ C₆H₅ H	poly(phenylethene) (polystyrene)	H H | | —C—C— | | C₆H₅ H /n	yoghurt cartons, packaging
tetrafluoroethene	F F \ / C=C / \ F F	poly(tetrafluroethene) or PTFE	F F | | —C—C— | | F F /n	non-stick coating in frying pans

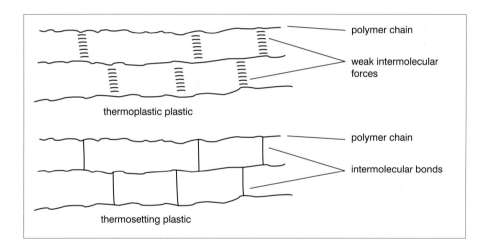

In thermoplastics the intermolecular forces are weak and break on heating. The plastic can be melted and re-moulded. In thermosetting plastics the intermolecular bonds are strong interlinking covalent bonds. The whole structure breaks down when these bonds are broken by heating.

Household waste

People produce a lot of waste, including sewage and rubbish they simply throw away.

As the Earth's population continues to increase, so will the problem of **household waste** and its **disposal**.

Some household rubbish is burnt, causing acid gas pollution and acid rain. Rubbish tips create their own problems:

- They are ugly and can smell.
- They can encourage rats and other pests.
- Methane gas produced by rotting material may build up in tips that are covered with soil – this gas is explosive.
- Covered-over tips cannot be used for building on because the ground settles.

We can reduce the amount of material in our dustbins by **recycling** or **reusing** materials and not buying **highly packaged** materials.

Natural macromolecules

There are many natural large, long-chain molecules (macromolecules) found in nature, i.e. in plants and animals.

The food we eat contains many of these macromolecules and we will look at three of these in more detail in this section. These macro molecules are the main constituents of the foods we eat: **proteins**, **fats** and **carbohydrates**.

PROTEINS

These macromolecules have been formed by condensation polymerisation of amino acids.

Amino acids have a carboxylic acid group on one end and an amine group on the other,

H_2N - ☐ - COOH

The ends of the molecules react together to form an amide link,

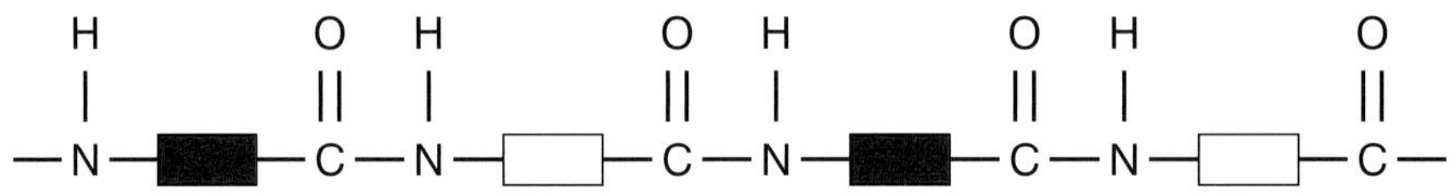

This is the same linkage found in nylon, but the amino acid molecules are different from the molecules used in nylon.
Proteins can be broken down to amino acids by **hydrolysis** ("reaction with water"). The protein is boiled in dilute acid to be hydrolysed.

FATS

Fats are natural macromolecules made by the reaction between molecules with an alcohol group (-OH) and molecules with a carboxylic acid group (-COOH) to form an ester link:

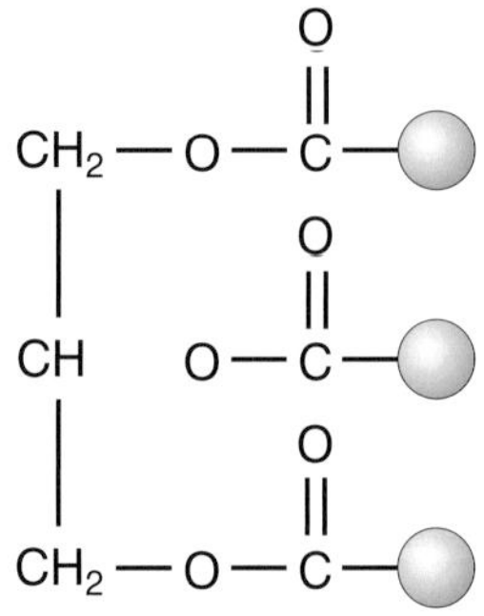

This is the same linkage as found in Terylene but, as with nylon and proteins, using different monomer molecules. Fats can be hydrolysed back to acids and alcohol by breaking the ester link. If fats are hydrolysed using sodium hydroxide then soaps are made.

CARBOHYDRATE

Carbohydrates contain carbon, hydrogen and oxygen atoms. Starch is an example of carbohydrate macromolecules. It is made of sugar molecules (the monomers) joined together by condensation polymerisation.

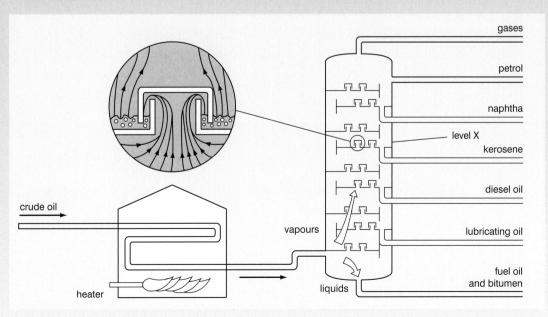

SUGAR MOLECULES   STARCH

The carbohydrate linkages in complex carbohydrates, e.g. starch can be broken down by hydrolysis using acids to form simple sugars.

Fermentation is a technique for turning sugars into ethanol (see page 153).

The products of the hydrolysis of proteins and carbohydrates can be separated and identified using paper chromatography. The products are colourless so need spraying with a locating agent to be seen on the chromatogram (see page 13).

REVIEW QUESTIONS

Q1 a How was crude oil formed?
     b Why is crude oil a non-renewable fuel?

Q2 The diagram shows a column used to separate the components present in crude oil.
     a Name the process used to separate crude oil into fractions.
     b What happens to the boiling point of the mixture as it goes up the column?
     c The mixture of vapours arrives at level X. What now happens to the various parts of the mixture?

The table shows some of the properties of the crude oil components:

Component	Boiling point (°C)	How runny?	Colour	How it burns
A	up to 70	very	colourless	easily, blue flame
B	70 to 150	fairly	pale yellow	fairly easily, a smoky flame
C	150 to 230	not very	dark yellow	difficult to light, a very smoky flame

d Another component was collected between 230 °C and 300 °C.
   What would it be like?

e Component A is used as a fuel in a car engine.
   Suggest why component C would not be suitable as a fuel in a car engine.

Q3 The cracking of decane molecules is shown by the equation $C_{10}H_{22} \rightarrow Y + C_2H_4$
   a Decane is a hydrocarbon. What is a hydrocarbon?
   b What conditions are needed for cracking?
   c Write down the molecular formula for hydrocarbon Y.

Q4 Reforming is an important process in refining oil.
   a What happens in the reforming process?
   b Give one example of when reforming is needed.

Q5 What is meant by each of the following?
   a homologous series
   b structural isomerism.

Q6 Draw two isomers of each of the following hydrocarbons:
   a hexane, C_6H_{14}
   b butene, C_4H_8

Q7 Why do isomers have different boiling points?

Q8 In the laboratory fermentation experiment to make ethanol from sugar using yeast, why is it important that
   a the reaction is kept at 20–30ºC and not higher than that temperature range?
   b oxygen from the air cannot enter the reaction flask?

Q9 Give the structural formula of two isomers of butanol, C_4H_7OH.

Q10 What is 'esterification'?

Q11 How would you test an unknown liquid to show it is a solution of a carboxylic acid?

Q13 Explain the difference between addition polymerisation and condensation polymerisation.

Q14 What is an
   a amide link?
   b ester link?

Q15 What are the monomers in proteins?

Q16 What is the link between monomers in proteins?

Q17 What is the meaning of "hydrolysis'?

Q18 What is made when fats are hydrolysed?

Q19 Sugar can be changed into ethanol using yeast.
a What is this process called?
b What method of separation is used to extract the ethanol from the mixture?

Examination questions are on page 170.

More questions on the CD ROM

EXAMINATION QUESTIONS

Q1 Poly(ethene) is a plastic which is made by polymerizing ethene, C_2H_4.

a) Which one of the following best describes the ethene molecules in this reaction? Put a ring around the correct answer.

alcohols   alkanes   monomers   polymers   products   [1]

b) The structure of ethane is shown below.

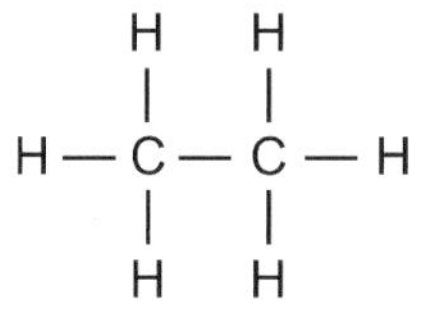

$$\begin{array}{c} \quad H \quad\; H \\ \quad | \quad\; | \\ H-C-C-H \\ \quad | \quad\; | \\ \quad H \quad\; H \end{array}$$

Explain, by referring to its bonding, why ethane cannot be polymerized.

_____ [1]

c) Draw the structure of ethene, showing all atoms and bonds.

[1]

d Ethene is obtained by cracking alkanes.

i Explain the meaning of the term cracking.

_____

_____ [1]

ii What condition is needed to crack alkanes?

_____ [1]

iii Complete the equation for cracking decane, $C_{10}H_{22}$.

$$C_{10}H_{22} \rightarrow C_2H_4 + \text{..}_____$$ [1]

e Some oil companies 'crack' the ethane produced when petroleum is distilled.

i Complete the equation for this reaction.

$$C_2H_4 \rightarrow C_2H_6 + \text{..}_____$$ [1]

ii Describe the process of fractional distillation which is used to separate the different fractions in petroleum.

_____

_____

_____

_____ [2]

iii State a use for the following petroleum fractions.

petrol fraction _____

lubricating fraction _____ .   [2]

Q2 Enzymes are biological catalysts. They are used both in research laboratories and in industry.

a Enzymes called proteases can hydrolyse proteins to amino acids. The amino acids can be separated and identified by chromatography. The diagram shows a typical chromatogram.

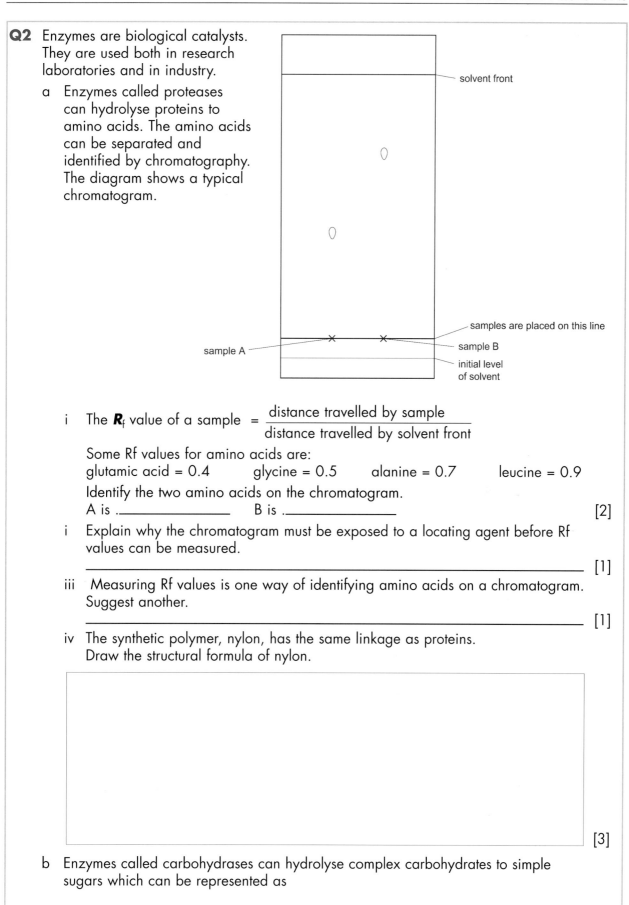

solvent front

samples are placed on this line

sample B

initial level of solvent

sample A

i The **R**$_f$ value of a sample $= \dfrac{\text{distance travelled by sample}}{\text{distance travelled by solvent front}}$

Some Rf values for amino acids are:

glutamic acid = 0.4   glycine = 0.5   alanine = 0.7   leucine = 0.9

Identify the two amino acids on the chromatogram.

A is ._____   B is ._____   [2]

i Explain why the chromatogram must be exposed to a locating agent before Rf values can be measured.

_____ [1]

iii Measuring Rf values is one way of identifying amino acids on a chromatogram. Suggest another.

_____ [1]

iv The synthetic polymer, nylon, has the same linkage as proteins. Draw the structural formula of nylon.

[3]

b Enzymes called carbohydrases can hydrolyse complex carbohydrates to simple sugars which can be represented as

HO ─|‾‾‾‾|─ OH

Draw the structure of a complex carbohydrate.

[2]

c   Fermentation can be carried out in the apparatus drawn below. After a few days the reaction stops. It has produced a 12% aqueous solution of ethanol.

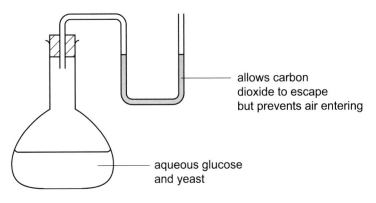

allows carbon dioxide to escape but prevents air entering

aqueous glucose and yeast

i   Complete the equation.

$C_6H_{12}O_6 \rightarrow$ _____ + _____
glucose   ethanol   carbon dioxide   [2]

ii   Zymase catalyses the anaerobic respiration of glucose. Define the term respiration.

_____

_____ [2]

iii Suggest a reason why the reaction stops after a few days.

_____ [1]

iv   Why is it essential that there is no oxygen in the flask?

_____ [1]

v   What technique is used to concentrate the aqueous ethanol?

_____ [1]

Q3 The structures of some compounds found in plants are shown below.

A	B	C	D	E

a   Which two of these compounds are unsaturated hydrocarbons?

_____ [1]

b Which two of these compounds contain a carboxylic acid functional group?
_____ [1]

c Write the molecular formula for compound D.
_____ [1]

d Draw the structure of the product formed when compound A reacts with bromine. Show all atoms and all bonds.

[1]

e Strawberry fruits produce compound **A** (ethene) naturally. A scientist left some green strawberry fruits to ripen. The scientist measured the concentration of ethene and carbon dioxide produced by the strawberry fruits over a ten day period. The graph below shows the results.

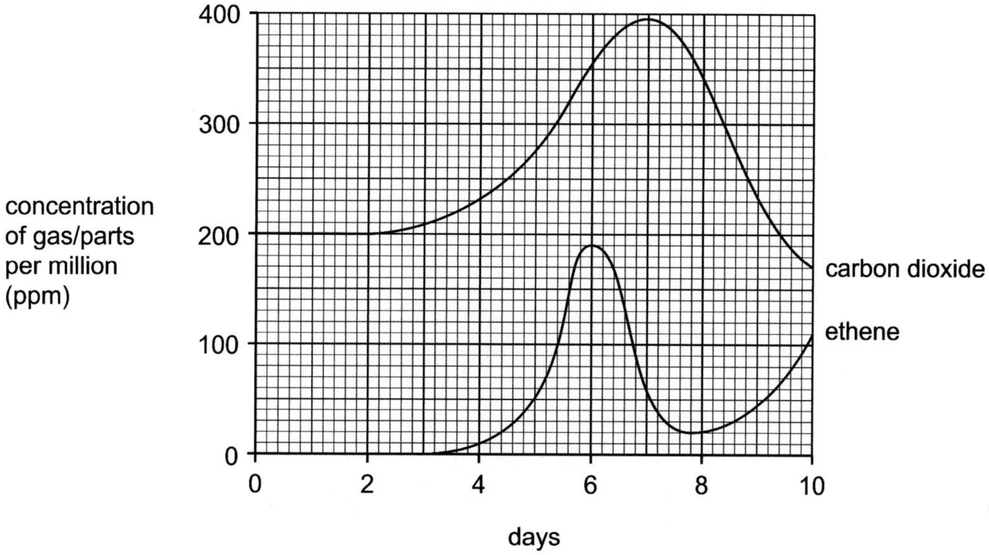

i Between which two days does the rate of ethene production increase most rapidly?
_____ [1]

ii What is the name given to the process in which carbon dioxide is produced by living organisms?
Put a ring around the correct answer.

acidification   combustion   neutralization   respiration   [1]

iii Carbon dioxide concentration over 350 ppm has an effect on ethene production by the fruits.
What effect is this?   [1]
_____ [1]

iv Ethene gas spreads throughout the fruit by a random movement of molecules.
What is the name given to the random movement of molecules?
Put a ring around the correct answer.

aeration   diffusion   evaporation   ionisation   [1]

v Ethene gas promotes the ripening of strawberry fruits.
Ripening of strawberries is slowed down by passing a stream of nitrogen over the fruit.
Suggest why this slows down the ripening process.

_____ [1]

vi Enzymes are involved in the ripening process. What is an enzyme?

_____
_____ [2]

f Plants make a variety of coloured pigments. A student extracted red colouring from four different plants, R, S, T and U. The student put a spot of each colouring on a piece of filter paper. The filter paper was dipped into a solvent and left for 30 minutes. The results are shown below.

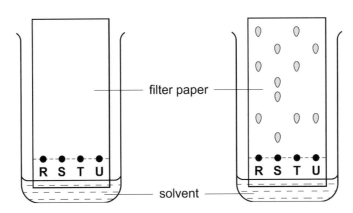

i   What is name given to the process shown in the diagram?

_____ [1]

ii Which plant contained the greatest number of different pigments?

_____ [1]

iii Which two plants contained the same pigments?

_____ [1]

Q4 The simplest alcohol is methanol.
a It is manufactured by the following reversible reaction.

$$CO\ (g) + 2H_2\ (g) \rightleftharpoons CH_3OH\ (g)$$
300 °C
30atm

i   Reversible reactions can come to equilibrium. Explain the term **equilibrium**.

[1]

ii At 400 °C, the percentage of methanol in the equilibrium mixture is lower than at 300 °C. Suggest an explanation.

[2]

iii Suggest two advantages of using high pressure for this reaction.
Give a reason for each advantage.

advantage	
reason	

advantage	
reason	

[5]

b i Complete the equation for the combustion of methanol in an excess of oxygen.

$\boxed{}$ CH_3OH + $\boxed{}$ $O_2 \rightarrow$ $\boxed{}$ + $\boxed{}$ [2]

ii Complete the word equation.

methanol + ethanoic acid $\rightarrow$ $\boxed{}$ + + $\boxed{}$ [2]

iii Methanol can be oxidised to an acid. Name this acid.

[1]

Q5 Polymers are extensively used in food packaging. Poly(dichloroethene) is used because gases can only diffuse through it very slowly. Polyesters have a high thermal stability and food can be cooked in a polyester bag.

a i The structure of poly(dichloroethene) is given below.

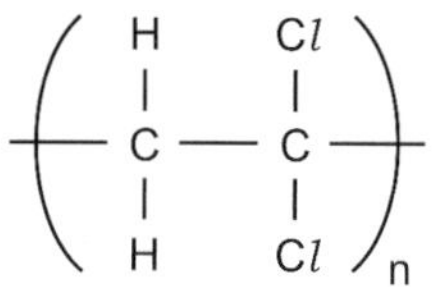

$$\left(\begin{array}{c} H \quad\quad Cl \\ | \quad\quad\quad | \\ -C - C - \\ | \quad\quad\quad | \\ H \quad\quad Cl \end{array}\right)_n$$

Draw the structural formula of the monomer.

[1]

ii Explain why oxygen can diffuse faster through the polymer bag than carbon dioxide can.

[2]

b) i A polyester can be formed from the monomers $HO\text{-}CH_2CH_2\text{-}OH$ and $HOOC\text{-}C_6H_4\text{-}COOH$. Draw the structure of this polyester.

[2]

i Name a naturally occurring class of compounds that contains the ester linkage.

[1]

iii Suggest what is meant by the term thermal stability.

[1]

c i Describe two environmental problems caused by the disposal of plastic (polymer) waste.

[2]

ii The best way of disposing of plastic waste is recycling to form new plastics. What is another advantage of recycling plastics made from petroleum?

[1]

Q6 The alkenes are a homologous series of unsaturated hydrocarbons.
  a The table below gives the names, formulae and boiling points of the first members of the series.

name	formula	boiling point/°C
ethene	C_2H_4	-102
propene	C_3H_6	-48
butene	C_4H_8	-7
pentene	C_5H_{10}	30
hexene		

    i   Complete the table on the previous page by giving the formula of hexene and by predicting its boiling point.   [2]

    ii   Deduce the formula of the alkene which has a relative molecular mass of 168. Show your working.

[2]

b Describe a test that will distinguish between the two isomers, but-2-ene and cyclobutane.

test	
result with but-2-ene	
result with cyclobutane	

[3]

c Alkenes undergo addition reactions.

    i   What class of organic compound is formed when an alkene reacts with water?

[1]

    ii   Predict the structural formula of the compound formed when hydrogen chloride reacts with but-2-ene.

[1]

    iii   Draw the structure of the polymer formed from but-2-ene.

[2]

Q7 Organic substances have many uses.

a Match the substances in the boxes on the left with the descriptions in the boxes on the right. The first one has been done for you.

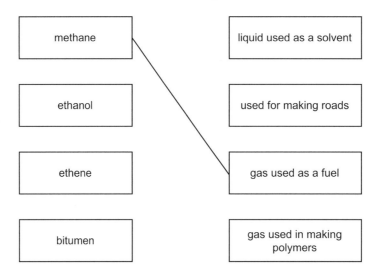

[3]

b Which one of the following would be least likely to be obtained from the fractional distillation of petroleum? Put a ring around the correct answer.

bitumen   ethane   ethanol   methane   [1]

c Some reactions of organic compounds are shown below.

A $n\ CH_2 = CH_2 \rightarrow +\ CH_2 - CH_2 +\ n$

B $C_3H_8 + 5O_2 \rightarrow 3CO_2 + 4H_2O$

C $C_6H_{12}O_6 \rightarrow 2CO_2 + 2C_2H_5OH$
glucose

D $C_8H_{18} \rightarrow C_2H_{14} + C_2H_4$

i Which one of the reactions, A, B, C or D, shows fermentation?

_____

ii Which one of the reactions, A, B, C or D, shows polymerization?

_____

iii Which one of the reactions, A, B, C or D, shows combustion?

_____

iv Which one of the reactions, A, B, C or D, shows cracking?

_____ [4]

d The hydrocarbon C8H18 is an alkane.

i What is meant by the term hydrocarbon?

_____

ii Explain why this hydrocarbon is an alkane.

_____ [2]

Q8 In 2003, Swedish scientists found high levels of acrylamide in starchy foods that had been cooked above 120°C. Acrylamide, which is thought to be a risk to human health, has the following structure.

$$\begin{array}{c} H \\ \diagdown \\ H \diagup \end{array} C = C \begin{array}{c} H \\ \diagup \\ \diagdown \\ CONH_2 \end{array}$$

a i It readily polymerises to polyacrylamide. Draw the structure of this polymer.

[2]

   ii Starch is formed by polymerisation. It has a structure of the type shown below. Name the monomer.

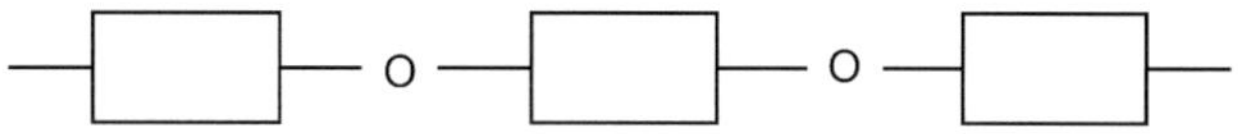

_____ [1]

   iii What are the differences between these two polymerisation reactions, one forming polyacrylamide and the other starch?

_____

_____ [2]

b Acrylamide hydrolyses to form acrylic acid and ammonium ions.
   i Describe the test for the ammonium ion.
   test   _____
   result _____

_____ [2]

   ii Given an aqueous solution, concentration 0.1 mol / dm , how could you show that acrylic acid is a weak acid.

_____

_____ [2]

c The structural formula of acrylic acid is shown right. It forms compounds called acrylates.

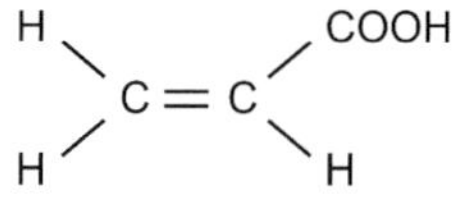

   i Acrylic acid reacts with ethanol to form the following compound.

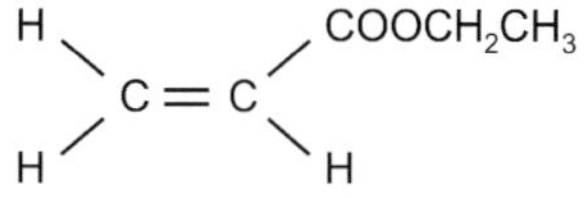

   Deduce the name of this compound. What type of organic compound is it?
   name   _____
   type of compound _____ [2]

   ii Acrylic acid is an unsaturated compound. It will react with bromine. Describe the colour change and draw the structural formula of the product of this addition reaction.
   colour change _____
   structural formula of product

[2]

EXAM PRACTICE AND ANSWERS

Exam practice and answers

Read each question carefully; this includes looking in detail at any **diagrams, graphs** or **tables**. Remember that any information you are given is there to help you to answer the question. Underline or circle the **key words** in the question and **make sure you answer the question that is being asked** rather than the one you wish had been asked!

Make sure that you understand the meaning of the '**command words**' in the questions. For example:
- '**Describe**' is used when you have to give the main feature(s) of, for example, a process or structure;
- '**Explain**' is used when you have to give reasons, e.g. for some experimental results;
- '**Suggest**' is used when there may be more than one possible answer, or when you will not have learnt the answer but have to use the knowledge you do have to come up with a sensible one;
- '**Calculate**' means that you have to work out an answer in figures.

Look at the **number of marks** allocated to each question and also the **space provided** to guide you as to the length of your answer. You need to make sure you include at least as many points in your answer as there are marks, and preferably more. If you really do need more space to answer than provided, then use the nearest available space, e.g. at the bottom of the page, making sure you write down which question you are answering. **Beware of continually writing too much because it probably means you are not really answering the questions.**

Don't spend so long on some questions that you don't have time to finish the paper. You should spend approximately **one minute per mark**. If you are really stuck on a question, leave it, finish the rest of the paper and come back to it at the end. Even if you eventually have to guess at an answer, you stand a better chance of gaining some marks than if you leave it blank.
In short-answer questions, or multiple-choice type questions, **don't write more than you are asked for.** In some exams, examiners apply the rule that they only mark the first part of the answer written if there is too much. This means that the later part of the answer will not be looked at. In other exams you would not gain any marks, even if the first part of your answer is correct, if you've written down something incorrect in the later part of your answer. This just shows that you haven't really understood the question or are guessing.

In calculations always show your working. Even if your final answer is incorrect you may still gain some marks if part of your attempt is correct. If you just write down the final answer and it is incorrect, you will get no marks at all. Also in calculations you should write down your answers to as many **significant figures** as are used in the question. You may also lose marks if you don't use the correct **units**.

In some questions, particularly short-answer questions, answers of only one or two words may be sufficient, but in longer questions you should aim to use **good English** and **scientific language** to make your answer as clear as possible.

If it helps you to answer clearly, don't be afraid to also use **diagrams** or **flow charts** in your answers.

When you've finished your exam, **check through** to make sure you've answered all the questions. Cover over your answers and read through the questions again and check that your answers are as good as you can make them.

- This Unit gives you invaluable guidance on how to answer exam questions well.
- It contains some sample students' answers to typical exam questions, followed by examiner's comments on them, showing where the students gained and lost marks. Reading through these will help you get a very clear idea of what you need to do in order to score full marks when answering questions in your GCSE Chemistry exam.
- There are also some typical exam questions for you to try answering. Model answers are given at the back of the book for you to check your own answers against. There are also examiner's comments, highlighting how to achieve full marks.

HOW SHOULD I ANSWER EXAM QUESTIONS?

- Look at the number of marks. The marks should tell you how long to spend on a question. A rough guide is a minute for every mark. The number of marks will indicate how many different points are required in the answer.
- Look at the space allocated for the answer.
  If only one line is given, then only a short answer is required, e.g. a single word, a short phrase or a short sentence. Some questions will require more extended writing and for these four or more lines will be allocated.
- Read the question carefully. Students frequently answer the question they would like to answer, rather than the one that has actually been set! Circle or underline the key words. Make sure you know what you are being asked to do. Are you choosing from a list? Are you using the periodic table? Are you completing a table? Have you been given the formula you will need to use in a calculation? Are you describing or explaining?

EXAM QUESTION AND STUDENT'S ANSWER (PAPER 2)

1 Read the following instructions for the preparation of hydrated nickel(II) sulphate ($NiSO_4$ $7H_2O$), then answer the questions which follow.

1 Put 25 cm^3 of dilute sulphuric acid in a beaker.

2 Heat the sulphuric acid until it is just boiling then add a small amount of nickel(II) carbonate.

3 When the nickel(II) carbonate has dissolved, stop heating, then add a little more nickel carbonate. Continue in this way until nickel(II) carbonate is in excess.

4 Filter the hot mixture into a clean beaker.

5 Make the hydrated nickel(II) sulphate crystals from the nickel(II) sulphate solution.

The equation for the reaction is
$(NiCO_2(S) + H_2SO_4(aq) \rightarrow HISO_4(aq) + CO_2(g) + H_2O(l)$

a) What piece of apparatus would you use to measure out 25 cm^3 of sulphuric acid?

measuring cylinder ✓ (1) [1]

b) Why is the nickel(II) carbonate added in excess?

to make sure some is left over ✗ [1]

c) When nickel(II) carbonate is added to sulphuric acid, there is a fizzing.

Explain why there is a fizzing.

CO_2 made ✓ (1) [1]

d) Draw a diagram to describe step 4.
You must label your diagram.

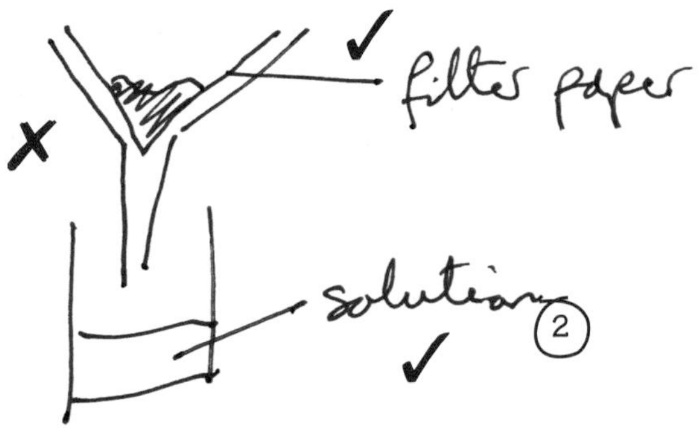

[3]

e) After filtration, which one of the following describes the nickel(II) sulphate in the beaker?
Put a ring around the correct answer.

crystals **(filtrate)** ✓ **precipitate** **water** [1]

f) Explain how you would obtain pure dry crystals of hydrated nickel(II) sulphate from the solution of nickel(II) sulphate.

Evaporate the solution to remove some water. Leave to crystalise. ✔

Filter crystals off and dry. ✔   ②   [2]

g) When hydrated nickel(II) sulphate is heated gently in a test tube, it changes colour from green to white.

i) Complete the symbol equation for this reaction.

$NiSO_4.7H_2O(s) \rightleftharpoons NiSO_4(s) + $ *$7H_2O$* ✗ _____ [1]

ii) What does the sign $\rightleftharpoons$ mean?

An eqilibrium reaction ✔   ①   [1]

iii) How can you obtain a sample of green nickel(II) sulphate starting with white nickel(II) sulphate?

Add water ✔   ①   [1]

⑨/12

More questions
on the CD ROM

HOW TO SCORE FULL MARKS

a) A burette or 25.00 cm³ pipette would have been equally acceptable.

b) The excess solid is added to ensure all the acid has reacted to make the salt. This is a standard procedure in making soluble salts from insoluble solids.

c) Correct: 'carbon dioxide' is equally acceptable (see (g) in the equation giving clue to 'fizzing').

d) A mark has been lost for failing to label the solid in the filter paper.

e) Correct response.

f) Both marks have been gained for a correct description of solution → evaporation → crystallisation.

g) i) '7H₂O' is correct, but (l) has been omitted (see 'symbol equation' mentioned in the question).

ii) Correct: also acceptable would be 'reversible reaction' or 'forward rate = backward rate' or 'reaction goes both ways'.

iii) The candidate has correctly seen the clue in $\rightleftharpoons$ i.e. will go backwards with H₂O.

QUESTION TO TRY

I The table below shows the composition of the mixture of gases coming from a typical car exhaust.

gas	% of the gas in the exhaust fumes
carbon dioxide	9
carbon monoxide	5
oxygen	4
hydrogen	2
hydrocarbons	0.2
nitrogen oxides	0.2
sulphur dioxide	less than 0.003
gas X	79.6

a) State the name of the gas X.

_____ [1]

b) The carbon dioxide comes from the burning of hydrocarbons, such as octane, in the petrol.

i) Complete the word equation for the complete combustion of octane.

octane + _____ → carbon dioxide + _____ [2]

ii) Which **two** chemical elements are present in hydrocarbons?

_____ [1]

iii) To which homologous series of hydrocarbons does octane belong?

_____ [1]

c) Suggest a reason for the presence of carbon monoxide in the exhaust fumes.

_____ [1]

d) Nitrogen oxides are present in small quantities in the exhaust fumes.

Complete the following the following equation for the formation of nitrogen dioxide.

$N_2(g)$ + _____ $O_2(g)$ → $NO_2(g)$ _____ [1]

e) Sulphur dioxide is an atmospheric pollutant which is only found in small amounts in car exhausts.

i) What is the main source of sulphur dioxide pollution of the atmosphere?

_____ [1]

ii) Sulphur dioxide is oxidised in the air to sulphur trioxide. The sulphur trioxide may dissolve in rainwater to form a dilute solution of sulphuric acid, H_2SO_4.

State the meaning of the term oxidation.

_____ [1]

iii) Calculate the relative molecular mass of sulphuric acid.

_____ [1]

iv) Sulphuric acid reacts with metals such as iron.

Complete the following word equation for the reaction of sulphuric acid with iron.

sulphuric acid + iron $\rightarrow$ _____ + _____

_____ [2]

v) What effect does acid rain have on buildings made of stone containing calcium carbonate?

[1]

More questions on the CD ROM

Answers are on page 201

EXAM QUESTION AND STUDENT'S ANSWER (PAPER 3)

1 a) Two of the gases in air are nitrogen and oxygen. Name **two** other gases present in unpolluted air.

Neon and argon ✓ ✓ ② [2]

b) Two common pollutants present in air are sulphur dioxide and lead compounds. State the source and harmful effect of each.

sulphur dioxide

source	burning fossil fuels ✓	①
harmful effect	causes 'acid rain' ✓	①

[2]

lead compounds

source	burning petrol ✗	
harmful effect	brain damage ✓	①

[2]

c) Respiration and photosynthesis are two of the processes that determine the percentage of oxygen and of carbon dioxide in the air.

i) name another process that changes the percentage of these two gases in air.

burning carbon fuels ✓ ① [1]

ii) The equation for photosynthesis is given below.

$6CO_2 + 6H_2O \rightarrow C_6H_{12}O_6 + 6O_2$

This is an endothermic reaction.

Complete the reaction for respiration.

$C_6H_{12}O_6 + 6O_2 \rightarrow$ 6CO_2 _____ + 6H_2O ✓ ①

This is an endothermic_____ reaction. ✓ [2]

d) The rate of photosynthesis of pond weed can be measured using the following experiment.

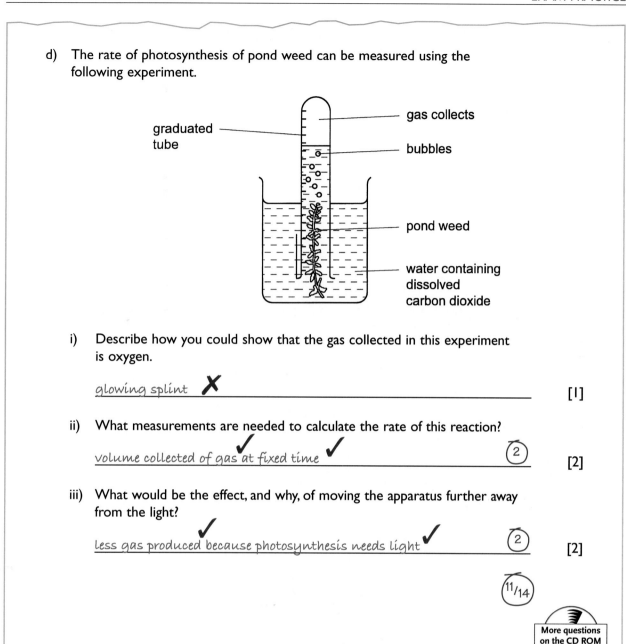

graduated tube — gas collects

— bubbles

— pond weed

— water containing dissolved carbon dioxide

i) Describe how you could show that the gas collected in this experiment is oxygen.

glowing splint ✗   [1]

ii) What measurements are needed to calculate the rate of this reaction?

volume collected of gas at fixed time ✓ ✓   ② [2]

iii) What would be the effect, and why, of moving the apparatus further away from the light?

less gas produced because photosynthesis needs light ✓ ✓   ② [2]

⑪/14

More questions on the CD ROM

HOW TO SCORE FULL MARKS

a) Correct response – also acceptable would be names of any noble gases or carbon dioxide or water vapour.

b) Fossil fuels containing sulphur, which burns to the oxide and forms 'acid rain', is an important environmental issue.

The first mark has not been given for 'lead' because the word leaded has been omitted (we now use the word unleaded petrol).

c) i) Correct response - also acceptable would be 'destroying forests' because forests produce oxygen through photosynthesis.

ii) The candidate has correctly spotted the reversal of the chemical equation. It should be 'exothermic' since the reaction has been reversed.

d) i) This is an incomplete test. It is essential to mention the positive result of the test. In this case 'relights a glowing splint'.

ii) The use of time is essential in following any rate, in this case cm^3/s for the gas.

iii) Correct response about light and photosynthesis.

QUESTION TO TRY

2 The simplest alcohol is methanol.

a) It is manufactured by the following reversible reaction.

$$CO(g) + 2H_2(g) \rightleftharpoons CH_3OH(g)$$
300°C
30 atm

ii) Reversible reactions can come to equilibrium. Explain the term *equilibrium*.

_____

_____ [1]

ii) At 400°C, the percentage of methanol in the equilibrium mixture is lower than at 300 °C. Suggest an explanation.

_____

_____ [2]

iii) Suggest two advantages of using high pressure for this reaction. Give a reason for each advantage.

advantage	
reason	

advantage	
reason	

b) i) Complete the equation for the combustion of methanol in an excess of oxygen.

☐ CH$_2$OH + ☐ O → ☐ + ☐ [2]

ii) Complete the word equation.

methanol + ethanoic acid → ☐ + ☐ [2]

iii) Methanol can be oxidised to an acid. Name this acid.

☐ [2]

Answers are on page 202

EXAM QUESTION AND STUDENT'S ANSWER (PAPER 6)

I An experiment was carried out to find the pH of samples of soil from a farmer's field.

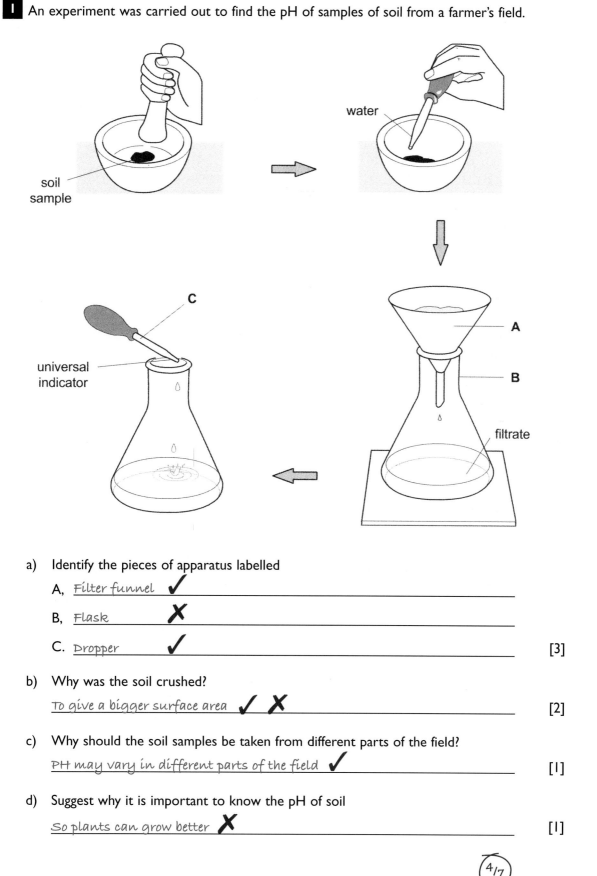

a) Identify the pieces of apparatus labelled

    A, _Filter funnel_ ✓

    B, _Flask_ ✗

    C. _Dropper_ ✓   [3]

b) Why was the soil crushed?

    To give a bigger surface area ✓ ✗   [2]

c) Why should the soil samples be taken from different parts of the field?

    PH may vary in different parts of the field ✓   [1]

d) Suggest why it is important to know the pH of soil

    So plants can grow better ✗   [1]

4/7

HOW TO SCORE FULL MARKS

a) A. Correct response.

   B. This is a 'conical flask' so the answer given was incomplete.

   C. Correct response – 'dropping pipette' is also an acceptable answer.

b) Only one mark was scored here because the student did not go on to explain that the water was dissolving some of the solids from the soil.

c) Correct response.

d) The student needed to explain that different plants grow better in different types of pH soil.

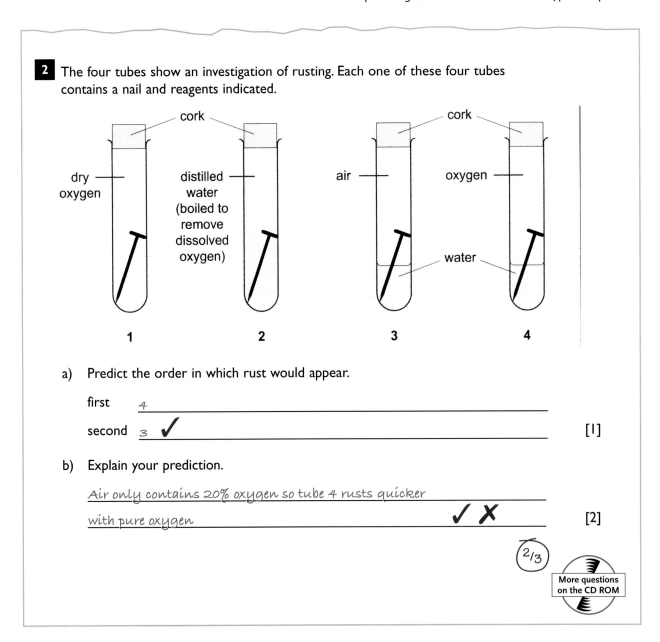

2 The four tubes show an investigation of rusting. Each one of these four tubes contains a nail and reagents indicated.

a) Predict the order in which rust would appear.

   first   4 _____

   second 3 ✔ _____   [1]

b) Explain your prediction.

   Air only contains 20% oxygen so tube 4 rusts quicker

   with pure oxygen   ✔ ✗   [2]

   (2/3)

   More questions on the CD ROM

HOW TO SCORE FULL MARKS

a) Correct response – rusting requires both oxygen/air and water so tubes 1 and 2 would rust much slower.

b) The comment is correct but the student has not gone on to explain the need for water to be present for rusting.

Marks could also be gained by making comments about tubes 1 and 2, i.e. absence of water or oxygen.

QUESTIONS TO TRY

I Lead bromide was placed in a tube and connected to an electrical circuit as shown below.

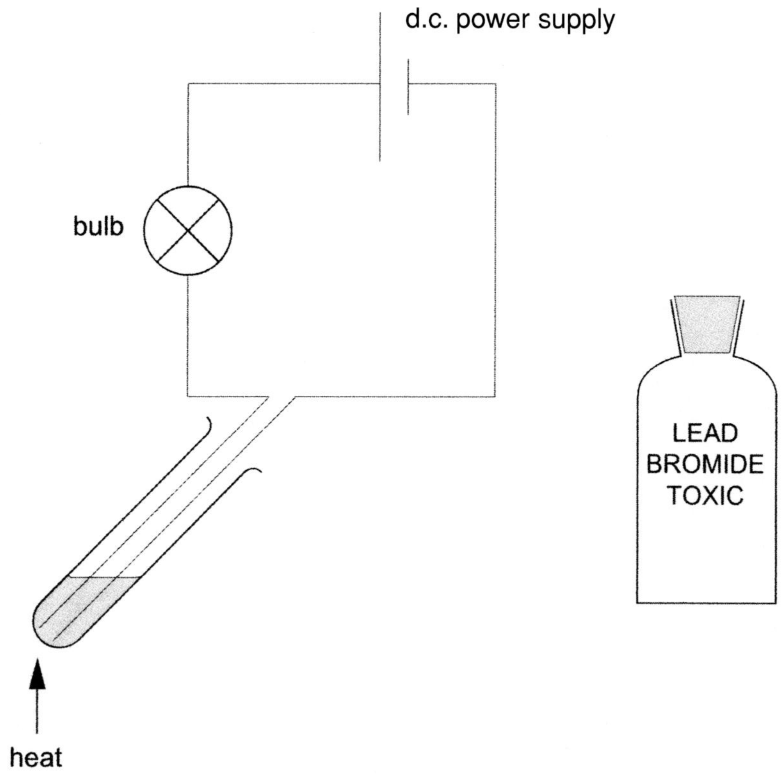

d.c. power supply

bulb

heat

LEAD
BROMIDE
TOXIC

The lead bromide was heated until molten. A brown gas was given off.
a)   State one other expected observation

_____   [1]

b)   i)   Suggest a suitable material for the electrodes.

_____

ii)   Indicate on the diagram the negative electrode (cathode).

_____   [2]

c)   Name the brown gas. At what electrode will the gas be given off?

name   _____

electrode   _____   [2]

d)   Why is this experiment carried out in a fume cupboard?

_____   [1]

2 Copper oxide was reacted with hydrogen using the apparatus shown below.

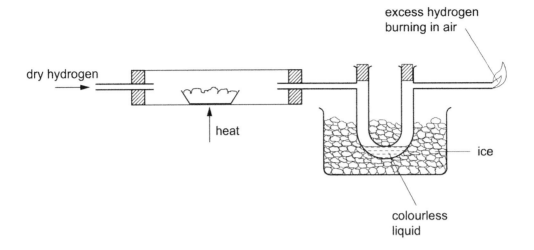

a) Indicate on the diagrams with an arrow where the copper oxide is placed.

_____   [1]

b) The colour of the copper oxide would change from _____

to _____   [2]

c) What is the purpose of the ice?

_____   [2]

3 Describe a chemical test to **distinguish** between each of the following pairs of substances. An example is given.

potassium chloride and potassium iodide

test: add aqueous lead(II) nitrate

result: potassium chloride gives a white precipitate, potassium iodide gives a yellow precipitate.

a) water and ethanol

test   _____

result with water   _____

result with ethanol   _____   [2]

b) sulphuric acid and aqueous sodium sulphate

test _____

result with sulphuric acid _____

result with aqueous sodium sulphate _____ [2]

c) hydrochloric acid and nitric acid

test _____

result with hydrochloric acid _____

result with nitric acid _____ [2]

More questions
on the CD ROM

ANSWERS AND SOLUTIONS

PRINCIPLES OF CHEMISTRY

1 The particulate nature of matter

Q1 Gas. The particles are moving faster and are further apart.

Q2 The forces between atoms in the aluminium must be greater than those in sodium.

Q3 The movement of gas/liquid particles from one place to another.

Q4 Matter is made of tiny, indivisible particles which are in constant motion in gases and liquids.

Q5 Gas particles are moving faster or liquid particles are moving more slowly.

Q6 Ammonia – it is the lighter molecule.

2 Experimental techniques

Q1 Paper chromatography.

Q2 88/89/90/91

Q3 Salt water freezes below 0°C so the ice changes to water.

3 Atoms, elements and compounds

Q1 Changes into another isotope.

Q2 Nucleus.

Q3 alpha, beta, gamma.

Q4 Copper and zinc.

Q5 They have a similar giant covalent structure based on the tetrahedral shape (four bonds).

4 Stoichiometry

Q1 a $NaCl$

Na (group 1) combining power 1, Cl (group 7) combining power 1.

b MgF_2

Mg (group 2) combining power 2, F (group 7) combining power 1. 2, 1, cross over = $Mg_1 F_2$ = MgF_2.

c AlN

Al (group 3) combining power 3, N (group 5) combining power 3. 3, 3, cancel = $Al_1 N1$ = AlN

d Li_2O

Li (group 1) combining power 1, O (group 6) combining power 2.

e CO_2

C (group 4) combining power 4, O (group 6) combining power 2. 4, 2, cancel = $C_1 O_2$ = CO_2.

Q2 a Fe_2O_3

Fe combining power 3, O (group 6) combining power 2.

b PCl_5

P combining power 5, Cl (group 7) combining power 1.

c $CrBr_3$

Cr combining power 3, Br (group 7) combining power 1.

d SO_3

S combining power 6, O (group 6) combining power 2. 6, 2, cancel = $S_1 O_3$ = SO_3.

e SO_2

S combining power 4, O (group 6) combining power 2. 4, 2, cancel = $S_1 O_2$ = SO_2.

Q3 a K_2CO_3

K combining power 1, CO_3 combining power 2.

b NH_4Cl

NH_4 combining power 1, Cl (group 7) combining power 1.

c H_2SO_4

H combining power 1, SO_4 combining power 2.

d $Mg(OH)_2$

Mg (group 2) combining power 2, OH combining power 1. Don't forget the brackets.

e $(NH_4)_2SO_4$

NH_4 combining power 1, SO_4 combining power 2. Don't forget the brackets.

Q4 a $C + O_2 \rightarrow CO_2$

This doesn't need balancing!

b $4Fe + 3O_2 \rightarrow 2Fe_2O_3$

Remember that balancing numbers must always go in front of symbols and formulae.

c $2Fe_2O_3 + 3C \rightarrow 4Fe + 3CO_2$

One maths trick to use here is to realise that the number of oxygen atoms on the right-hand side must be even. Putting a '2' in front of Fe_2O_3 makes the oxygen on the left-hand side even too.

d $CaCO_3 + 2HCl \rightarrow CaCl_2 + CO_2 + H_2O$

Note that the carbonate radical does not appear on both sides of the equation.

Q5 a $Ca^{2+} + CO_3^{2-} \rightarrow CaCO_3$

b $Fe^{2+} + 2OH^- \rightarrow Fe(OH)_2$

c $Ag^+ + Br^- \rightarrow AgBr$

The symbols and charges must balance on each side of the equation. State symbols could be used,
e.g. $Fe^{2+}(aq) + 2OH^-(aq) \rightarrow Fe(OH)_2(s)$
$Ag^+(aq) + Br^-(aq) \rightarrow AgBr(s)$.

Q6 a $Al^{3+} + 3e^- \rightarrow Al$

b $Na \rightarrow Na^+ + e^-$

c $2O^{2-} \rightarrow O_2 + 4e^-$

d $2Br^- \rightarrow Br_2 + 2e^-$

At the cathode positive ions gain electrons. At the anode negative ions lose electrons. Remember that symbols and charges must balance.

Q7 a 2 moles

Moles = mass/A_r = 56/28 = 2

b 0.1 mole

Moles = mass/A_r = 3.1/31 = 0.1

c 0.25 mole

Moles = mass/M_r = 11/44 = 0.24

d 0.5 mole

Moles = mass/M_f = 50/100 = 0.5
Note: Calcium carbonate is an ionic compound so the correct term is relative formula mass.

Q8 a 48 g

Mass = moles × A_r = 2 × 24 = 48 g

b 4 g

Mass = moles × M_r = 2 × 2 = 4 g

c 9.8 g

Mass = moles × M_r = 0.1 × 98 = 9.8 g

Q9 $TiCl_4$

	Ti	Cl
mass/A_r	25/48	75/35.5
moles	0.52	2.1
ratio	0.52/0.52 = 1	2.1/0.52 = 4.04

formula is $TiCl_4$

Q10 a NaBr

0.1 mol Na reacts with 0.1 mol Br, i.e. ratio 1:1.

b CO_2

0.05 mol C reacts with 1.6/16 = 0.10 mol O, i.e. ratio 1:2.

c FeCl

0.2 mol Fe reacts with 7.1/35.5 = 0.2 mol Cl, i.e. ratio 1:1.

Q11 4 g

2Na = 2 moles = 46 g. 2NaOH = 2 moles = 80 g. The scaling factor is ÷ 20.

Q12 a 560 tonnes

Fe_2O_3 = 1 mole → 160 tonnes. 2Fe = 2 moles → 112 tonnes. The scaling factor is × 5.

b 144 litres at room temperature and pressure

Fe_2O_3 = 1 mole → 160 g. $3CO_2$ = 3 × 24 = 72 litres. The scaling factor is × 2.

Q13 2.33 g

$BaCl_2$ = 1 mole = 1000 cm³ (1 mol dm⁻³). $BaSO_4$ = 1 mole = 233 g.
First scale by 5. 1000 cm³ (0.2 mol dm⁻³) and 46.6 g.
Second scale by 20. 50 cm³ (0.2 mol dm⁻³) and 2.33 g.

PHYSICAL CHEMISTRY

5 Electricity and chemistry

Q1 Ions cannot move.

Q2 a cathode – sodium
anode – chlorine

b cathode – hydrogen
anode – chlorine

Q3 cathode – the fork
anode – (pure) silver

Q4 $Ag^+ + e \rightarrow Ag$
$2I^- + 2e \rightarrow I_2$

6 Chemical changes

Q1 **a** Energy = $40 \times 4.2 \times 32 = 5376$ J.

b Energy = $5376/0.2 = 26\,880$ J/g.

Use the formula energy = mass $\times 4.2$ $\times$ temperature change.

Q2 **a** The reaction is exothermic.

b More energy is released when bonds are formed than is used to break the bonds in the first place.

In an energy level diagram, if the products are lower in energy than the reactants the reaction change is exothermic. Remember that the overall energy change = energy needed to break bonds – energy released on forming bonds.

Q3 More energy is released when the H—Cl bonds are made than is needed to break the H—H and Cl—Cl bonds. The overall energy change is therefore exothermic.

Again this refers to the balance between bond breaking and bond forming. Always refer to the specific bonds involved.

7 Chemical reactions

Q1 Not all collisions provide enough energy for the reaction to take place.

Energy is needed to break chemical bonds so that the atoms, molecules or ions can rearrange and form new bonds. Remember that collisions that do have sufficient energy are referred to as effective collisions.

Q2 Reaction A.

Reaction A has a lower activation energy than reaction B. This means that there will be more effective collisions and so the rate of reaction will be higher. If you are still not clear about this idea of an 'energy barrier', look again at the explanation of activation energy in the collision theory section.

Q3 **a** Carbon dioxide

Remember that marble has the chemical name calcium carbonate. The carbon dioxide is released from the carbonate ion.

b (i) 20 cm^3; (ii) 16 cm^3; (iii) 13 cm^3; (iv) 0 cm^3.

$20 - 0 = 20$; $36 - 20 = 16$; $49 - 36 = 13$; $70 - 70 = 0$. Don't forget the units of volume.

c The volume of gas produced in each 10 second interval decreases as the reaction proceeds. This means the rate of production of gas decreases.

The rate of reaction is measured in terms of the volume of gas produced in a certain amount of time. If you wanted to calculate rates in these time intervals you would need to divide the volume of gas produced by the time taken. So between 0 and 10 seconds 20 cm^3 of gas was collected giving a rate of $20/10 = 2$ cm^3/s. Between 20 and 30 seconds the rate was 1.3 cm^3/s.

d As the reaction proceeds there are fewer particles of hydrochloric acid and calcium carbonate to collide with each other. Therefore there will be fewer collisions and hence fewer effective collisions.

Don't forget to mention the idea of 'effective collisions' (see page xx). This is a key idea in this chapter. If you want to impress the examiner use the correct names for the particles, e.g. in this reaction collisions occur between hydrogen ions (H$^+$ ions) and carbonate ions (CO$_3{}^{2-}$ ions). see page 66

e Measuring the change in mass as the reaction proceeds.

The carbon dioxide gas will escape, causing a decrease in mass of the reaction container.

Q4 As the temperature increases, the kinetic energy of the reacting particles also increases. The particles will therefore be moving faster and will collide more frequently. In addition, there will be more energy transferred in the collisions and so more are likely to be effective and lead to a reaction.

Don't forget to mention the energy of the collision. Many students only mention the increased number of collisions.

Q5 **a** (i) Experiment 1; (ii) the reaction finishes more quickly because the curve levels out soonest.

A better answer would mention the gradient of the curve – e.g. the gradient of the curve at the beginning of the reaction is the steepest.

b (i) Experiment 3; (ii) the largest chips have the smallest surface area and so the lowest rate of reaction.

The curve for experiment 3 has the lowest gradient at the beginning of the reaction. If you got this wrong check the section on surface area again.

c (i) 7.5 minutes (approximately); (ii) the reaction finished because the marble was used up.

Try to read off the graph as accurately as you can. In an examination you will be allowed a small margin of error. In this example 7.3 to 7.7 minutes would be acceptable. The question says that the hydrochloric acid was 'an excess'. This means that there was more than would be needed. Therefore the reaction must have finished because the marble was used up. Always look for the phrase 'an excess' or 'in excess'.

d The same mass of marble was used in each experiment.

As the acid is in excess the amount of marble will determine how much carbon dioxide is produced.

e The curve would be steeper (have a higher gradient) at the beginning of the reaction but would reach the same plateau height.

Increasing the temperature will increase the rate of the reaction but will not change the amount of carbon dioxide produced. If you are still in doubt about this read the section on temperature again.

Q6 a A catalyst is a substance that alters the rate of a chemical reaction but does not change itself.

Remember that whilst most catalysts speed up reactions some slow them down.

b A catalyst provides another route for the reaction with a different activation energy.

Think of activation energy as an energy barrier that prevents reactants changing into products.

Q7 The film is coated in a layer of different silver halides. When light falls on the film, the silver ions are converted to silver.

Q8 A reaction is in equilibrium when the number of reactant and product molecules do not change.

You might remember that at equilibrium the rate of the forward reaction equals the rate of the backward reaction.

Q9 a The rate changes (usually increases).

Catalysts are usually used to increase reaction rate.

b No effect.

A catalyst does not change the position of equilibrium.

Q10 Mg is oxidised.
ZnO is reduced.
ZnO is the oxidising agent.
Mg is the reducing agent.
Magnesium changes oxidation number from 0 to +2.
Zinc changes oxidation number from +2 to 0.

8 Acids, bases and salts

Q1 Neutral oxides do not react with oxides or alkalis/bases, amphoteric oxides react with both acids and alkalis/bases.

Q2 a A substance that changes colour to show if a solution is acidic, neutral or alkaline (basic).

Litmus as red, purple or blue is linked to acidic; neutral and alkaline need to be remembered as conditions shown by an indicator.

b The numbers 1 to 14 linked to the strengths of acids and alkalis (bases).

pH 1 to 6 is strongly acidic to weakly acidic, pH 7 is neutral and pH 8 to 14 is weakly alkaline to strongly alkaline.

c Each colour from Universal Indicator has a pH number.

Remember pH 1–2 is maroon/red, pH 7 is yellow-green and pH 13–14 is blue/purple.

Q3 a An acid that totally dissociates into ions, so releasing all its available H^+ ions.

This is 'strong' as opposed to 'weak' (partial dissociation).

b $H_2SO_4(aq) \rightarrow 2H^+(aq) + SO_4^{2-}(aq)$

For a strong acid you need to use the arrow symbol, $\rightarrow$.

c pH = 1 to 2

Strong acids are in this range on the pH scale, and maroon/red as UI colours.

Q4 $LiOH(aq) \rightarrow Li^+(aq) + OH^-(aq)$

Lithium is in group 1, the same as sodium and potassium, so is a strong alkali. This needs the arrow symbol for complete dissociation to ions.

Q5 a Only partially dissociates into ions.

As opposed to 'strong' which is complete dissociation to ions.

b $HCOOH(aq) \rightleftharpoons HCOO^-(aq) + H^+(aq)$

Methanoic acid is monobasic (one H^+) and, since it is weak, there is an equilibrium shown by the $\rightleftharpoons$ sign.

Q6 a B. Its pH is less than 7.

Remember that how an atom reacts depends on its outermost electrons.
Remember that the acidic oxide will also react with an alkali.

b A and B. Both react with an acid.
'A' has a pH of 7 because it doesn't dissolve in water.

c (i) Neutralisation

Copper oxide is a base. The reaction of a base with an acid is neutralisation.

c (ii) Copper oxide + sulphuric acid → copper sulphate + water

Remember that acid + base → salt + water.

c (iii) $CuO(s) + H_2SO_4(aq) \rightarrow CuSO_4(aq) + H_2O(l)$

No extra balancing is required here.

c (iv) A.

Copper(II) oxide is insoluble in water and so the mixture will have a pH of 7.

Q7 a $K_2SO_4(aq) + 2H_2O(l)$

alkali + acid → soluble salt + water

b $MgCl_2(aq) + H_2O(l)$

acid + base → soluble salt + water

c $Ba(NO_3)_2(aq) + CO_2(g) + H_2O(l)$

acid + metal → soluble salt + hydrogen

d $ZnCl_2(aq) + H_2(g)$

acid + metal → soluble salt + hydrogen

e $ZnCO_3(s) + 2KCl(aq)$

soluble salt + soluble salt → insoluble salt + soluble salt
The issue is which of the two salts is insoluble. You need to remember that in this method it is usually sodium or potassium salts that are used as one of the reactants – sodium and potassium salts are almost always soluble.

Q8 Put some dilute sulphuric acid into a beaker and add copper(II) oxide until it is in excess. Filter the mixture through a filter paper in a funnel to remove the excess copper(II) oxide. The liquid collected in an evaporating dish is copper(II) sulphate solution.

The evaporating dish is put on a gauze on a tripod and heated with a Bunsen burner to evaporate some of the water. The hot solution is poured into the dish to cool, and crystals of the salt are formed. The dish is left until all the water evaporates and only the crystals are left.

The information in the question about the reagents and the salt show this is the preparation of a soluble salt, i.e. crystals.
acid + base → soluble salt + water

Q9 a $H_2SO_4(aq) + Zn(s) \rightarrow ZnSO_4(aq) + H_2(g)$

Zinc is a metal, so the method is:
acid + metal → soluble salt + hydrogen
Sulphuric acid forms sulphate.

b $HCl(aq) + KOH(aq) \rightarrow KCl(aq) + H_2O(l)$

To make a chloride requires hydrochloric acid, and the KOH being a solution means it is an alkali, not just a base.
The method is:
acid + alkali → soluble salt + water

c $2HNO_3(aq) + CuCO_3(s) \rightarrow Cu(NO_3)_2(aq) + CO_2(g) + H_2O(l)$

Nitrates are made from nitric acid, and the carbonate shows which of the 5 methods to use.
acid + carbonate → soluble salt + carbon dioxide + water

d $MgCl_2(aq) + 2KCO_3(aq) \rightarrow MgCO_3(s) + 2KCl(aq)$

The reactants are two soluble salts, and so is the product potassium chloride. So magnesium carbonate must be an insoluble salt for it to be possible to separate it, as a precipitate.
The method is:
soluble salt + soluble salt → insoluble salt + soluble salt

e $2HCl(aq) + ZnO(s) \rightarrow ZnCl_2(aq) + H_2O(l)$

The zinc oxide is a solid, and oxides are bases. The method uses hydrochloric acid to make the chloride, so the general method is:
acid + base → soluble salt + water

Q10 'Corrosive' means it can damage the skin, so gloves should be worn when handling it. Because it is 'highly flammable' it gives off vapours (evaporates easily) so it should be used in a fume cupboard so that it does not catch fire.

You cannot give the safety precautions needed without explaining the specific effects indicated by the hazard symbols.

Q11 Put a piece of damp blue litmus paper which will go first red (it is acidic), then white (it is a bleach).

The tests for gases need to be learnt. The test for chlorine is the least well known by students!

Q12 To test for the cation, add sodium hydroxide solution and a white precipitate will be formed. If the precipitate dissolves when excess sodium hydroxide solution is added, Al^{3+} is present. If it does not dissolve in excess, then Mg^{2+} or Ca^{2+} is present. Perform a flame test on the solution – a brick red colour identifies Ca^{2+}; if not a red colour, it is Mg^{2+}.

Q13 The colours show that the white solid is zinc carbonate and the gas is carbon dioxide.

Zinc carbonate (white/yellow/white) and copper carbonate (green/black) are specifically identified by their distinctive colour changes on heating/cooling.

INORGANIC CHEMISTRY
9 The periodic table

Q1 **a** b

Group 4 is the fourth major column from the left.

b a

This is the second row.

c d

The noble gas family is group 0.

d c

Transition elements are in the middle block.

e b

Metalloids are found near the 'staircase' on the right side of the periodic table, which separates metals from non-metals.

f d and f

These are on the right of the 'staircase'. If you included b you would not be penalised.

g d

Gases are non-metals and so have to be on the right side. f is a possibility but in groups 5, 6 and 7 elements near the bottom of the group are solids.

Q2 They contain the same number of electrons in the outer electron shell.

Remember that how an atom reacts depends on its outermost electrons.

Q3 **a** Caesium.

Remember that the reactivity of metals increases down a group.

b To prevent the metal reacting with air and water.

These are highly reactive metals. They oxidise rapidly without heat being needed.

c Caesium.

The melting point gives a measure of hardness. Melting point decreases down the group.

d On cutting, the metal is exposed to the air and rapidly oxidises.

Tarnishing is another word for oxidation.

e When added to water they react to produce an alkali.

The metal hydroxides formed in the reactions are alkalis.

f Sodium is less dense than water.

Density increases down the group. The more reactive metals would not float but their reaction is so violent that the metal usually flies out of the water!

g (i) rubidium + oxygen → rubidium oxide
$$4Rb(s) + O_2(g) \rightarrow 2Rb_2O(s)$$

Rubidium behaves in the same way as sodium but more violently.

g (ii) caesium + water → caesium hydroxide + hydrogen
$$2Cs(s) + 2H_2O(l) \rightarrow 2CsOH(aq) + H_2(g)$$

The reaction of the group 1 metals with water produces the metal hydroxide (an alkali) and hydrogen.

g (iii) potassium + chlorine → potassium chloride $2K(s) + Cl_2(g) \rightarrow 2KCl(s)$

Potassium chloride is a salt with an appearance very similar to sodium chloride, common salt.

Q4 **a** Fluorine

Unlike groups of metals, reactivity decreases down the group.

b Bromine

Bromine is the only liquid non-metal.

c Iodine

Astatine would be expected to be a solid but it is radioactive with a very short half-life so it is difficult to confirm this prediction.

d They only need to gain one electron in order to have a full outer electron shell. Other non-metals need to gain more than one electron.

Remember that reactivity depends on the number of electrons in the outer electron shell.

e (i) sodium + chlorine → sodium chloride
$$2Na(s) + Cl_2(g) \rightarrow 2NaCl(s)$$

e (ii) magnesium + bromine → magnesium bromide $Mg(s) + Br_2(l) → MgBr_2(s)$

The halogen elements react with all metals. They form salts, called fluorides, chlorides, bromides and iodides.

e (iii) hydrogen + fluorine → hydrogen fluoride $H_2(g) + F_2(g) → 2HF(g)$

Hydrogen fluoride will have very similar properties to the more familiar hydrogen chloride. Its solution in water, hydrofluoric acid, is highly corrosive.

Q5 a (i) Very pale yellow. (ii) Brown. (iii) Brown. (iv) Colourless.

Bromine is more soluble in water than iodine but it is very difficult to distinguish between dilute solutions of the two. Sometimes a solvent like cyclohexane is added. The bromine is brown in the cyclohexane, the iodine is violet.

b On mixing the pale yellow solution with the colourless solution, a brown solution is formed.

Observations are what you see, smell or hear. You don't see bromine; you see a brown solution.

c ✗ ✓ ✓
✗ ✗ ✓
✗ ✗ ✗

The more reactive halogen will displace (take the place of) the less reactive halogen. Chlorine will displace bromine from sodium bromide because it is more reactive. Iodine cannot replace chlorine or bromine as it is less reactive than both of them.

d Bromine + sodium iodide → iodine + sodium bromide
$Br_2(aq) + 2NaI(aq) → I_2(aq) + 2NaBr(aq)$

Bromine is more reactive than iodine and so will displace it from the solution. In this reaction it would be difficult to see a change as both the bromine and iodine solutions are brown. Using cyclohexane would confirm that a reaction had taken place.

Q6 a They are harder, have higher densities, higher melting points and are sonorous (any two).

Potassium chloride is a salt with an appearance very similar to sodium chloride, common salt.

b A catalyst is a substance that changes the speed of a chemical reaction without being changed itself.

Catalysts and their effects on rates of reaction are covered on Chapter 7.

c The alkali metals have only one electron in the outer electron shell. Transition metals have more than one electron in the outer electron shell.

Reactivity is principally related to the number of electrons in the outer electron shell. Metals lower down a group are also more reactive than those higher up, but this is of secondary importance.

Q7 a A – sodium, B – copper, C – calcium.

The sodium and calcium can be identified from the flame test information. Only one of the compounds contains a transition metal (forms a coloured compound).

b The hydroxides of the group 1 metals are soluble in water and would not form a precipitate.

Calcium is in group 2. Calcium hydroxide is only sparingly soluble in water and so a precipitate forms.

c $Cu^{2+}(aq) + 2OH^-(aq) → Cu(OH)_2(s)$

The important part of the compound is the copper ion. The non-metal ion or radical does not play a part in the reaction – it is a spectator ion.

Q8 Noble gases have full outer electron shells and so do not need to gain or lose electrons in a reaction.

Remember that metals want to lose electrons and form positive ions, whereas non-metals often try to gain electrons and form negative ions. Details of ionic bonding are given on page 22.

Q9 a more reactive/reactivity increases

b less reactive/reactivity decreases

Q10 Metals lose electrons, non-metals gain electrons.

Q11 Lose electrons more easily/more shielding of nucleus by electron levels/more electron levels.

10 Metals

Q1 a Iron oxide + carbon → iron + carbon dioxide

In the blast furnace much of the reduction is done by carbon monoxide.

b Reduced. Reduction is the loss of oxygen. The iron oxide has lost oxygen, forming iron.

Reduction and oxidation always occur together. In this reaction the carbon is oxidised.

c The limestone reacts with impurities, forming a slag that floats to the top and is removed from the furnace.

Of the three raw materials in the blast furnace (coke, iron ore, limestone) this is the easiest one to forget.

Q2 They have better properties, for example they might be stronger.

Q3 Foreign atoms break up the regular structure of the metal and jumble up the atoms.

Q4 a $2KNO_3 \rightarrow 2KNO_2 + O_2$

b $Mg(OH)_2 \rightarrow MgO + H_2O$

c $2Cu(NO_3)_2 \rightarrow 2CuO + 4NO_2 + O_2$

Q5 Aluminium is covered by a thin layer of unreactive aluminium oxide.

Q6 Zinc blende is ZnS.

Q7 Copper is used for cooking pans because it is a good heat conductor with a high melting point.

11 Air and water

Q1 Air is liquefied under pressure and cooling. Liquid air is fractionally distilled to obtain the oxygen (as a liquid, kept under pressure).

Q2 Reaction of iron with oxygen and water.

Q3 a Galvanising/sacrificial protection.

b Zinc is more reactive than iron, so if the zinc coating is breached to expose the iron, the zinc corrodes in preference to the iron.

12 Sulphur

Q1 The reaction:
$SO_3(g) + H_2O(l) \rightarrow H_2SO_4(l)$

is very exothermic. The heat makes the acid vaporise into a dangerous 'acid mist'.

13 Carbonates

Q1 Limestone can be converted into quicklime, and quicklime into slaked lime. All three materials have a wide variety of uses.

This is the basis of the huge amounts quarried. There is no need to give a specific use in this answer.

Q2 a $CaCO_3(s) \rightarrow CaO(s) + CO_2(g)$

b $CaO(s) + H_2O(l) \rightarrow Ca(OH)_2(s)$

Both equations are pivotal to the topic and need to be thoroughly learned. State symbols are essential.

Q3 a Pass the gas though limewater. If the limewater turns cloudy/milky, the gas is carbon dioxide.

b $Ca(OH)_2(aq) + CO_2(aq) \rightarrow CaCO_3(s) + H_2O(l)$

The limewater test for CO_2 is a key chemical test, and the cause of the cloudy/milky colour is the formation of insoluble calcium carbonate (limestone) as a precipitate, i.e. a solid formed in a solution.

Q4 Limestone is used to neutralise the acidic gases, e.g. sulphur dioxide produced by burning fossil fuels. The equation is:
$CaCO_3 + H_2SO_4 \rightarrow CaSO_4 + H_2O + CO_2$

This would be a 2 marks question, giving the 'clue' that the equation is also needed. Limestone to neutralise acidity is the key for the first mark, with the second mark for the chemical equation. Note that $H_2O + SO_2 \rightarrow H_2SO_3$, 'sulphurous acid' is first formed. It then oxidises in the air to sulphuric acid.

ORGANIC CHEMISTRY
14 Organic chemistry

Q1 a Small sea creatures died, their bodies settled in the mud at the bottom of the oceans and decayed. They were compressed over a period of millions of years and slowly changed into crude oil.

Remember the process involves compression and takes place over millions of years. Do not confuse crude oil with coal, which is formed from plant material.

b It takes millions of years to form. Once supplies have been used up they cannot be replaced.

A common mistake is to say 'it cannot be used again'. No fuel can be used again but some, such as trees (wood), can be regrown quite quickly. Wood is therefore renewable.

Q2 **a** Fractional distillation.

There is often a mark for 'fractional' and a mark for 'distillation'.

b The boiling point of the fractions decreases.

Remember the column is hotter at the bottom than at the top.

c Components that have boiling points just above the temperature of X will condense to a liquid. Components which have boiling points below the temperature of X will remain as vapour and continue up the column.

If a vapour is cooled below its boiling point it will condense.

d The component would be not very runny (it would be viscous), very dark yellow/orange in colour, very difficult to light and very smoky when burning.

Again the clues are in the table. A fuel needs to ignite easily and be 'clean'.

e It would not ignite easily. It would produce a lot of soot when burning.

In a question like this, the clues to the answer will be in the table. Always give as full an answer as possible. Four points can be scored using the last three columns of the table.

Q3 **a** A compound containing carbon and hydrogen atoms only.

Don't miss out the word 'only'. A lot of compounds contain carbon and hydrogen but are not hydrocarbons (e.g. glucose, $C_6H_{12}O_6$).

b High temperature, catalyst.

'Catalytic crackers' are used at oil refineries.

c C_8H_{18}.

The equation must balance so the number of carbon atoms must be 10 – 2, the number of hydrogen atoms 22 – 4.

Q4 **a** Larger straight-chain molecules are broken down into smaller molecules that are re-joined to form branched-chain molecules.

You need to recognise the difference in the changes to molecules during reforming as compared to cracking.

b High-grade petrol is mainly branched-chain molecules because they catch fire at the correct temperature in the combustion chamber.

It is important to know that straight-chain molecules catch fire more readily than branched-chain molecules.

Q5 **a** Members of the same family which differ by one carbon atom each time, i.e. $-CH_2-$ is added.

b Molecules with the same number and type of atoms but arranged in different ways.

Questions on alkanes and alkenes will almost always ask you for one of these terms – sometimes both of them.

Q6 **a** Two isomers of hexane:

and

b Two isomers of butene:

and

Comment It is always easiest to draw the long straight-chain isomer, then to take a $-CH_3$ off one end and put it somewhere else in the, now shorter, chain.
Don't forget to count the C's and H's to make sure they add up to the original formula.

Q7 The molecules have intermolecular forces between them. The longer the chain the greater these are, so the boiling points increase with length of chain.

Sometimes, this idea is tested by giving you two or three isomers and asking you to say which would have the highest boiling point, when you should identify the molecule with the longest carbon chain.

Q8 **a** Yeast contains an enzyme that converts sugar to ethanol. Enzymes work at a low optimum temperature. If the temperature rises above 30 °C, the enzyme is denatured and the reaction stops.

b Oxygen from the air would oxidise the ethanol to ethanoic acid ('vinegar'). This is 'spoilage'.

As an oxidation process, changing alcohols to carboxylic acids, is a fundamental part of the chemistry syllabus.

Q9 Two isomers of butanol:

and

As with the isomers of hydrocarbons, the simplest way is the best in such questions. Start with the –OH group at the end of the longest straight carbon chain and then put it on another carbon atom in the chain.

Q10 The reaction between an alcohol and a carboxylic acid to form an ester.

This is a basic reaction of alcohols and carboxylic acids. Esters are vital components of perfumes.

Q11 Dip in Universal Indicator paper – it will show a pH of 4 to 6.

This is the easiest way to recognise that a solution is a weak acid. However, you need to recognise that these compounds are weak acids, so will react with carbonates (e.g. Na_2CO_3) or hydrogencarbonates (e.g. $NaHCO_3$) to give off CO_2 (turning limewater cloudy/milky).

Q12 A large molecule made of smaller molecules joined together.

Q13 'Addition' involves identical monomer molecules containing a carbon double bond. 'Condensation' involves two different monomer molecules reacting together with functional groups to form the macromolecules.

Q14 a –CO–NH–

b –CO–O–

Q15 Amino acids

Q16 Amide

Q17 Reaction with water

Q19 Soap

Q20 a Fermentation

b Fractional distillation

15 Exam Practice

Q1 a Nitrogen (1)

The percentage of gases in the air need to be remembered. 'About 80%' is nitrogen.

b i) oxygen (1) → water (1)

ii) hydrogen and carbon (both needed) (1)

Octane is a hydrocarbon so contains hydrogen and carbon. Combustion = reaction with oxygen. Hydrocarbons burn to make carbon dioxide and water.

iii) Alkanes (1)

The ending of hydrocarbon names are clues: 'ane' = alkane, 'ene' = alkene.

c Incomplete combustion of the octane/petrol or burns in insufficient oxygen/air.

In sufficient oxygen, carbon dioxide would be made. The words 'incomplete' or 'insufficient' referring to oxygen/air are essential for the mark.

d 2, 2 (both needed) (1)

Balancing chemical equations is an important skill.

e i) burning fossil fuels (1)

ii) adding oxygen (1)

Fossil fuels often contain sulphur and oxidation is a standard term to learn.

iii) 98 (1)

This needs the use of the periodic table at the ed of the paper, i.e. H = 1, S = 32 and O = 16, i.e. $2 + 32 + (4 \times 16) = 98$

iv) iron sulphate (1), hydrogen (1)

This is one of the equations for making salts, i.e. acid + metal → a salt + water.

Sulphuric acid produces sulphates'.

v) Erodes/attacks/corrodes them (1) accept 'reacts and wears them away' etc.

This is another equation that needs to be learnt:

acid + carbonate → a salt + water + carbon dioxide.

QUESTION AND STUDENT'S ANSWERS (PAPER 3)

Paper 3 (page 186)

Q1 a (i) Reversible reaction or 'rate forward' = rate backward' or 'amounts of reactants and products do not change at equilibrium'. (1)

The definition of equilibrium is often asked and should, therefore, be an easy mark to gain.

(ii) The forward reaction is exothermic (1) so increasing temperature moves equilibrium to the left/towards reactants (1)

The effect on an equilibrium of changes in temperature, pressure and catalysts is Le Chatelier's Principle and needs to be understood.

(iii) EITHER ORDER:

a. Increase rate of reaction (1)

b. Particles closer together so more chance of collisions (leading to reactions). (1)

a. More CH_3OH/product made (1)

b. Left hand side has more molecules than right hand side/this is high pressure side and rhs is low pressure side (1)

Increased pressure means equilibrium moves to right/product (1)

This is another application of the effect of pressure on an equilibrium involving gases. The other issue is increasing pressure affecting rate.

b (i) 2, 3, $2CO_2$, $4H_2O$ (2)

A difficult equation to balance because of the oxygens. You need to be logical and use the method for balancing taught.

(ii) methyl ethanoate(1) water (1)

This is:
alcohol + carboxylic acid → an ester + water

The issue is the name of the ester, i.e. it is not 'ethyl methanote' because the acid is ethanoic'.

(iii) methanoic (acid) (1)

This is the oxidation of an alcohol to a carboxylic acid.

QUESTION AND STUDENT'S ANSWERS (PAPER 6)

Paper 6 (page 189)

Q1 a Bulb lights up or silver metal on an electrode. (1)

b i) Carbon or platinum (1)

ii) A (–) sign drawn on the right hand side electrode in the tube. (1)

The electrolysis of lead bromide is specifically mentioned in the syllabus. Ionic solids, like lead bromide, only conduct when molten ('bulb lights up') and in this case lead ('silvery metal') and bromine ('brown gas') are formed at the electrodes.

c Bromine (1)

Anode (1)

Lead is a metal so forms cations (+) which go to the cathode (–). Bromine forms anions (–) which go to the anode (+).

d bromine vapour is toxic. (1)

The danger is given away by the word 'toxic' on the diagram of the bottle.

Q2 a An arrow pointing to the pot above the word 'heat'. (1)

b black (1) to brown (1).

This is a specified experiment in the syllabus, i.e. the reduction of copper(II) oxide with hydrogen'

hydrogen + copper(II) oxide → copper
(black)   (brown)
+ water

The colour of copper(II) oxide should be learned.

c Water is formed in the reaction (1) which comes over as steam so needs cooling to collect it. (1)

The reaction produces water in the form of steam because of the heat in the reaction tube.

Q3 a Anhydrous copper(II) sulphate (1)

Water – changes from white to blue

Ethanol – no change (1)

These types of questions can be challenging. The technique requires a good knowledge of the properties of the substances being identified. Equally acceptable would be anhydrous cobalt chloride as a test.

b Add Universal Indicator paper (1)

Sulphuric acid – goes red/maroon

Sodium sulphate – goes green (1)

In this case, the acidity test is best, e.g. equally acceptable would be adding a metal, e.g. zinc or a carbonate both of which would produce 'bubbles'/'effervescence'. Sodium sulphate solution is neutral.

c Add silver nitrate solution (1)

Hydrochloric acid – a white precipitate

Nitric acid – no change (1)

Silver nitrate solution is the test for halide ions, i.e. chloride ions in hydrochloric acid.

The University of Cambridge Local Examinations Syndicate bears no responsibilty for the example answers to questions taken from its past question papers which are contained in this publication.

PRINCIPLES OF CHEMISTRY

1 a i   A is methane.
      ii   B and E are giant structures.
      iii A and C are hydrocarbons.
      iv   B.
      v   B and E have very high melting points.

   b i   The structure is graphite.
      ii   Diamond or buckminsterfullerene are other forms of carbon.

   c The simplest formula for substance B is NaI.

   d Substance D is a compound, because two different atoms are bonded together.

2 a The clay can be separated from the river water by filtration.

   b The river water is acidic, so litmus paper turns red.

   c i   The steel is an alloy.
      ii   Water is a liquid at room temperature.
      iii Copper and iron are both elements.
      iv   Natural gas is a fuel.

   d The main substance in natural gas is methane.

   e The normal temperature of boiling water is 100°C.

   f i   Calcium had the greatest concentration in the water.
      ii   Na → Na$^+$ + e$^-$.

   g i   When butane burns in excess air the products are carbon dioxide and water.
      ii   Carbon monoxide (CO).

3 Experiment 1: final 10.6.
   Experiment 2: initial14.9 final 36.1
   Differences Experiment 1:10.6
   Experiment 2: 21.2

   a The chemical reaction is neutralisation.

   b i   Experiment 2.
      ii   Experiment 2 has twice the volume of acid than Experiment 1.
      iii The likely explanation is that M is more concentrated than N.

   c It is likely that the volume of solution would be 21.2 cm^3. The explanation is that there is twice as much calcium hydroxide solution.

   d To obtain more accurate results you could use a pipette instead of a measuring cylinder use a pipette.

4 a Concentrated means that there is or little water.

   b The pH is likely to be less than 7.

   c A suitable experiment would be paper chromatography. Apply a spot of the drink to the paper and use a solvent such as water. You should see two yellow spots.

5 a To measure the acid you should use a measuring cylinder.
   b The nickel(II) carbonate is added in excess so that all of the sulphuric acid is used up.

   c The fizzing is because carbon dioxide gas is given off.

   d On the diagrams there should be labels of filter funnel, filter paper and beaker.

   e The correct answer is filtrate.

   f To obtain pure dry crystals you would evaporate off some of the water and allow it to crystallise in a warm place.

   g i   7H$_2$O
      ii   The sign means equilibrium or a reversible reaction.
      iii To obtain green nickel(II) sulphate from white you would add water.

6 The correct words are: dilute filter saturated cool blue sulphate.

7 a They both have a valency of 2 because Group II metals will lose 2 electrons.

      Group VI elements will gain 2 electrons.
   b SCl$_2$ There should be 8 electrons around both chlorine atoms. 8 electrons around sulphur with 2o and 2x.

c i Ions cannot move in the solid state but can in the liquid state.

ii There are no ions in sulphur chloride as it is covalent but strontium chloride is ionic.

8 a i $Zn(OH)_2 \rightarrow ZnO + H_2O_{\neq}$

ii When solid sodium hydroxide is heated it would melt.

b When copper(II) nitrate is heated you would observe a blue solid turning into a black solid and a brown gas being evolved.

Moles of $Fe_2(SO_4)_3$ 0.025
Moles of Fe_2O_3 0.025
Mass of iron(III) oxide formed   4 g
Moles of SO_3 produced   0.075
Volume of sulphur trioxide at rtp   0.075 x 25 = 1.8 dm³

PHYSICAL CHEMISTRY

1 a The diagram should show a random arrangement, with the molecules far apart.

b pH 9

c i NH_3
ii Bonding in ammonia is covalent.
iii Ammonia has a low boiling point because there are only weak forces between particles.

d i H_2SO_4.
ii Nitrogen   Soil.

e Ammonia evaporates from ammonia solution, and there is diffusion around the room. The particles of ammonia move freely and fast and when they reach the girl she can smell the ammonia.

f i The oxygen comes from the air.
ii 2.
iii The symbol means a reversible reaction or equilibrium.
iv It shows the reaction is exothermic.

2 a i Iron + sulphuric acid → iron sulphate + hydrogen
ii Put a lighted splint into the tube and see if there is a pop.

b i Cathode
ii It allows conduction so that ions can move through the solution.
iii The iron object is coated with a layer of copper.
The rod of copper loses copper and gets smaller.

iv Test for copper(II) ions is to add aqueous sodium hydroxide. Result is a light blue precipitate, insoluble in excess.

c Chromium is used to because it protects the iron so that it does not rust.

d Most reactive iron → chromium → copper   Least reactive

3 a i CH_3–CH==CH_2
ii Make sure you have drawn the correct repeating unit and shown the continuation at the ends.
iii The monomer will react with bromine because it has a double bond.

b i The mixture was filtered to remove the solid fibres.
iii Silver atoms to silver ions is oxidation because silver atoms have lost electrons.
iii The white precipitate is silver chloride.

c i You can give the name and formula of any ester. For example terylene with an ester linkage or a fat.
ii Alcohol.

d i An acid loses a proton and a base accepts a proton.
ii A weak acid is only partly ionised in solution.

4 a The electrodes should be correctly labelled on the rods.

b When the circuit is switched on there will be bubbles at the positive electrode, and bubbles at the negative electrode. The bulb lights up, smells of bleach and there is a greenish gas.

c i Chlorine.
ii To test, use litmus paper.
The paper will turn white and become bleached/colourless.

5 The results should be: 15, 45, 61, 73, 74, 80 and 80.

a On the graph all points should be plotted correctly and there should be a smooth curve.

b The volume of acid from the graph should be between 10.5 and 11.5 cm³.

c The volume of hydrogen from the graph should be between 29.5 and 30.5 dm³.

6 a i Fertilisers increase growth and crop yield.
   ii Potassium.
   iii Phosphate.

b To test for nitrate ions, add sodium hydroxide solution and aluminium foil, warm and then test the gas evolved with red litmus paper. The result is that the litmus will turn blue.

c i The reaction is neutralisation.
   ii NH_3

d The 2nd and 4th boxes should be ticked.

7 The 3rd box down should be ticked.
b i Electrolysis is the decomposition of a substance using electricity.
   ii Hydrogen is produced at the negative electrode, the cathode.
   iii Graphite could be used for the electrode.

c i An electron would make a chloride ion.
   ii To test, acidify with nitric acid and add silver nitrate solution. The result should be that a white precipitate is seen.

d 2

e i 2550 kg
   ii 3.6%

f i Unsaturated Catalyst Saturated

g Hydrogen can be used for balloons.

8 b i Increase
   ii Zinc
      COND and a correct reason – such as it loses electrons more easily or it is more reactive.
      Need both zinc and reason for the mark.
   iii From the more reactive to the less reactive NOT just from zinc to lead.

INORGANIC CHEMISTRY

1 a i Diatomic means the molecule contains two atoms.
   ii State means physical state, i.e. whether it is solid, liquid or gas.

b i Last column: gas; liquid; solid.
   ii Colour of bromine is red/brown/orange.
   iii From the table, the boiling point of iodine will be between 130 and 210 (°C).

c Iodine + potassium chloride.

d i The diagram should show 8 electrons in each shell and the atoms bonded.
   ii Chlorine is used for: water purification or treatment, killing bacteria, bleaching agent (for paper), making refrigerants, making hydrochloric acid, and other uses listed in the chapter.

e i A is an element.
   ii C, HCl forms hydrochloric acid.
   iii It contains ions which are free to move.

f i Astatine is in Period 6.
   ii Astatine has 85 protons.
   iii Isotopes are atoms with the same number of protons and different number of neutrons.
   iv Astatine contains 125 neutrons.

2 a i Down the group the colour changes and gets darker.
   ii The physical state changes from gas to liquid to solid.
   iii Fluorine is likely to be a colourless or very light-coloured gas.

b To distinguish between the two you could add chlorine water. The result with bromide would be a yellow or orange colour and with iodide would be dark crystals.

c $I_2 + 3Cl_2 \rightarrow 2ICl_3$.

d Chlorine would diffuse faster because it has a lower density and lighter molecules.

3 a i Carbon dioxide + water.
   ii For a test you could add (acidified) barium chloride(aq) and the result would be a white precipitate.
   iii You could show the water has a high concentration of hydrogen ions by seeing that universal indicator or litmus paper turns red (aq).

b i $H_2S + 2O_2 \rightarrow H_2SO_4$.
   ii It should be removed from petrol because it is poisonous and when burnt can form acid rain.
   iii The diagram should show 2H to 1S with 8e around sulphur atom and 2e per hydrogen atom.

c i The catalyst is vanadium(V) oxide, V_2O_5.
   ii Temperature of 400 to 500°C is used.
   iii By adding it to (concentrated) sulphuric acid then adding water.

d 79.1g $CaSO_4$ = 0.58 moles.
   20.9 g H_2O = 1.16 moles
   x = 2.

4 a i The main ore of aluminium is bauxite.
ii Cryolite is used to reduce the melting point and improve electrical conductivity.
iii At the anode carbon dioxide or carbon monoxide or fluorine can be given off.

b i Aluminium has the greater tendency to form ions.
ii As the reaction proceeds the solution goes colourless and copper is formed.
iii Aluminium reacts slowly because it is covered with an unreactive oxide layer.

c reaction   no reaction
reaction   reaction

d i $2Al(OH)_3 \rightarrow Al_2O_3 + 3H_2O$
ii Aluminium nitrate $\rightarrow$ aluminium oxide + nitrogen dioxide + oxygen

5 a Stand   Pipette   Bunsen burner.

b When water is added hydration takes place. The reaction is exothermic.

6 a The density increases down the group.
b Rubidium is predicted to boil between 670 and 714°C.

c The radius of a caesium atom is likely to be between 0.260 and 0.300 nm.

d Lithium would react less rapidly.

e Properties of metals: conduct heat, conduct electricity, malleable, ductile, shiny, sonorous.

f i The other product is sodium hydroxide
ii Test for hydrogen is to put in a lighted splint. The result is that there will be a pop.

g i The positively charged particle is a proton.
ii These atoms are called isotope(s).
iii There are three nucleons in tritium.
iv Radioactivity can be used as a radioactive tracer or in treating cancer.

7 a X is nitrogen.

b i Octane + oxygen $\rightarrow$ carbon dioxide + water.
ii Hydrocarbons contain carbon and hydrogen.
iii Alkanes.

c Carbon monoxide is the product of incomplete combustion.

d i $N_2 + 2O_2 \rightarrow 2NO_2$.
ii NO_2 cause breathing difficulties and illness because it dissolves in water in the lungs.

e i The main sources is burning coal or other fossil fuels.
ii Oxidation means addition of oxygen
iii The M_r of sulphuric acid is 98
iv Sulphuric acid + iron $\rightarrow$ iron(II) sulphate.
v Acid rain erodes calcium carbonate

8 a Other gases in air are carbon dioxide, water vapour, noble.

b Sulphur dioxide source: burning fossil fuels harmful effect: acid rain.
Lead compounds source: car exhausts harmful effects on health.

c i Combustion also changes air composition.
ii $6CO_2 + 6H_2O + 6O_2 \rightarrow 6CO_2 + 6H_2O$.
This is an exothermic reaction.

9 a i Correct equation with a more reactive metal.
ii Electron loss.
iii Because they can accept electrons or take electrons away from...
iv Silver or silver(I).

b i Increase.
ii Zinc.
COND and a correct reason – such as it loses electrons more easily or it is more reactive. Need both zinc and reason for the mark.
iii From the more reactive to the less reactive NOT just from zinc to lead.

10 a Insoluble particles/solids/dirt trapped/ caught on stones.
NOT: filter reacts with insoluble impurities.
NOT: impurities unqualified.
Water passes through/filtered OWTTE.

b i Kill bacteria/germs, disinfect water OWTTE.
ii Neutralises acidity/water.
ALLOW: reacts with acids in water.
iii Calcium hydroxide.
NOT: formula.
iv Neutralising acid soils/neutralising acidic (industrial) waste/making bleaching powder/removing acidic gases/in Solvay process/in recovery of ammonia/making limewater/in water softening/for making plaster/for mak ing mortar/controlling soil acidity.
NOT: neutralising acids unqualified.
NOT: making cement

c   i   100.
        °C (conditional on 100).
    ii Anhydrous cobalt chloride/anhydrous
        copper sulphate (or correct colours).
        NOT: cobalt chloride/copper sulphate
        unqualified.
        Turns pink/blue (respectively).
    iii Any suitable, e.g. washing/cleaning/
        drinking/cooking.

d   B.

e   Ethanol.
    NOT: alcohol.

f   Potassium hydroxide; hydrogen.
    NOT: symbols.

11 a Chlorine, argon, potassium, bromine, iodine.
     ALLOW: symbols.

b   Chlorine, potassium, argon, bromine, iodine.
    ALLOW: symbols

c   2nd box down ticked.

d   Chlorine, bromine, iodine.
    ALLOW: symbols

e   i   Potassium/K.
    ii Argon/Ar.

f   1st and 4th boxes ticked.

g   i   High (boiling point).
    ii Conducts/is high.

h   Potassium loses an/one electron/loses outer
    shell.
    Chlorine gains an/one electron/outer shell
    becomes complete.
    ALLOW: potassium loses two electrons
    + chlorine gains two electrons.
    ALLOW: e.g. 2.8.8.1 •2.8.8.
    Any indication of sharing electrons = 0.

ORGANIC CHEMISTRY

1 a The ethene molecules are monomers.

b   Ethane cannot be polymerised because it
    does not have a double bond.

c   Refer back to the chapter for a diagram.

d   i   Cracking means breaking down of
        long-chain hydrocarbons into smaller
        molecules.
    ii A high temperature is needed.
    iii C_8H_{18}..

e   i H_2..
    ii Fractional distillation creates a
        temperature gradient in fractionating
        column so that the smaller/lighter
        molecules (rise) higher in the column
        and different fractions condense at
        particular places depending on their
        boiling points.
    iii Petrol is used as fuel.
        Lubricating fraction: used for lubricating
        oils.

2 a i   A is glutamic acid and B is alanine.
    ii The locating agent must be used
        because the acids are colourless.
    iii You can also identify amino acids by
        comparing them with with known acids
        or references.
    iv The picture should show an amide
        linkage and continuation at the ends.

b   Refer back to the chapter for the structure.

c   i $C_6H_{12}O_6 \rightarrow 2C_2H_5OH + 2CO_2$.
    ii Respiration means giving out energy.
    iii The reaction stops because glucose is
        used up or yeast is 'killed' by ethanol.
    iv If there was any oxygen it would
        oxidise alcohol to acid or to ethanoic
        acid to carbon dioxide and water.
    v   The ethanol can be concentrated by
        fractional distillation.

3 a A and D are unsaturated hydrocarbons.
   b C and E contain a carboxylic group.
   c Compound D is C_5H_{10}.

d   The diagram should show the correct
    formula for 1,2-dibromoethane and all
    atoms and bonds.

e   i   Between days 5 and 6.
    ii Respiration.
    iii It decreases ethene production.
    iv Diffusion.
    v   It slows down the ripening process
        because it removes the ethene.
   vi   An enzyme is a biological molecule, a
        protein and it acts as a catalyst.

f   i   The diagram shows chromatography.
    ii S contained the greater number of
        pigments.
    iii R and T contained the same pigments.

4 a i   Equilibrium means there is no change in
        concentration of reagents.
    ii It must be lower because the back
        reaction is endothermic or the forward
        reaction is exothermic.
    iii Advantage: increased rate.
        Reason: because molecules collide
        more frequently.
        Advantage: increased yield.
        Reason: high pressure favours side with
        few molecules.

b i $2CH_3OH + 3O_2 \rightarrow 2CO_2 + 4H_2O$.

    ii Methyl ethanoate + water.

    iii Methanoic acid.

5 a i Refer to the chapter for the correct structure.
$CH_2 = CCl_2$.

      ii Oxygen can diffuse faster because it has a lower M_r or density.

  b i Refer to the chapter, this has an ester linkage:
$-OOC-C_6H_4-COOCH_2CH_2O-$

      ii Fats or lipids contain the ester linkage.

      iii Thermal stability means that it does not decompose easily with heated.

  c i Plastic waste does not decompose and gives off poisonous gases when burnt.

      ii An advantage of recycling plastics is to save energy.

6 a i Hexene: C_6H_{12}.
Predicted boiling point between 60 and 65°C.

      ii The alkene is $C_{12}H_{24}$.

  b A test is to add bromine water or potassium manganate(VII) and the result with butene is that it goes from brown/orange/yellow to colourless and with cyclobutane it remains brown/orange/yellow.

  c i Alcohol is formed.

      ii $CH_3 - CH_2 - CHCl - CH_3$

      iii $- CH(CH_3) - CH(CH_3) -$

7 a Ethanol – solvent.
Ethene – polymer.
Bitumen – roads.

c i C.

   ii A.

   iii B.

   iv D.

d i (compound) containing only carbon and hydrogen.
NOT: it contains carbon and hydrogen.

   ii Has only single bonds/has general formula Cn2n + 2.
NOT: it is saturated.

8 a i Correct repeat unit.
COND evidence of polymer chain.

      ii Glucose or maltose.

      iii Addition (polymerisation)or no other product.
Except polymer.
Condensation (polymerisation) or polymer and water.

  b i Sodium hydroxide.
COND ammonia or alkaline gas or litmus red to blue.
If aluminium added wc = O_2+.

      ii Measure pH.
More than 1 and less than 7 or correct colour, e.g. orange or yellow.
NOT red.
NOT green.
OR add magnesium or calcium carbonate.
Weak acid reacts slowly.

  c i Ethyl acrylate.
Ester or alkene.

      ii Brown to colourless (NOT clear).
correct formula for acid NOT ester.

GLOSSARY

Oil refinery, Malaysia

Potash mining, Canada

Singaporean silver coin

Diamonds are allotropes

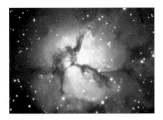

Nebula gases

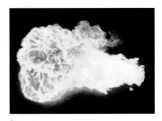

Burning

acid Substance with a pH less than 7. Acid molecules in solution release hydrogen ions, H^+.

activation energy Energy needed to start a chemical reaction.

alcohol Molecule with an –OH group attached to a chain of carbon atoms.

alkali Soluble substance with a pH greater than 7. Alkalis usually release hydroxide ions, OH^-, in a solution.

alkali metal A Group 1 element.

alkane Hydrocarbon where the carbon atoms are bonded together by single bonds only.

alkene Hydrocarbon that contains a single carbon-carbon double bond.

alloy A solid mixture of two or more metals.

amphoteric A substance that will react with both an acid and a base.

allotrope The different physical forms in which a pure element can exist.

anhydrous Literally means 'without water' – a compound with no water of crystallisation.

anode A positively charged electrode in electrolysis.

atom The smallest particle of an element. Atoms are made of protons, electrons and neutrons.

atomic number Number of protons in an atom.

Avogadro's constant The number of particles in one mole of a substance. It is 6.023×10^{23}

base Substance that neutralises an acid to produce a salt and water.

boiling point The temperature of a boiling liquid – the highest temperature that the liquid can reach and the lowest temperature that the gas can reach.

Brownian movement The random movement of tiny particles such as those in smoke caused by the bombardment of surrounding small molecules.

boiling Group of electrical cells.

burning The reaction of a substance with oxygen in a flame.

catalyst A chemical that is added to speed up a reaction, but remains unchanged at the end.

cathode A negatively charged electrode in electrolysis.

cell, chemical A device for turning chemical energy into electrical energy.

chemical change A change that is not easily reversed because new substances are made.

combustion The burning of a fuel in oxygen, also in air.

concentration Amount of chemical dissolved in 1 litre of solvent.

covalent bond Bonding between atoms that depends on the sharing of electrons.

cracking Forming shorter alkanes and alkenes from longer alkanes using high temperatures and pressures.

decomposition Chemical change that breaks down one substance into two or more.

density The mass, in kilograms, of one metre cube of a substance.

electrode The carbon or metal material that is given an electrical charge in electrolysis reactions.

electrolysis This involves breaking down a compound containing ions by the passage of an electric current. The compound must either be melted or dissolved in water.

electron Negatively charged particles with a negligible mass that form the outer portion of all atoms.

element A substance that cannot be broken down into other substances by any chemical change.

endothermic Type of reaction in which energy is transferred in from the surroundings.

enzyme Chemical that speeds up certain reactions in biological systems, e.g. digestive enzymes speed up the chemical digestion of food.

equilibrium reaction Chemical reaction where the forward and backward reactions are both likely, shown as: $X \rightleftharpoons Y$.

evaporation Liquid changes to gas at a temperature lower than the boiling point.

exothermic Type of reaction in which energy is transferred out to the surroundings.

fermentation Chemical decomposition by micro-organisms, e.g. yeast.

filtrate The clear solution produced by filtering a mixture.

formula mass (Mr) The sum of the atomic masses of the atoms in a formula.

fossil fuel Fuel made from the remains of decayed animal and plant matter compressed over millions of years.

fraction A collection of hydrocarbons that have similar molecular masses and boil at similar temperatures.

fractional distillation Separating fractions of a mixture by distilling. The process depends on the differences in boiling points of the fractions.

freezing Changing a liquid to a solid at the melting point.

group A vertical column of elements in the Periodic Table.

Copper oxidation

Chemical change; nylon

Fireworks, China

Environmental pollution

Gold leaf

Waterfall, Thailand

Saudi Arabia, refinery

Dried fish, Thailand

Indian lattice pattern

Molten lead

Neon lights, Hong Kong

Norwegian oil platform

halogens Group 7 elements (F, Cl, Br, I, At). They have one electron missing from their outer shell.

homologous series Molecules with the same functional group but with different lengths of carbon chain.

hydrated Literally means 'containing water' – hydrated salts contain water of crystallisation.

ion A charged atom or molecule.

ionic bonding Bonding that involves the transfer of electrons to produce electrically charged ions.

isomer A compound having the same molecular formula but different structures.

isotope Atoms of the same element that contain different numbers of neutrons. Isotopes have the same atomic number but different mass numbers.

lattice Regular arrangement of atoms or ions in a three-dimensional structure.

melting Changing a solid into a liquid at the melting point.

molar Containing one mole per litre.

mole An amount equal to the number of atoms in 12g of ^{12}C.

molecule A group of two or more atoms covalently bonded together.

monomer A small molecule that can be joined in a chain to make a polymer.

neutron Particle present in the nucleus of atoms that have mass but no charge.

noble gas Group 0 elements (He, Ne, Ar, Kr, Xe, Rn). They have full outer electron shells.

non-renewable Fuel that cannot be made again in a short time span.

nucleus, atomic The tiny centre of an atom made from protons and neutrons.

ore A mineral from which a metal may be extracted.

organic chemistry The study of covalent compounds of carbon.

organic molecules Carbon based molecules.

oxidation This happens when a substance gains oxygen in a chemical reaction. Oxidation is the loss of electrons.

percentage yield Fraction of substance produced (actual yield) in a chemical process compared to the possible predicted yield.

period Row in the Periodic Table, from an alkali metal to a noble gas.

pH scale Measure of the acidity (lower than 7) or alkalinity of a solution (greater than 7). It is a measure of the concentration of hydrogen ions in a solution.

photochemical A reaction affected by light.

photosynthesis A reaction that plants carry out to make food.

physical change A change in chemicals that is easily reversed and does not involve the making of new chemical bonds.

polymer Large molecule made up from smaller molecules. Polythene is a polymer made from ethene.

polymerisation Making polymers from monomers.

precipitation The formation of an insoluble solid when two solutions react together.

products The chemicals that are produced in a reaction.

proton Positively charged, massive particles found in the nucleus of an atom.

rate of reaction How fast a reaction goes in a given interval of time.

reactant The chemicals taking part in a chemical reaction. They change into the products.

reactivity series A list of elements showing their relative reactivity. More reactive elements will displace less reactive ones from their compounds.

reduction When a chemical loses oxygen. Reduction is the gain of electrons.

Relative Atomic Mass (Ar) A number comparing the mass of one mole of atoms of a particular element with the mass of one mole of atoms of other elements. One mole of C is 12.

Relative Molecular Mass (Mr) The sum of the relative atomic masses of each of the atoms in one mole of a substance.

reversible Describes a reaction that can go backwards as well as forwards.

salt Compound made from the reaction of an acid and a base.

saturated Describes an organic compound that contains only single bonds.

shell A grouping of electrons around a nucleus. The first shell in an atom can hold up to 2 electrons, the next two shells can hold up to 8 each.

solution This is formed when a substance dissolves into a liquid. Aqueous solutions are formed when the solvent used is water.

solvent The liquid in which solutes are dissolved.

speed of reaction How fast a reaction goes in a given interval of time.

state symbols These denote whether a substance is a solid (s), liquid (l), gas (g) or is dissolved in aqueous solution (aq).

transition metal Elements found between Group 2 and 3 in the Periodic Table. Often used as catalysts and often make compounds that have coloured solutions.

universal indicator Indicating solution that turns a specific colour at each pH value.

unsaturated Describes carbon compounds that contain double bonds.

volatile Easily turning to a gas.

yield Amount of substance produced from a chemical reaction.

Grass, Bali

Polymer container

Bridge repainting

Space shuttle

States of matter

Planets in space

Index